MEMORIES OF RAF WITCHFORD

Barry & Sue Aldridge

Copyright 2013 by Barry & Sue Aldridge

First published in 2013 by

Milton Contact Ltd

A CIP catalogue record for this book is available from

The British Library

ISBN: 978-0-9571959-6-7

2nd Printing

Printed in United Kingdom

Milton Contact Ltd

3 Hall End, Milton, Cambridge, UK.

CB24 6AQ

www.miltoncontact.co.uk

Publisher's Note

This book forms part of and is an extension of the RAF Witchford Display of Memorabilia. It contains a wealth of material and information, much of which has come through generous donations and contributions of items, pictures and stories relating to the history of the site and the people who served there.

We have incorporated this information within the book in good faith that we have permission to use it in this way, in support of the RAF Witchford Display of Memorabilia. Where external newspaper cuttings, letters, reports and images have been used, we have sought permission of the copyright owners, where they could be identified.

Errors and omissions in seeking permission are likely; we are dealing with artefacts, photos, letters and cuttings spanning the past 70 years that were given to Barry. Donors may have passed away and unfortunately, Barry is no longer able to tell us how and from whom he received the materials and information beyond his brief notes at the time.

Therefore, if we are in error with any particular item, our sincerest apologies; please let us know, and we will amend for any future editions.

Dr Chris Thomas, Milton Contact Ltd., Publisher

Acknowledgements

We wish to thank everyone who supported us in writing this book and to the many who gave help, loaned and donated items of memorabilia to the RAF Witchford Display of Memorabilia in Grovemere House on Lancaster Way Business Park – formerly RAF Witchford airfield.

Sue would especially like to thank Dr. Chris Thomas, Jane Thomas and Elizabeth Lane for their encouragement, guidance and support to her after Barry became too unwell to finish the book. Without them I doubt this book would have taken off.

And of course, our family who were behind us all the way.

Frank Allen
Amory Civil Engineering
B. & T. Motor Repairs
Graham Barber
Trevor Benton
Eric Billson ex 115 Sq.
Denis Calvert
City of Ely Council
Harry Durham ex 115 Sq.
Eric Fairclough
Fensure Plumbing Merchants Ltd.
Nigel Fyffe
Ken Gregory ex 115 Sq.
L. Handley Carpenter, Joiner & Builder
Daphne & Leon Hogg
Chris Jakes
Brian Jordan Builders
Roy Kent
George Lavender
Giuseppe Lombardi
Jim McGillivary ex 115 Sq.
Jim Mitchell
N. & C. Glass
Page Plumbing & Heating

Alpha Glass Windows
Graham Austin
Ron Ball
Madge Baxter
David Brand
R.S. Button Joinery
Cambridge Collection
Dalgety
Jack & Dot Eames
Fen Signs
Martin Fuller

Gas Services (Soham)
H.R. Halls
Grovemere House

Aubrey Howell ex 115 Sq.
J.C.G. Builders
Frank Kanarens ex 115 Sq.
Elizabeth Lane
Bryan Lely
Anne Mathews
Smiley & Cherry Mildwater
Murfitts Builders
John Osborne
Mike Petty

Colin Pratley
Royal Air Force Association members
Bill & Maureen Robbins

Harry Rossiter ex 115 Sq.
Frank Rutter ex 115 Sq.

75 Squadron Association members
Bob Smith Heating & Plumbing
Terry & Jean Strawson
Jack Tarran
Dr. Chris Thomas
Daphne Valentine ex 115 Sq.
R. & H. Wale Ltd
Charles Wyatt
Witchford Parish Council
Jim Woodbine
Ken Wooton

Alan Richardson Builders
Royal Naval Association members
Rogerson Plumbing & Heating
Archibald Russell ex 115 Sq.
115 Squadron Association members
Neil Stephens

Pip & Audrey Stowell
Roy Sutton
Sidney & Margot Thatcher
Jane Thomas
David & Yvonne Thorne
Charles Wernham ex 115 Sq.
Philip Williams ex 115 Sq.
Sam Wood ex 115 Sq.
Ray Woodbine
Dick Young

and all those kind people who have given us help in many ways over the last few years to keep the RAF Witchford Display of Memorabilia open.

Foreword from Sue

The reason for Barry writing this book is because there were so many airfields in this region during World War II and two right on our doorstep, RAF Witchford & RAF Mepal. For many years he had thought that there were no visual records on these two airfields and it was when he got involved with organising the exhibition in Ely Museum on World War II, then helping to excavate the remains of the Lancaster which crashed in Coveney, that he felt he wanted to find out more about these brave men who had lost their lives and also about the airfields. So in 1996 he started to research and started to write notes down for writing a book. Having his own Plumbing & Heating business it wasn't easy to spend a lot of time on it but he always said, "When I retire I can concentrate on 'the book' and get it published".

Sadly, Barry became unwell and had to give up work in 2010. His health deteriorated in 2012 through Alzheimer's and after 10 weeks in hospital, he moved into Soham Lodge Nursing Care home in October 2012.

I decided all Barry's (and my) hard work and time must not be wasted; this was local history and must be written down for future generations to read, so myself with three other helpers who have given me great support and encouragement, decided to finish the book off for Barry and get it published.

This book is dedicated to all those who lost their lives during World War II, especially those from RAF Witchford and RAF Mepal.

The profit from the sale of the books will go to the RAF Witchford Display of Memorabilia and Soham Lodge Nursing Care Home Residents' Fund.

Sue Aldridge.

Dedication by Barry

During the many years I have spent researching the incident I have corresponded with relatives and ex 115 Squadron members in New Zealand, Australia, Canada, South Africa and of course the United Kingdom. With their help and encouragement I have decided to write the story of the Witchford Intruder Incident. Some facts will never be known but I hope this book will go a long way towards telling the story of how 14 brave airmen lost their lives in a field known as Ashwell Moor at the foot of Coveney Hill, not far from Ely Cathedral and so close to the safety of their home airfield at Witchford.

I dedicate this book to their memory:

Lancaster KO-R LL667 MK II
Pilot Officer John (Jock) Birnie
Pilot Officer Arnold Feldman
Sergeant Edwin Kerwin
Sergeant Jack Ferguson
Sergeant William James McMillan
Flight Sergeant David Lloyd Jones
Sergeant George Edward Bailey

Lancaster A4-JLL867 MK I
Flight Lieutenant Charles Eddy MBE
Flying Officer Albert Smith
Flight Sergeant Harold Edward Pugh
Warrant Officer Henry Bennis
Sergeant William Leslie Murphy
Sergeant Alfred Frank Langridge
Flight Sergeant Peter Maddox

Barry Aldridge

Contents

PART 1: RAF Witchford

A first encounter with Witchford airfield

On one of those long hot summer school holidays we all seem to remember from our youth, I and three school chums wandered aimlessly down St. Johns Road in Ely, Cambridgeshire. The year was 1955, a time when parents could safely let their children roam and be almost sure that apart from getting into mischief, no harm would come to them.

Quite often Jim Green, Richard Barrowclough, Godfrey (Nonny) Clark and I would equip ourselves with a bottle of pop and a few biscuits and go off in search of adventure, down the droves of West Fen. On this occasion minus pop and biscuits we decided on a new route.

Passing the playing field formerly known as Mill Pits, we continued down St. Johns Road. On our left we came to Mill Cottages. This was where the made up road ended and the drove began. St. Johns Road in the early part of the century had been called Mill Road, once boasting two windmills.

Photo of windmill in Mill Road, Ely (now St. Johns Road) Photo taken around 1900

The rough unmade drove we were now entering had once been a route into Ely, leaving the main Cambridge Road near Little

Thetford. Within a few hundred yards we would come across the reason this route was now impossible. Soon the drove ended as we had now come to the point where the main Ely to Witchford Road cut across the drove.

On the other side of the road was the reason the drove no longer continued towards Little Thetford. There in front of us was the disused former RAF Witchford airfield. Completed in 1943 it had swept away many farms and also the remainder of the drove we had been following.

We crossed the road and entered one of the old crash exits. The main entrance being in the village itself. It was here that two of the three runways met like the point of a triangle. We took the right-hand runway and headed down towards a grey building, way in the distance to our right.

I can still remember how still and eerie it all seemed, on that hot day, with only the sound of several larks joining our boyish chatter. I also remember how cold that grey building felt when we entered and climbed the stairs of the old control tower. The windows were all smashed. There were three small rooms and one large room which had several cables dangling from the wall. None of us felt comfortable in this building and although none of us would admit to the other, I am sure we were all a bit scared. Of what, I do not know, but we did not stay long and soon left in search of another adventure. Little did I know that forty two years later I would get involved with Witchford airfield again. Now I look back and wish I had owned a camera and taken it on that day.

Like many other wartime airfields, nearly all traces of RAF Witchford have disappeared, including the control tower on whose balcony the King and Queen and the young Princess Elizabeth stood on 5th July 1944, during a Royal visit to Witchford. One of the three hangars still exists. It has been reclad and is now occupied by one of the many businesses that now occupy the site of the former airfield.

Former airfield hangar

One nice touch is that the names of the aircraft that once flew from here are remembered. The Business Park is called Lancaster Way and roads leading off are Stirling Way and Wellington Way.

On 21st May 1989, a memorial was unveiled and dedicated to the men of 115 Squadron who lost their lives in World War II. The memorial is situated just inside the entrance to the Business Park, at the point where two of the three runways met, forming the point of a triangle.

The Beginning of War

War began on Sunday September 3rd 1939.

A peal of bells was heard. Everyone listened to their wireless as Prime Minister, Neville Chamberlain, broadcast to the nation. Another speaker read Government notices about places of entertainment closing until further notice; how gas masks should always be carried and what people should do in an air raid. Sirens were heard. Boys started getting call up papers and soon left for their regiments. Some women joined the Auxiliary Territorial Services (A.T.S.).

National registration day was 29th September 1939, when every household had a form to fill in giving names of everyone living in the house.

Identity cards were then issued to everyone and food offices issued Ration Books to every household.

The lane in the photo on the next page was once a country lane leading to Bedwell Hey Farm and was also the entrance to the airfield of RAF Witchford during WWII.

The photo was taken near the airfield's Admin Centre and the village. The Sentry box can be seen to the left of the picture, complete with its 'Witchford Guard', which is surprising considering the high security of the time, when most signposts had been removed.

Bedwell Hey Lane Witchford on a cold and frosty morning in 1944

The Construction of Witchford Airfield

With the Battle of Britain over by the end of 1940, the Government could see the need for more airfields to enable our increasing Bomber Force to carry the war to the heart of Germany. All over East Anglia, farm land was being purchased ready for the contractors to move in, such was the case with the land between Witchford and Ely.

The Air Ministry Airfields Board was responsible for the selection of suitable sites. The requirements were that the land was reasonably flat and free from obstructions and between 50 and 600 feet above sea level.

The land between the small Cathedral City of Ely and the village of Witchford appeared to meet these requirements, as did land surrounded by the nearby villages of Sutton, Witchford and Mepal where RAF Mepal would be constructed at the same time as Witchford. Reconnaissance engineers were sent in to carry out a site inspection which would include checking the type of soil and drainage (although drainage would prove to be a problem). After a few days the engineers' investigations were complete and the site considered suitable for the construction of an airfield.

The next stage was the requisition of the land required, under the Emergency Powers (Defence) Act of 1939. Civilian building contractors were then invited to tender for the work.

Wartime airfields needed to be constructed quickly so high standard brick buildings, as used on pre-war airfields, were too labour intensive. Instead prefabricated buildings which could be erected quickly, such as Nissen huts and the T Type hangars, were used. Witchford and the many other airfields of its type were usually ready for operations within eighteen months of the first soil being turned. The achievement of turning muddy fields into operational airfields in such a short time can only be admired. So from the land which Hereward the Wake defended against the Normans, Witchford airfield was constructed to enable our bombers to launch attacks against another aggressor.

In 1941 Witchford, a quiet village with a population of just over four hundred situated 2 ½ miles from Ely, saw the influx of about two thousand five hundred workmen, a large proportion of which were free state Irish. The main contractors were Holland, Hannen and Cubit, who before the war were mainly house builders in the London area. At first some of the workmen were billeted with the villagers, but some being of a rather rough and ready appearance were inclined to get into bed with their work clothes on, including their boots. This did not go down too well, but huts were quickly erected to accommodate the workmen and generally they got on well with the people of Witchford. Some husbands were apprehensive about the safety of their wives and daughters after dark, especially as the navvies got drunk on a Saturday night. On Sunday morning they had usually sobered up in time to catch the buses, laid on by the contractor, to take them to church in Ely.

To construct the airfield, four farms and six farm cottages were demolished. Hundreds of lorries carried gravel onto the site, these were sometimes owned by van dwellers or men unfit for Military Service. They were paid either by the day or sometimes by the cubic yard. Draglines and excavators were brought to help with the digging out, as trees and hedges were pulled up and runways staked out. The earth was shovelled up and moved in huge dumpers. Goods trains arrived at Stretham Station carrying tons of brick rubble from buildings demolished in the Blitz in London. This was rolled out and used as a base for the concrete which was to be eight inches thick. Stretham Station was situated in Grunty Fen some distance from the village from which it took its name. Its distance from the village of Stretham was probably why the station was not well used by the residents of the village, but its position would be ideal for the new RAF Witchford airfield. Not only for bringing in some of the construction materials, but later when the airfield became operational, bombs were brought in by rail to the station, unloaded and transported only a short distance to the bomb dump.

The water supply to Witchford was a problem, so a new main was laid from Ely Water Tower to a new Braithwaite Tower constructed on the airfield. Another job was to lay a temporary pipe-line from Braham drain and to put an engine there to pump the water to temporary storage tanks. Although the construction of the runways was of prime importance, other smaller sections of the complex had also commenced. The Mess sites were being constructed on the northern side of the village. Where the village college now stands was (site 4) the Officers Mess and the generator which in the event of a power cut would be able to re-light the runway lights within three minutes.

The WAAF Quarters (site 11) were built in the Common Road and Sedgeway. On the west side of Sedgeway was (site 2 communal) the Institute and NAAFI Staff Quarters, the Gymnasium, the Chapel and Squash courts. Various shops were located here including Tailors, Barbers, Shoemakers, Grocery and local produce store.

Site 9 was constructed further up into the village, at the back of the Baptist chapel. This was where most of the contractor's buildings were sited, later to become Sergeants Quarters, Airmen Quarters, Ablutions blocks and a fuel compound.

Marroway Lane, a soft road, was made up and became site 5 communal. At first this was also used as a contractor site, and then became Sergeants and Officers Quarters with the necessary Latrines and Ablution blocks.

In total sites 2 to 14 were all situated well away from the airfield and well dispersed. This invasion of men and machinery must have been a big shock to the quiet life of the inhabitants of Witchford and the surrounding villages. Even the residents of the small Cathedral City of Ely had not seen anything like the influx of people arriving in the area. One of the major complaints made by the villagers during the construction work was about mud. As can be imagined with construction work of this magnitude, the main street became a mud bath. This was at its worst in January and February, when the mud in some places was six inches deep. After protests the contractors had to put mechanical sweepers on the road to sweep the mud to the road sides, where it was scooped up with shovels and hard labour.

The problems did not stop here, for the roads were still in a terrible state and when the March winds arrived and everything dried up, the dust storms started where the mud finished. To make things worse there was also a problem with cement.

Major construction work needs concrete and mortar and they are made up of a mixture of sand and cement, and with cement being a light grey powder it drifted easily in the wind. Much of it whipped up from the constant stream of lorries delivering the cement to the various sites. Much to the annoyance of the villagers, nearly every household gained a thin film of grey dust inside and out.

The aerodrome comprised one main runway 2,010 yards long x 50 yards wide, and two other runways laid to form a triangle, one at 1,408 yards long x 50 yards wide and one at 1,415 yards long x 50 yards wide. These runways were connected to a perimeter track from which branched dispersal points, dotted around the airfield, so that in the event of an attack by enemy aircraft, all Squadron aircraft would not be caught in one place.

The Bomb Stores site was constructed near Bedwell Hey Farm, this was a large area laid out to accommodate the bombs which used to arrive at Stretham Station by the train load. They were then transferred via Grunty Fen Road and through Witchford Main Street, which was not an ideal situation. Later, at the suggestion of local man Frank Allen, a short piece of road was constructed northwards of Stretham Station to the bomb dump, which shortened the journey and kept the trailer loads of bombs away from built up areas.

Witchford Main Street circa 1930s, before the arrival of the contractors who built Witchford airfield. Photo from the Cambridgeshire Collection

The same view 1998. The entrance to the airfield (Bedwell Hey Lane) was in the far distance where the white building can be seen on the right hand side of the photo.

Frank Allen was to be of help to the RAF again when most of their bomb carrying trailers became unusable. The problem with the bomb trailers was caused when the bombs were unloaded from the waggons at Stretham Station and loaded onto trailers. WAAFs were driving the Coles` cranes used for the unloading. They had no difficulty in lifting the bombs, but the lowering was controlled by a hand operated brake which not only required skill but strength to ensure a smooth decent of the bombs. Unfortunately, many of the bombs came down hard on the wooden planking of the trailers, causing many of them to be put out of action.

The Allen family lived on the left hand corner as you turned into Bedwell Hey Lane, which up until the construction of the airfield had led to Bedwell Hey Farm and on to the village of Little Thetford, across the A10 Ely to Cambridge Road. Once the construction of the airfield began, the lane was severed by the runways and the Witchford end of Bedwell Hey Lane became the main entrance to the airfield. Apart from living on the corner of the lane where it joined Main Street, the Allen family also had their builder's yard and workshops here.

One day Frank Allen was approached by one of the Armourers who asked if he had any timber to repair the trailers (At this time timber was in short supply). Mr Allen asked the Armourer what had happened to all the trees which had been removed to make way for the runways. The Armourer replied that they were all stacked to one side of the airfield. Mr Allen said that if the trees were transported to his yard, he had the machinery to cut them into one and a quarter inch thick planks, which could then be bolted on to the trailers. This was done, and the trailers were soon back in use.

Frank Allen's name will appear several times in this book. Frank sadly died aged 89 years in 1997. His knowledge and help in the writing of this book has been invaluable. A kind man and a great character, he will be greatly missed by the people of Witchford. Several pages of the stories he related will be found later in this book.

Control Tower

Sadly I have been unable to find a complete photograph of Witchford's` Watch Tower or Control Tower as they are more commonly known.

Below is a photograph of nearby Mepal's Control Tower which was identical to the one at Witchford and was demolished shortly after this photo was taken.

Photo of Mepal Control Tower
Photo: David Thorne

RAF Administration staff started to arrive at Witchford early in 1943, before the construction work had finished. A Guard room and barriers were set up in Bedwell Hey Lane and M.P.s (Military police) were on duty night and day. Other exits and entrances were well guarded.

The Administration site had been constructed on the right hand side of the lane before you reached the guard room. After passing the Guard room you would enter the Technical site. On your right was the Fire party hut and a short distance to your left was the Fire tender house. Now most of the site was on your left, with the exception of the works servicing buildings, and further on, the Flight offices. The rest of the Technical site curved round the back of one of the T2 type hangars, and included buildings such as, the Photographic block, Gas Defence centre, Crew lockers and drying room, Squadron offices, Dinghy shed, Fuel compound and Parachute stores etc. – a total of well over one hundred and fifty buildings.

There were three hangars; two were situated just off the perimeter track adjacent to the 1,415 yard long runway, one of which was a B1 type and the other a T2. The third, another T2, was situated adjacent to the perimeter track which ran alongside the 2,010 yard long runway. The B1 hangar was first introduced in 1942, and could accommodate all the RAF aircraft types. The two T2 hangars have long since been demolished at Witchford, but the B1 remains, and is presently used by one of the many businesses on Lancaster Way Business Park.

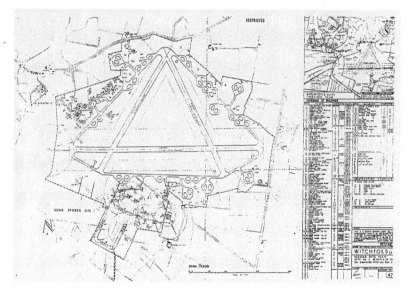

Map of site plan

The arrival of Witchford airfield and likewise nearby Mepal which was constructed and opened at the same time, would affect the lives of local people, just as other airfields were affecting others in towns and villages throughout Eastern England.

Even Ely Cathedral had been affected by the arrival of the two local airfields, as a red navigation light had been fitted at the top of the West Tower. The Bishop of Ely was somewhat concerned about the light on two counts, one the colour of the light on a religious building and two, whether it would make the Cathedral a target for German aircraft. He was assured by the C.O. at Witchford that the light had to be red and it would only be switched on when absolutely necessary.

I think that Bishop Wynn's comments on the red light were somewhat tongue in cheek, showing that the church had a sense of humour.

1944 – As dusk descends, two of Witchford's 115 Squadron's Lancasters are seen here in the Type T2 hangar situated on the west side of the airfield. Photo: Henry McCartney

This photograph was taken from a Lancaster in late 1944 by Corporal Douglas West of RAF Witchford's photographic section. The Cathedral must have been a welcome sight to crews returning from operations in the early hours of daylight. In the hours of darkness during take off and landings, a red navigation light on top of the west tower would be switched on.

At first glance, not much seems to have changed since 1944, but the Gas Works (top far right), the Corn Exchange on the Market Place (far left) and the Brewery have long since gone.

Aerial view of Ely

In order to be able to identify one airfield from another from the air, a two letter code system was used. These letters were displayed on the ground as 10 feet high white letters near the control tower in the signals square. The two letters used were usually taken from the airfield's name, ie. RAF Mepal's letters were M P. With so many airfields being built, a repeat of letters would eventually be inevitable, so several deviations were made, as with Witchford's , whose Pundit code (as the letters were known) were E L and were taken from the name of nearby Ely.

Another system had to be found for identification during the hours of darkness and this was done by a beacon that flashed in red light the identity letters in Morse code. Witchford and Mepal airfields became operational at the same time, July 1943. Mepal airfield was situated about three miles further along the

B142 (now A142) from Witchford and six miles from Ely. The airfield had three villages on it's boundries: Sutton, Witcham and Mepal. Although the airfield was closer to Sutton and most of the domestic sites and entrance in Witcham, the airfield could not be named after them, as airfields already existed with similar sounding names. So Mepal was the obvious choice.

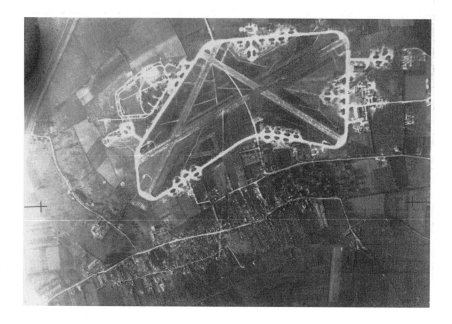

Above – Aerial photo of RAF Mepal. Sutton village can be seen at the bottom and Mepal village just off the top. Witcham village, where the main entrance to the airfield was situated, is just off the top right of the photo. All of the domestic buildings were also in this area.

The photograph was taken from a 75 Squadron Lancaster piloted by Colin Burch in the spring of 1944.

When the building of Witchford and Mepal was completed, only 1.4 miles separated Site 13 at Mepal (the sick quarters) and Site 5 at Witchford (Officers and Sergeants quarters). The circuits of the airfields also overlapped and it was a credit to ground control and skill of the pilots that collisions were not common place, although it did happen on one occasion, luckily without tragic results. Landing at the wrong airfield also happened on a few occasions when tired crews returned in poor visibility.

Aerial view of RAF Witchford airfield 1944

With major construction work, accidents can always happen and the airfield at Witchford was no exception.

On one occasion when the trees were being removed to make way for the runways, a heavy earth moving machine was employed to pull them up by the roots with a wire rope. Suddenly the rope snapped snaking across the ground like a scythe, cutting both legs off one of the workmen.

On another occasion, a hut-full of Irish workmen were overcome by coke fumes from the stove in their hut when they were asleep. After this, instructions were given that some windows must be left open at all times.

On a further occasion, some of the navvies returning from an evening drinking session, accidently burned down their canteen.

Madge Baxter, formerly Leonard, remembers the arrival of the contractors who were to construct the airfield.

Our village was built mainly on either side of the long Main Street and like most villages it was fairly quiet.

In 1937 my parents decided to have a bungalow built on the land opposite to the house we rented from Mrs. Dolby. When the bungalow was completed they decided to turn it into a small shop. There was one other shop in the village at this time called 'Tricker's Stores'.

War had been declared in 1939 but it was 1941 when the quiet of the village was broken with the arrival of thousands of construction workers. At first we had no idea what was happening but rumour soon went round that they had come to build an airfield.

Soon huts were erected to accommodate the workers who were mainly Irish. You can imagine the shock to the village, and many husbands were concerned about wives' and daughters' safety after dark, with so many strange men around.

The Main Street soon became quite a mess with mud and dust everywhere. For myself and my parents at the shop it was the start of a new life. Every night when the Irishmen left off work they would call at the shop for bread, tobacco and other goods. I remember we used to order over 200 loaves per day.

The workmen would get off the bus and queue from the shop doorway to the road. We had to lock the back gate otherwise they would come in the back door as well, but they were really a lovely crowd. As they came into the shop they would say, " 1oz Bacci Missie and a loaf".

Some nights when we cycled home from the pictures in Ely, the roads would be crowded with Irishmen walking back to their huts in Witchford. Dad was worried about me cycling home so I started to use the bus instead.

When the airfield and domestic sites were completed and the RAF had moved in, our trade increased and the shop had to be extended.

Although the war was on, we met some very nice people and I often wonder if any of these boys in blue or the Irishmen, remember Leonard's Stores.

The Cinema / Theatre and Ballroom at RAF Witchford

When 513 Squadron was disbanded without Stirlings ever becoming operational, several buildings became surplus to requirements. Site No. 3 (Mess site) off Common Road was no exception and the group of buildings numbered 219 were soon put to a new use.

The Cinema / Theatre took up one part of the group of linked buildings with the Ballroom taking up another. The Cinema / Theatre was completed in late 1943 and the Ballroom in early 1944.

These two photographs show views of both ends of the Cinema / Theatre.

The artistic talents of RAF Witchford's airmen can be seen on the wall behind the stage. The band can be seen on the far left of the stage.

The Cinema / Theatre had tiered seating with a more comfy seated, roped off area for the officers. Many plays and variety acts were performed on this stage with the Station Concert Party making their debut appearance on the theatre's completion. The Cinema screen was located in the roof section behind the curtain. It could be raised when there was a stage show. The sound speakers were a bass one as big as a very large sideboard and a tweeter which was hinged to the top of the front edge. It could be folded into the base cabinet when not in use, and they could be wheeled away for safe keeping.

The Ballroom: looking from the bandstand towards the entrance hall that was linked to the Cinema / Theatre. Half way down the hall was a raised area. The photo was taken after the asphalt floor was laid. Note the glitter ball.

As everyone takes partners for the next dance

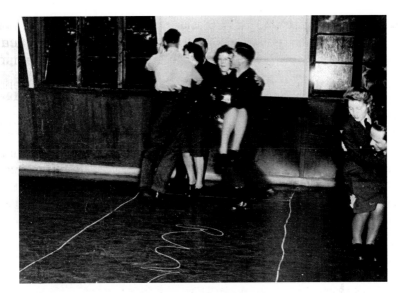

'Crossing the River'

This photograph shows a game being played called `Crossing the River`. When the music stopped you had to pick your partner up and carry her over the river (Chalk markings on the floor indicate the river). If the music stopped and you were still in the river you were out of the game.

The Debut of the Station Concert Party

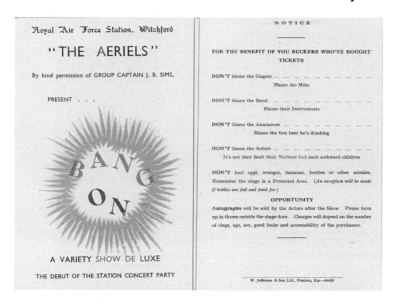

Royal Air Force Station, Witchford

"THE AERIELS"

By kind permission of GROUP CAPTAIN J. B. SIMS,

PRESENT . . .

BANG ON

A VARIETY SHOW DE LUXE

THE DEBUT OF THE STATION CONCERT PARTY

NOTICE

FOR THE BENEFIT OF YOU SUCKERS WHO'VE BOUGHT
TICKETS

DON'T blame the Singers ... ...
Blame the Mike

DON'T blame the Band ... ...
Blame their Instruments

DON'T blame the Announcer ... ...
Blame the free beer he's drinking

DON'T blame the Actors ... ...
It's not their fault their Mothers had such awkward children

DON'T hurl eggs, oranges, bananas, bottles or other missiles.
Remember the stage is a Protected Area. (*An exception will be made
if bottles are full and paid for.*)

OPPORTUNITY

Autographs will be sold by the Actors after the Show. Please form
up in threes outside the stage door. Charges will depend on the number
of rings, age, sex, good looks and accessibility of the purchasers.

W. Jefferson & Son Ltd., Printers, Ely—44426

Front and back cover of a variety show programme

Photo of the company. Centre of photo is Section Officer
Jacqueline Freeman-Mathews.

PROGRAMME

1. The Gang salutes you .... The Company
2. Busy Bee ...... Ernie, Archie and Bobbie
3. The Barrack Room Piano ...... Freddy
4. Four Nice Girls ...... Shirley, Joyce, Joanne and Irene
5. All Star Broadcast ...... Archie
6. Three Shades of Blue ...... Fred, Jack and Ellis
7. Witchford Dramatic and Pub. Crawling Society in :—
   (a) Mother of Two ...... ⎱ Jacqueline, Ernie, Jock and
   (b) One in every Unit ...... ⎰ the Fun Section
8. Electric Melodies ...... Jim
9. An Odd Spot of Bother ...... Ernie, Maxie and Archie
10. A little bit o' Irish ...... Paddy
11. Parson's (k)nose ...... Jock

INTERVAL

12. The Aerolites' Dance Orchestra
13. Maxie mixies it ...... Maxie
14. Top Hat and Tails ...... Shirley and Joanne
15. Good Advice ...... Joyce
16. Slightly Sophisticated ...... Rollanda
17. More Mystery ...... Ernie, Maxie and Archie
18. Old Favourites ...... Dicky
19. Agony Column ...... Ernie, Maxie and Jacqueline
20. Accordeonly Yours ...... Eric
21. Meet the Gang ...... The Company

THE KING

This Programme may be subject to slight alteration

THE COMPANY

The 'Aerolites' Dance Orchestra

Leader	L.A.C. Jock Robinson
Saxophonist	A.C. Ken Barkham
Drums	A.C. Freddie Winstone
Piano-Accordian	L.A.C. Eric Dennant
	Cpl. Len Levitt
Vocalists	L.A.C.W. Bobby Roberts

F/O. Roy Lawrence	Compere
Cpl. Ernie Warner	Comedy Sketches
Cpl. Archie Pidcock	Impressionist
L.A.C. Maxie Malloy	Comedian
S/O. Jacqueline Freeman-Mathews	Sketches
L.A.C. Dicky Bird	Ballads
L.A.C. Paddy Higgins	Ballads
L.A.C. Ellis Goldstone	
Cpl. Jack Curtis	Three in Harmony
Cpl. Fred Cooper	
L.A.C.W. Shirley Sanderson ⎫	
Cpl. Irene Lambart ⎬	Dancers
A.C.W. Joanne Bradley ⎭	
Cpl. Jim Dolan	Guitar
Sgt. Joyce Barron	Dancer and Monologues
Sgt. 'Alex' Alexander	Illusionist
Sgt. Jock Davies	Lesson
L.A.C. Michael McVitty	Accompanist

PRODUCTION	By all means possible
Stage Management	By accident
Technical advice	Gas and Fire Section
Lighting	Coal, Gas & Coke Co. Ltd.
Perfume	Lifebuoy
Gowns	Deep Sea Diving Suit Co. Ltd.
Make-up	British Camouflage Co. Ltd.

Inside of a variety show programme

The Initial Opening of RAF Witchford as recorded in the Station Records.

On the 7th June 1943, an initial opening party of eighteen NCOs left RAF Mepal where it had been formed under the command of Squadron Leader J. Blackmore. The party arrived at Witchford at 19.00 hours. The last meal of the day having been taken at Mepal, Squadron Leader Blackmore was to take command of RAF Station Witchford, while at the same time retaining command of RAF Mepal until relief was due to be posted in on the 28th.

Both Witchford and Mepal were to temporarily work as Satellite Stations for RAF Waterbeach. The opening up party took over accommodation at No. 3 Dormitory site which was 100% complete with linoleum laid, flush lavotories, blackouts and running water all installed. The main Guardroom was temporarily set up, while another Nissan hut was used as a General Office, Orderly room, Disciplinary NCO and Transport.

8/6/43

The first unit routine orders and station standing orders were published. No. 6 Dormitory site was taken over, equally complete as No. 3. At No. 2 site, comprising Officers and Sergeants messes and airmen's dining hall, the Picquet Post (temporarily used as Officers Mess), Fuel compound and shower baths for all three messes, were all ready for immediate use.

10/6/43

A considerate amount of Barrack room furniture arrived by road, by day and night. All Barrack equipment being temporarily stored in half of the airmen's dining hall and the Sergeant's Mess dining hall, prior to distribution to all of the various sites.

11/6/43

Technical equipment commenced to arrive, this being housed in the main stores. RAF Witchford held it's first pay parade.

13/6/43

Squadron Leader Blackmore moved his quarters from Mepal to Witchford.

21/6/43

First WAAF Personnel began to arrive and were accommodated at No. 6 Dormitory site.

22/6/43

A fitting party of one Sergeant and three airmen commenced fitting the T.R.9. in the Watch Office.

23/6/43

The swill contract was signed by Ely Butcher Mr. William Rayment.

24/6/43

Colonel Cutlack, a Director of the Ely Brewery, was contacted by the C.O. and an adequate supply of beer etc. was promised for the Officers and Sergeants Messes, ready for when the squadrons arrived. Pilot Officer W. Skinner Fire Officer from RAF Waterbeach inspected all fire fighting appliances, hydrants etc. on the station.

27/6/43

Fifty nine Personnel and one Officer of an anti-aircraft flight of the RAF Regiment arrived.

28/6/43

A G.P.O. Letter box was erected and ready for use in a central place convenient to all Mess sites and the institute.

30/6/43

A considerate quantity of RAF comforts arrived in the form of games, books and wireless sets. Comments were made in the Station Operation book regarding the general state of the site.

Positioning of Dormitory and Mess sites

These are pleasantly situated to the north of the village of Witchford and about three miles from the City of Ely. No site is more than a quarter of a mile from the village and the main road, with Mess sites considerably nearer. All sites are approached by the conventional concrete roads, which were originally pleasant country lanes. The rural amenities have fortunately not however been spoiled by contractors' construction work and hedges and trees have not been interfered with or demolished. This considerably enhances the pleasant atmosphere which pervades the entire site. The sleeping quarters are all placed in a convenient semi-circle around the Mess site, so that distances to be traversed are not excessive. All these features add to the comfort and wellbeing of all personnel generally. All sites so far taken over are well constructed and finished. A YMCA mobile van visits the site three mornings per week.

The strength of the Station is:

RAF	Officers	1
	Sergeants	2
	Other ranks	31
RAF Regiment	Officers	1
	Sergeants	3
	Other ranks	60
WAAF	Corporals	1
	Other ranks	9

The Officers and Sergeants Messes have clear glass fitted in the essential rooms so that a view of the surrounding countryside may be enjoyed, whilst the anti-rooms have been well positioned so as to obtain the maximum sun and light.

The Station Commander at the RAF General Hospital in Ely has invited all personnel to attend dances, concerts and other forms of entertainment, held in the Welfare hut.

The village of Witchford has already been equipped with full postal facilities prior to the arrival of the opening up party, by the foresight of the Head Postmaster at Ely.

Sick Parade

This is now held at RAF Mepal, only three miles away, thereby saving the long journey to RAF Waterbeach.

Education

The Education Officer from RAF Waterbeach visits the station each Tuesday afternoon for the benefit of all airmen.

Recreation

A Recreation hut and games room has been set up on No. 3 Dormitory site where wireless, daily newspapers and a variety of indoor games are available. A consignment of books has been loaned by the County Library at March. These books will be changed from time to time, whilst 200 volumes have been received from the RAF Comforts Fund.

Showers / Baths

These are available for all on Mess site No. 2, thus saving bathing parades to RAF Waterbeach. These are limited to three days per week in order to economise on fuel.

NAAFI

NAAFI supplies are to be sent over twice weekly from RAF Waterbeach.

Gradually, day by day and bit by bit, RAF Station Witchford was fast approaching becoming an operational airfield. On 6th July 1943 Wing Commander Alexander and several specialist officers from 196 Squadron at Leconfield in Yorkshire, arrived at Witchford to inspect the airfield and facilities prior to their squadron's move to this new airfield later in the month. Also making an inspection on this day was Squadron Leader D. Stafford-Clark, Senior Medical Officer at

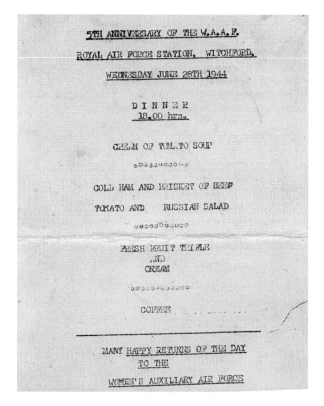

5TH ANNIVERSARY OF THE W.A.A.F.

ROYAL AIR FORCE STATION, WITCHFORD.

WEDNESDAY JUNE 28TH 1944

D I N N E R
18.00 hrs.

CREAM OF TOMATO SOUP

COLD HAM AND BRISKET OF BEEF

TOMATO AND   RUSSIAN SALAD

FRESH FRUIT TRIFLE
AND
CREAM

COFFEE

MANY HAPPY RETURNS OF THE DAY
TO THE
WOMEN'S AUXILIARY AIR FORCE

The NAAFI and the WAAF's Anniversary menu

Waterbeach, who had arrived to inspect the station's sewage works and sick quarters etc.

7/7/43

Squadron Leader J.E. Day (organisation Headquarters 3 Group) Exning and Flight Lieutenant Poston (electrical engineer) from 3 Group, visited the station.

9/7/43

Squadron Leader J. Healy and other engineer officers from RAF Waterbeach made a complete inspection of the station from the maintenance point of view.

10/7/43

The Station Commander Group Captain G.I.L. Saye OBE DFC held a conference in the officers mess relating to the state of readiness of the station for occupation by 196 Squadron on the 19th of July inst.

The following officers were present at the meeting:

The Senior Administration Officer (Witchford), Signals Officer, Intelligence and Mechanical Transport Officer, all from Waterbeach. Also present at the meeting was the Resident Engineer, Mr. C.P. Coleman, the M & E Supervisor Mr. S.S. Copsey and the contractor's agent. It was found that the station was in an extremely good state of readiness to receive an operational squadron, considering the early take-over and only a few minor points were found necessary to be accelerated. This was mainly due to the energy of the resident engineer and the excellent co-operation he had received from his Clerk of Works and the Contractors on the construction side, and on the RAF side, to the vigilance of the Station Commander from RAF Waterbeach and the extremely fine work accomplished by his Senior Signals and Equipment Officers, Flight Lieutenant E.A. Fawcet and Flight Lieutenant C.W. Gains respectively.

15/7/43

Thirteen crews left Leconfield for Conversion Units at Waterbeach, Stradishall and Woolfox Lodge.

16/7/43

WAAF Personnel moved from No. 6 Dormitory to No. 2 WAAF site.

17/7/43

The squadron's heavy equipment was loaded onto the train at Beverly while all personnel were engaged in packing etc. Pilot Officer C. Priestley arrived for signals duties from Headquarters 3 Group Exning. Squadron Leader Wigfall and Flight Lieutenant Luff arrived at Witchford with an advance party numbering 32 Personnel of 196 Squadron from Leconfield.

23/7/43

Aircrew personnel consisting of a few incomplete crew members went to 1651 Conversion Unit at Waterbeach, apart from the Commanding Officer and the navigation gunnery, bombing and signal leaders. All aircrew are now away at one conversion unit or another.

24/7/43

During the past week there has been nothing to report, owing to the aircrew personnel being away at various conversion units and some of the maintenance crews being away at Waterbeach.

25/7/43

Pilot Officer C.H. Hinkel arrived on posting from RAF Sunburgh for meteorological duties. The remainder of 4787 A.C. Flight (works) comprising of one Warrant Officer, one Sergeant and forty other ranks arrived from RAF Bassingbourn. Section Officer M.J.A. Harris who arrived on the 21st ceased to be attached and returned to 3 Group Headquarters.

26/7/43

Section Officer L. Nimmo-Watson arrived on attachment from 3 Group Headquarters for WAAF duties. There was much activity throughout the new airfield and its domestic sites in preparation for the station to become operational. Medical Officer Flight Lieutenant J. Bryson had arrived at Witchford on the 11/7/43 to take charge of the station sick quarters and recorded on the 16/7/43 that parts of the station sick quarters were now ready for use. The consulting room was equipped with six beds and an area had been screened off for treatment room. After 196 Squadron arrived at Witchford he carried out an inspection of the entire camp which he found to be generally satisfactory. The feeding arrangements were good and the water supply was pure. A test taken later gave a satisfactory report. On all the living sites, sanitation is by water carriage system, and although the plant was not complete, it was coping well.

On 12/8/43 the Senior Medical Officer for 3 Group also arrived and carried out an inspection of the station sick quarters, airmen's mess and the sewage works.

A film on V.D. was shown to all male personnel on the camp on the 18/8/43, resulting in a slight increase in the average sick parade for a few subsequent mornings and in two cases the film led to the discovery of V.D.

On the last day of July 1943, Group Captain G.I.L. Saye OBE A.F.C. visited the station and interviewed Mr. Pratt (part 2 Clerk of Works) about the readiness of the station.

August saw 196 Squadron returning from various conversion units where they had converted from the Wellington to the Stirling MK II with which the squadron would now be fully equipped.

The Aircraft Arrive

196 Squadron – The First Squadron Moves to Witchford

The 196 Squadron was originally formed at Driffield on the 7th November 1942 moving to Leconfield on the 22nd December 1942 as part of 4 Group commencing operations in February 1943. The squadron was equipped with Wellington IIIs and Xs and flew 33 bombing and 23 mining operations from Leconfield, totalling 517 sorties for a total of 13 aircraft lost. The squadron moved from Witchford on the 18th November 1943 to take up glider towing and transport duties outside Bomber Command at Leicester East.

On the night of the 13th July 1943, 196 Squadron sent nine Wellington Bombers on a maximum effort to Aachen, from their Yorkshire base at Leconfield. All aircraft returned safely to base with the exception of one aircraft that landed at Harwell. This was the last time the squadron would operate from Leconfield and the last time they would fly Wellingtons.

The squadron was not required for operations on the 14th and, as orders had been received for the unit to move to RAF Witchford near Ely in Cambridgeshire on the 19th, all further flying for the squadron from Leconfield ceased. The original intention was to move the squadron personnel and a large quantity of its equipment by glider, but circumstances prevented this and the squadron moved to Witchford by road and rail.

Both Witchford and Mepal airfields were originally intended to become satellite airfields for RAF Waterbeach which was used as a training base, but before both airfields were completed it was decided to make Waterbeach an operational station again, so both airfields became sub stations of Waterbeach.

16/7/43

Witchford opened in June 1943 under 3 Group, but it was the 16th July before an advance party of thirty two from 196 Squadron left Leconfield in Yorkshire under command of Squadron Leader Wigfall. The following day the squadron's heavy equipment was loaded onto a train at Beverley, while all other personnel were engaged in packing at the airfield.

18/7/43

On a cloudy day on the 18th July the final preparations were made for the move.

19/7/43

196 Squadron moved by road, rail and air to Witchford which saw the arrival of it's first aircraft, Wellington Xs. The move was accomplished without incident. The Air Officer commanding Headquarters No. 3 Group, Air Vice Marshal R. Harrison C.B.E., A.F.C., Group Captain G.I.L. Saye OBE, A.F.C. and Wing Commander H.E. Hills OBE (S.O.A.) visited RAF Witchford during the morning, just prior to the arrival of No. 196 Squadron. They inspected the aerodrome and the messes and expressed entire satisfaction with the way in which the station had been opened. The main party of 196 Squadron commenced to arrive after lunch, some by special train to Ely Station (L.N.E.R.) and some by road. Most had arrived by 15.30 hours, when a hot meal was served to all ranks. The Sergeants Mess opened up; the first meal, being the above mentioned. Almost immediately 196 Squadron began converting to Stirlings IIIs.

20/7/43

Squadron Leader J. Blackmore who had been in command of the opening up party at Witchford on the 7th June, was informed by telephone by Wing Commander Hills OBE (S.O.A.) that he was to proceed to RAF Little Snoring to open up that station. Flying Officer D. Bishop was posted in from 1651 Conversion Unit for Armament duties.

21/7/43

One Sergeant and nineteen other ranks of 4787 A.C. Flight (works) arrived on attachment. Section Officer M.J.A. Harris arrived on temporary WAAF `G` duty from Headquarters N3 Group permanent pool.

22/7/43

Squadron Leader A.D. Drysdale arrived on attachment for S.A.O. Duties. Squadron Leader Blackmore proceeded to RAF Snoring in Norfolk. Two Stirling aircraft arrived at Witchford on allotment to 196 Squadron. Flight Officer K. Rolfe-Rogers, Senior WAAF Admin Officer from RAF Waterbeach inspected the WAAF accommodation.

23/7/43

On the 23rd July several incomplete aircrew members left to begin training with 1651 Conversion Unit at Waterbeach. Apart from the Commanding Officer, the Navigators, Gunnery, Bombing and Signal Leaders, all aircrews were away at one conversion unit or another. Between the 11th August and the 15th the aircrews began to return to Witchford. 196 Squadron began main force operations at the end of the month.

196 Squadron losses whilst at Witchford

24/8/43

196 began flying from Witchford with their III Stirlings on 24/8/43. Four aircraft took off from Witchford between 12.47 hours and 13.12.

Stirling III EH 952 ZO-A took off from Witchford at 12.47 hours on an air/sea rescue operation. The aircraft came down in the sea at 100km west of Esbjerg, Denmark where the crew were picked up by Danish fishing vessel. The crew of Sergeants P.W. Brett, R.A. Treadwell, E.W.J. Kerr, D.H. Canning, L.H. Huggins, D.F. Moore and E. Lawton had the unwanted distinction of losing the squadron`s first stirling bomber.

Stories of planes ditching in the sea have been told in 'The Goldfish Club', a book by Danny Danziger.

31/8/43

Stirling III EH 961 ZO-D took off at 20.37 hours operation to Berlin. The aircraft was shot down by a night fighter and crashed at 23.28 hours 9km south of Enschede, Holland. Sergeants J. Griffiths, G.P. Poynter, G.A. Sperring and G.S. Auld RCAF were all taken as POWs. Sergeant C.P. Pierce RCAF, Flying Officer D.L.P.Justice and Sergeant I. Llewellyn were all killed.

5-6/9/43

Stirling III EE 964 ZO-F took off at 20.00 hours operation Mannheim, crashed at Bachenau, cause unknown. Pilot Officer F. Norris, Flight Sergeant R.R. Whitaker RAAF, Sergeant G.W. Moss, Flight Sergeant T.C. Foster, Flight Officer K.A.C. Ayling, Sergeant F.J. Brown and Sergeant A.E.G. Price were all killed. Sergeant R.A. Newman was taken as POW.

5-6/9/43

Stirling III EE 973 ZO-U took off at 20.11 hours operation Mannheim, lost the starboard outer engine when it was hit by flak over Speyer. Crash landed at Witchford at 0.300 hours after a low level return. Squadron Leader D.M. Edmundson, Sergeant T.Y. Byrne, Pilot Officer R. Lawton, Sergeant H. Towers, Pilot Officer S. Yardley and Sergeant N.S. MacEwen were unhurt. Sergeant C.H.A. Redding was injured.

16-17/9/43

Stirling III EF 114 ZO-H took off at 20.13 hours operation Modane, crashed at Heurtevent, near Livarot, France, cause unknown. The crew of Flight Sergeant N.N. Wakeley RNZAF, Sergeant W.A. Gilbert, Pilot Officer H.A.N. Kitchen RCAF and Sergeants A.S. Taylor, S.T. Flatman, G.F. Pyott and G.E. Kane were all killed.

27-28/9/43

Stirling III BK 663 ZO-K took off at 19.54 hours operation Hannover. An electrical fault prevented the release of the bomb load. Further problems developed when the aircraft was hit by flak while crossing the Dutch Coast. The aircraft crash landing on land between Ely and the village of Stuntney while on approach to landing at Witchford. Sergeants F.W.J. Weaver, T.W. Perry, R.J. Rouse, H. Wooton, R.M. Oakes RAAF and

D.R.R. Pepall escaped unhurt, but Sergeant M. Stern was injured.

3-4/10/43

Stirling III EF 464 ZO-P took off 18.56 hours operation Kassel. Attacked by night fighter and turned back with engine problems, crashing at 21.43 hours, 4 miles from North Walsham, Norfolk. Flight Sergeant G.H. Kogel, Sergeants T.D. Wiliams, A.W. Clarke, R.L. George, J.A. Beattie and F. Reeves were injured. Sergeant T.L. Dickie was killed.

8-9/10/43

Stirling III EF 494 ZO-C took off 22.58 hours operation Bremen. Losing power from both starboard engines the pilot was forced to bring the aircraft down in the sea at Hemsby, Norfolk close to the beach. It was not until later that he discovered he had landed in the middle of a mine field. The crew of Pilot Officer P. Dyson, Sergeants P.A. Hooker, D.L. Northover, Warrant Officer C.B. Rattigan RCAF, Flight Sergeants D.G. Denning and J.L. Parker were unhurt. Flight Lieutenant R.N.P. Luff was injured and sent by ambulance to the RAF Hospital in Ely, Cambridgeshire, while the rest of the crew spent the night at a Wrens listening post close to where the aircraft came down.

Stirling III EH 960 ZO-X took off on a morning Airtest on 17/10/43. The Stirling crashed in the Wash following loss of control due to excessive vibration. There were no survivors from the crew of Flying Officer J.L. Deans DFC, Sergeant K.L. Walace, Flying Officer F. J. Chapman, Sergeants T. McDonnell and J.L. Lane, Flight Sergeant N. Butts DFM RCAF and Flight Lieutenant J.G. Griffith. Four of the crews have no known graves including Flight Lieutenant Griffith who had accompanied the crew in his capacity as a Squadron Engineering Officer to help detect the fault with the aircraft.

Fate and Stirling EH 960 ZO-X

Electrical Engineer Flight Lieutenant Douglas Humphery had a narrow escape concerning the above mentioned aircraft. But for a German air raid, it would have been he and not Flight Lieutenant Griffith who accompanied the crew of ZO-X on the ill fated air test. On the 16th October Flight Lieutenant Humphery went on a 24 hour leave to visit his mother at Broxborne in Kent. He was due to return early the next day for the air test of ZO-X which had developed a fault, which at the time was thought to be an electrical problem. On arriving at Broxborne station early the next morning he was informed that, due to an air raid on London that night, some trains had been cancelled. Douglas eventually arrived at Ely Railway Station at 11.00am instead of 9.00am, and he still had to cycle the 3 miles back to Witchford airfield. As he neared the airfield on the B142 an aircraft took off on the short runway and passed over his head, this aircraft was Stirling EH 960 ZO-X, the very one he should have been on. His place had been taken by Flight Lieutenant Griffith, a University graduate who was very keen to take any opportunity to fly. Douglas returned to his office and was informed, some 3 hours later that the Stirling had gone missing and that no trace of it could be found.

For 55 years Douglas Humphery still believed that no trace of the Stirling had ever been found, until I sent him a copy of the accident report which can be seen below.

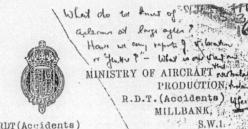

TELEPHONE: FRANKLIN 2211.

Extn. _____

Any communications on the
subject of this letter should be
addressed to :—
THE SECRETARY.

Our Reference G.36698/43/RDT(Accidents)

Your Reference _____

MINISTRY OF AIRCRAFT
PRODUCTION,
R.D.T.(Accidents)
MILLBANK,
S.W.1.

3rd January, 1944.

The Director,
Royal Aircraft Establishment,
South Farnborough,
Hants.

For the attention of S.M.E. Department.

Accident to Stirling III, EH.960

Stirling EH.960, 196 Squadron, R.A.F., was involved
in an accident on 17th October, 1943, in the following
circumstances:

It took off from Witchford on a 30 minute air test,
following action to eliminate excessive vibration reported
on a previous test after an engine change, and nothing more
was heard of the aircraft for some six weeks.   On
13th November, 1943, a signal was received at Air Ministry
from 196 Squadron reporting that the Salvage Officer at
Kings Lynn had salvaged the aircraft and identified two
of the occupants.

The Court of Enquiry was held on 17th October, 1943.
The C.I.(Accidents) has not investigated the accident.

The only substantial outcome of the investigation
is the following remarks by the Commanding Officer of the
Squadron:

"As a result of this Court of Enquiry no information

Part of EH 960 accident report

195 Squadron

Badge of 195 Squadron

195 Squadron did not arrive at Witchford but was in fact formed there or, as should correctly be said, reformed.

195 Squadron had originally been an Army Co-operation Squadron from 1942 until disbanded in February 1944. On the 1st October 1944, 195 was reformed as a Lancaster Squadron in 3 Group at Witchford. Instructions were received at RAF Witchford from Admin at 3 Group Headquarters for the formation of 195 Squadron to take place on the authority of Bomber Command letter BC/S 21717/13/ORG at RAF Witchford, under establishment scale LWE/BC/3245 to carry out duties of a heavy bomber squadron.

The new squadron was to be equipped with 16 plus 4 Lancaster MK III aircraft. Aircrew for the new squadron to be produced from 1 flight of No. 115 Squadron already located at RAF Station at Witchford, as a Nucleus and adding Squadron Headquarters and Personnel to complete a 2 Flight Squadron. Wing Commander D.H. Burnside DFC and Bar was appointed Commander of the new squadron.

On the 7th October 1944 the first three crews arrived from No. 3 Lancaster Finishing School, including Squadron Leader R.H.

Franklin as Flight Commander. The following day the new squadron Adjutant Flying Officer J. Gilchrist arrived to hold a conference with Station Commander Squadron Leader Day and Flight Lieutenant Hill from 3 Group on the formation of the squadron.

Over the next three days organising of billets, squadron headquarters, briefing room, orderly room and the collecting of office furniture all took place. On the 11th October 1944 RAF Witchford was visted by Wing Commander W.H.H. Shakespeare M.C. A.F.C. from No. 33 base and Squadron Leader Day from 3 Group to inspect progress. The next day Air Commodore H.H. Down A.F.C. Commanding Officer at No. 33 base, visited the new squadron along with its newly appointed Commanding Officer Wing Commander D.H. Burnside DFC. The 14th October 1944 saw eleven crews from 115 Squadron C Flight and Squadron Leader W.L. Farquharson Flight Commander transferred to 195 Squadron. 195 Squadron Pilots Squadron Leader R.H. Franklin. Pilot Officer Betty, Flight Lieutenant Thorne, Flying Officer Thompson and Sergeant Gilliam carried out duties of 2nd pilot on operations with 115 Squadron over Duisberg. On the following day Squadron Leader Franklin again carried out duties as 2nd pilot to Flying Officer Perry in a 115 aircraft on an operation to Wilhelmshaven. The Lancaster ME 692 A4-G and its crew were lost without trace. Such incidents made it difficult to separate 195 Squadron losses from 115 Squadron until the squadron became completely independent. Officers and Airmen continued to arrive and on the 17th October 1944 Wing Commander Burnside arrived to take up post as Commanding Officer of the new squadron.

Throughout October 195 Squadron pilots and crews either flew as complete crews with 115 Squadron on operations or 195 Squadron pilots flew with 115 Squadron crews as 2nd pilots. On the 19th October 1944 Pilot Officer J. Palmer flew as 2nd pilot to Flight Lieutenant Stechman in a 115 Squadron aircraft, ME 803 KO-D on an operation to Stuttgart.

Pilot Officer Palmer with his own crew also operated with 115 Squadron on the 21st October 1944 against Flushing, while Flying Officer Haig, Flying Officer Scott, Flying Officer Levens and Warrant Officer Hopkins carried out duties as 2nd pilots with 115 Squadron crews. 195 Squadron Aircrew continued to fly 115 Squadron aircraft on operations with 115 Squadron over the next few days.

On the 25th October 1944 115's C Flight, which had formed the nucleus of the new 195 Squadron, became 195's A Flight and moved over to new squadron offices. 195 Squadron were now to operate as an operational squadron. On the 26th October 1944 the squadron operated for the first time in its own right within Bomber Command, with ten aircraft on a G.H. operation over Leverkusen. All aircraft returned safely and the bombing was reported as accurate. The new squadron was now in business and continued to operate from Witchford until the 13th November when they left for their new base at Wratting Common. Further information on this squadron will follow later in this book.

ME 803 would eventually move over to 115's reformed C Flight in March 1945. The new C Flight would carry code letters I L. ME 803 was given the letter B as a call sign so carried the letters I L -B. This aircraft would go on to complete 105 operations.

513 Squadron

513 Squadron was formed at RAF Witchford on the 15th September 1943 when airmen and airwomen began arriving to form the Ground crews of the squadron. Stirlings, known to have been transferred to 513 Squadron from 196 Squadron, were BF 529, EF 116, EF 146 and EF 200.

EF 201, EF 205, EF 206 and EF 2011 were transferred from 75 Squadron. Aircraft code letters are believed to have been CS or JC, but there is no firm confirmation of this.

On 20th of September Flight Lieutenant F.G. Chapman reported on posting from Finningley for duty as Squadron Adjutant, followed five days later by Flying Officer K.W.H. Dixon who arrived for duty as Squadron Navigation Officer. By the end of the month the strength of 513 Squadron totalled 2 officers, 11 senior NCOs, 196 corporals and airmen and 27 airwomen.

October was a busy month with more personnel arriving from various squadrons. On the 21st of the month the first aircraft arrived when Stirling MKIII's EE 958 and EF 465 were transferred from nearby RAF Mepal. Five more aircraft arrived from Mepal three days later. Three more Stirlings, EF 216, EF 146 and B 529, were transferred from 196 Squadron already based at Witchford. On the same day Wing Commander G.E. Harrison arrived to take command of 513 Squadron. On 29th three crews arrived from 119 Squadron to help form one flight.

November saw the influx of more personnel and crews from 1665 and 1651 conversion units. Among those arriving from 1665 conversion unit, based at Woolfox Lodge, was Flight Sergeant Morrison and crew.

The squadron was disbanded on the 21st November 1943 without ever becoming operational. This is believed to be because 3 Group were withdrawing the Stirling and re-equipping with the Lancaster. Due to the short period between formation and disbandment, no badge was ever issued.

There seemed so little information available about this squadron, so I made an appeal in Bomber Command newsletter for information and was answered by former navigator Jim Mitchell. Jim served with 513 Squadron at Witchford for three weeks, having arrived from 1665 heavy conversion unit at Woolfox Lodge at the end of October 1943. The only entry in his log book regarding 513 Squadron is on the day after the squadron disbanded.

Jim's log book is signed by Squadron Leader Joll DFC DFM Officer commanding A Flight. Joll arrived at Witchford from 75 N.Z. Squadron based at Mepal to take over duties as a Flight Commander on the 14th November 1943. One day after Joll's arrival, instructions arrived from 3 Group Headquarters that 513 Squadron was to be disbanded with effect from the 21st November 1943. Almost immediately, 513 Squadron personnel were transferred to other stations and squadrons. Squadron Leader Joll was transferred to 1665 Conversion Unit on detachment pending posting to 1653 Conversion Unit on the 28th and, on the same day, 513 Squadron were instructed to proceed to No. 1653 on detachment on formation of that unit at Chedburgh. A rear party consisting of one officer, one flight sergeant and fifteen airmen were left at Witchford with instructions to move to Chedburgh on the 2nd December 1943. And so 513 formed and disbanded within three months.

The following comments were made in the Operation Book at Chedburgh:

It had been said that 513 Squadron by the reason of the 13 in the number was fated, never to take its place among the operational squadrons of Bomber Comand. Unlucky it certainly was, because the officers (in particular the section leaders) Airmen and Airwomen were very keen to make 513 Squadron one of the leading squadrons in the group. The majority of personel came from a famous 3 Group Squadron No. 75 (N.Z.) Squadron – and although they were loth to leave the unit, they soon settled down and gave their best. By the middle of November, training was fully organised and lectures were given on all manner of subjects by the specialist officers. Day flying was carried out when the weather was favourable and progress was made rapidly. Everyone was looking forward to the day when the first 513 Squadron aircraft would take off on operations, and a bitter disappointment was felt when the news was received that 513 Squadron was to disband. Immediately interest waned and overnight the squadron members became merely a collection of individuals awaiting disposal.

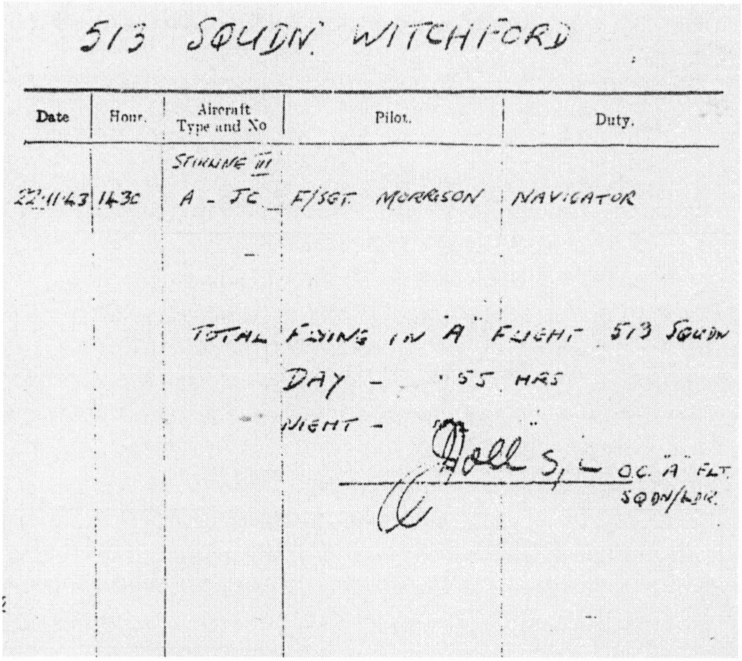

513 SQUDN. WITCHFORD

Date	Hour.	Aircraft Type and No	Pilot.	Duty.
		STIRLING III		
22·11·43	1430	A - JC	F/SGT. MORRISON	NAVIGATOR
		-		

TOTAL FLYING IN "A" FLIGHT 513 SQUDN

DAY - ·55 HRS

NIGHT -

Holl S, ← O.C. "A" FLT.
SQ DN/LDR.

Entry in Jim Mitchell's log book

Photograph of Squadron Leader Joll and crew while serving with 75 N.Z. Squadron at RAF Mepal. Squadron Leader Joll is 4th left in photo.

Compiling Officer. F/O. J. GILCHRIST.

R.A.F. Form 540			**OPERATIONS RECORD BOOK**	Page No. 1
See instructions for use of this form in K.R. and A.C.I., para 2849, and War Manual, Pt. II., chapter XX, and notes in R.A.F. Pocket Book.				MONTH No. of pages used for ...
			of (Unit or Formation) No. 195 Squadron, R.A.F.	

Place	Date	Time	Summary of Events	References to Appendices
WITCHFORD.			Headquarters No. 3 Group Admin. Instruction No 34, of 1944 received by R.A.F. STATION, WITCHFORD, covering the formation of No. 195 Squadron. This formation to take place on 1st. October, 1944 at R.A.F. STATION, WITCHFORD.	B1 - 2
	1.10.44		The official formation of No. 195 Squadron on the authority of Bomber Command letter BC/S.21717/13/ORG. dated 1st. October, 1944 at R.A.F. STATION, WITCHFORD, under establishment scale LWS/BC/3425, to carry out the duties of a Heavy Bomber Squadron armed with 16 plus 4 LANCASTER III Aircraft. Aircrew of No. 195 Squadron to be provided by one Flight from No. 115 Squadron already located at R.A.F. STATION, WITCHFORD, as a nucleus and adding Squadron Headquarters and personnel to complete a 2-Flight Squadron. Wing Commander D.H. BURNSIDE, DFC. and BAR, is appointed Commander of No. 195 Squadron.	
	7.10.44		ADMIN. The first 3 Crews arrive from No. 3 Lancaster Finishing School, including Squadron Leader P.H. FRANKLIN as Flight Commander.	
	8.10.44		ADMIN. Flying Officer J. GILCHRIST arrived as Squadron Adjutant. Conference with STATION COMMANDER, Squadron Leader DAY, and Flight Lieutenant HILL (No. 3 Group) on the formation of the Squadron.	
	9.10.44		ADMIN. Organising of Billets, Squadron Headquarters and Briefing Room.	
	10.10.44		ADMIN. Formation Of Squadron Orderly Room and Collecting of Office Furniture.	
	11.10.44		ADMIN. Visited by Wing Commander W.H.N. SHAKESPEARE. DC., AFC. (No. 33 Base) and Squadron Leader DAY (No. 3 Group). An additional crew posted to the Squadron.	
	12.10.44		ADMIN. Air Commodore H.E. DOWN. AFC. Commanding, No. 33 Base visited the Squadron. Wing Commander D.H. BURNSIDE. DFC. visited. 4 crews posted.	
	13.10.44		ADMIN. Three specialist officers arrived for duty.	

Copy of record book

115 Squadron

Badge of 115 Squadron

115 Squadron had been in 3 Group from the outbreak of war flying Wellingtons from Marham, Kinloss, Mildenhall and East Wretham, where on the 1st March 1943 they began conversion to the radial engine Lancaster MK II, becoming operational with this aircraft on the15th March 1943. 115 – a 2 Flight squadron – were the first to become fully equipped with the MK II Lancaster. By the time they moved to Little Snoring on the 5th August 1943 they had lost 17 MK II Lancasters and 13 Wellingtons whilst stationed at East Wretham. 95 Wellingtons had also been lost previous to this, either in action or due to crashes whilst the squadron was stationed at previous bases. Before the move to Witchford took place, 16 more MK I Lancasters would be lost.

On the 26th November 1943, 115 Squadron main party moved to RAF Witchford by road, whilst the Lancasters left Little Snoring on an operation to Berlin – the return to be their new base at Witchford. The 12 aircraft taking off from Little Snoring between 17.40 hours and 17.46 hours were as follows:

Lancaster MK II DS 777 KO-C	Captain Pilot Officer F. Blackwell
Lancaster MK II DS 827 KO-F	Captain Flight Lieutenant G.Y. Mackie
Lancaster MK II DS 678 KO-J	Captain Pilot Officer H.G. Hicks
Lancaster MK II DS 680 KO-L	Captain Flying Officer E.B. Woolhouse
Lancaster MK II DS 781 KO-W	Captain Flight Sergeant J. Lee
Lancaster MK II DS 667 KO-G	Captain Flight Sergeant R. Milgate
Lancaster MK II DS 728 KO-P	Captain Flight Lieutenant J.H. Christian
Lancaster MK II DS 766 KO-Q	Captain Flight Lieutenant R.L. Barnes
Lancaster MK II DS 661 KO-Z	Captain Flying Officer K. Harris
Lancaster MK II DS 773 KO-T	Captain Flying Officer D.L. Pirie
Lancaster MK II DS 734 KO-Y	Captain Pilot Officer A. Howell
Lancaster MK II DS 664 KO-K	Captain Warrant Officer E. Bouttier DFC

Flying Officer E.B. Woolhouse and his crew of Sergeant W. Bell Navigator, Flying Officer W.A. Mitchell Wireless Operator, Sergeant A. Baker Bomb Aimer, Sergeant H. Falls Mid Upper Gunner, Sergeant T. Monk Rear Gunner and Sergeant J. Pallanca Flight Engineer were killed. This crew would be recorded as 115 Squadron's first casualties whilst stationed at Witchford, although they did not return to their new base.

One other aircraft was forced to abandon the sortie and return to base after safely jettisoning its bombs. Two aircraft were unable to reach the target, one due to starboard engine trouble and the other to a hot engagement of flak. Both aircraft jettisoned bombs live on Limburg and Brandenburg respectively. 11 aircraft returned to Witchford safely.

Several of the returning crews had loaded their bicycles onto the aircraft rather than leave them at Little Snoring, this gave rise to the story, that had any of the Lancasters crashed on enemy territory and the bicycles found, the Germans would have thought that this was a new tactic for aircrew to bike home if they crashed.

On the 29th November 1943 C Flight was formed on the squadron. A and B Flights had always carried the squadron code letters of KO. The new C Flight aircraft would carry the leters A4. On the 25th March 1944 C Flight comenced conversion to Lancaster MK I and MK IIIs.

115 Squadron, who had only detached to Coastal Command for a short period in 1940, ended the war with one of the finest records of operational service in Bomber Command. The squadron carried out the first G trials in August 1941 and carried out the third highest number of bombing raids in Bomber Comand heavy squadrons. They carried out the most raids and dropped the most bombs in 3 Group, as well as carrying out the highest number of sorties in Bomber Command. They were believed to have dropped the second highest tonnage of bombs in the Command, carried out the most raids, flew the most sorties and suffered the most losses of any Wellington Squadron in Bomber Command.

Badge of Bomber Command

No.115 Squadron Battle Song

(To be sung to the tune of Lilli Marlene)

The Lancasters of Witchford, they're on their way,
Off to bomb the Jerries, they bomb them every day,
And when they wish to show their might
They bomb the sods by day and night,
The Lancasters of Witchford, the Lancs of 115.

Off we go from briefing, and leap into our kites,
Open up the throttle and roar into the night
We've left the flare path far behind,
It's bloody dark but we don't mind,
The Lancasters of Witchford, the Lancs of 115.

There's the bloody searchlights waving round the sky
Not much ruddy power, and not too bloody high,
I hope they don't start shooting till we're through,
They may get me and they might get you,
The Lancasters of Witchford, the Lancs of 115.

Now we're through the target, setting course for home,
Soon we'll see the Sandras waving o'er the drome,
That's if we don't go off the track,
And stop a crafty burst of flak,
The Lancasters of Witchford, the Lancs of 115.

Junkers off to starboard, Focke-Wulfe off to Port,
Gunner calls to skipper, "Range is getting short",
Prepare to corkscrew, starboard - - go,
We know our stuff and we're not too slow,
The Lancasters of Witchford, the Lancs of 115.

Now we're in the circuit, with a turn to land,
No intruders round us, ain't it bloody grand,
We fooled the hun once more tonight,
Dropped a load, right on the Reich,
The Lancasters of Witchford, the Lancs of 115.

When the war is over and there's no more ops to do,
We'll think of all our pals,
Those who didn't get through,
The pals who were with us through thick and thin,
So that we one day the War would win,
The Lancasters of Witchford, the Lancs of 115.

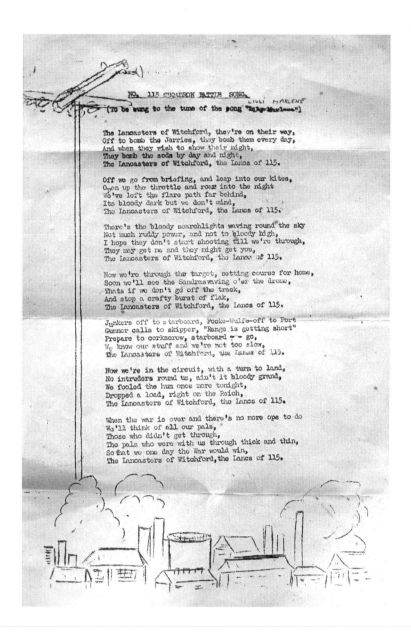

NO. 115 SQUADRON BATTLE SONG.
(To be sung to the tune of the song "Lilli Marlene")

The Lancasters of Witchford, they're on their way,
Off to bomb the Jerries, they bomb them every day,
And when they wish to show their might,
They bomb the sods by day and night,
The Lancasters of Witchford, the Lancs of 115.

Off we go from briefing, and leap into our kites,
Open up the throttle and roar into the night
We've left the flare path far behind,
Its bloody dark but we don't mind,
The Lancasters of Witchford, the Lancs of 115.

There's the bloody searchlights waving round the sky
Not much ruddy power, and not too bloody high,
I hope they don't start shooting till we're through,
They may get me and they might get you,
The Lancasters of Witchford, the Lancs of 115.

Now we're through the target, setting course for home,
Soon we'll see the Sandras waving o'er the drome,
Thats if we don't go off the track,
And stop a crafty burst of flak,
The Lancasters of Witchford, the Lancs of 115.

Junkers off to starboard, Focke-Wulfe-off to Port
Gunner calls to skipper, "Range is getting short"
Prepare to corkscrew, starboard -- go,
We know our stuff and we're not too slow,
The Lancasters of Witchford, the Lancs of 115.

Now we're in the circuit, with a turn to land,
No intruders round us, ain't it bloody grand,
We fooled the hun once more tonight,
Dropped a load, right on the Reich,
The Lancasters of Witchford, the Lancs of 115.

When the war is over and there's no more ops to do
We'll think of all our pals,
Those who didn't get through,
The pals who were with us through thick and thin,
So that we one day the War would win,
The Lancasters of Witchford, the Lancs of 115.

Total Wartime Operational Performance of the Squadrons that flew from RAF Witchford

196 Squadron – Raids Flown:

4 Group	Wellingtons	33 Bombing	23 Minelaying
Group	Stirlings	12 Bombing	18 Minelaying
Total		45 Bombing	41 Minelaying

= 86 Raids

Sorties and Losses:

4 Group	Wellingtons	517 Sorties	13 Aircraft lost
3 Group	Stirlings	166 Sorties	11 Aircraft lost
Total		683 Sorties	24 Aircraft lost

115 Squadron – Raids Flown:

3 Group	Wellingtons	332 Bombing	54 Minelaying	4
Leaflet				
3 Group	Lancasters	261 Bombing	27 Minelaying	
Total		593 Bombing	81 Minelaying	4
Leaflet	= 678 Raids			

Sorties and Losses:

	Wellingtons	3,075 Sorties	98 Aircraft lost
	Lancasters	4,678 Sorties	110 Aircraft lost
Total		7,753 Sorties	208 Aircraft lost

22 aircraft were also lost in accidents.

195 Squadron – Raids Flown:

3 Group	Lancasters	87 Bombing

Sorties and Losses:

	Lancasters	1,384 Sorties	14 Aircraft lost

1 aircraft lost in accident

Aircraft Losses of Squadrons while stationed at RAF Witchford

196 Squadron
Period stationed at Witchford – 19th July 1943 - 18th November 1943

Aircraft Type   Stirlings
Losses 11 MK IIIs   Total   11 *

115 Squadron
Period stationed at Witchford – 26th November 1943 - 10th September 1945

Aircraft Type   Lancasters
Losses 34 MK I   32 MK II   17 MK III   Total   83

195 Squadron
Period stationed at Witchford – 1st October 1944 - 13th November 1944

Aircraft Type   Lancasters
Losses 4 MK I   1 MK II   Total   5
1 other written off in accident

* Only 9 of the 11 aircraft lost by 196 Squadron can be accounted for in operational records. The other 2 aircraft may have been written off in accidents.

The Royal Visit and Investiture RAF Witchford 5th July 1944

The Royal Visit and Investiture at which Aubrey Howell and his navigator Ron Stewart were awarded their decorations was held on 5th July 1944.

While researching for Ely Museum War Year exhibition in early 1995, I had found the date of the investiture at the Public Records Office amongst 115 Squadron`s operational records, but two publications I had read stated the date as 10th July 1944 and several local Witchford villagers were positive the date was sometime during September 1944. So, believing in the old saying, ` If you want to know something always go to the top`, I duly wrote and posted off a letter to Buckingham Palace.

I received a reply to my letter, as can be seen below, on 18th April 1995. Apart from confirming that there was only one visit by the Royal family to Witchford on the 5th July 1944, the letter also solved another mystery and gave names of other Senior Officers who accompanied the Royal party on their visit. The letter is reproduced below by kind permission of Her Majesty Queen Elizabeth II.

The mystery of whether Air Chief Marshal Sir Arthur Harris attended the ceremony or not was solved in the letter as `Bomber` Harris`s name (as he was better known), had obviously been confused by some with Air Vice Marshal Harrison's name, who did attend the ceremony. It was also interesting to find that Fighter Pilot Wing Commander Peter Townsend, whose name was later to be linked romantically with Princess Margaret, attended as an equerry.

The Royal party had arrived at Ely Railway Station under strict security where they were received by the Station Master Mr. R.H. Aggas, with whom the King and Queen and Princess Elizabeth shook hands. Her Majesty the Queen chatted with Mr. Aggas for some minutes. As the Royal car drove through

THE ROYAL ARCHIVES

18th April 1995

Dear Mr. Aldridge,

I have been asked by Her Majesty The Queen to reply to your letter of 14 March.

The Royal visit to RAF Witchford took place on 5 July 1944, and our records show that this was the only visit there which King George VI made. They also visited other RAF stations that day and some USAAF stations the following day.

The only senior officer accompanying the Royal party named in our records is Air Vice-Marshal Richard Harrison, AOC No. 3 Group. They were also accompanied throughout by the King's Assistant Private Secretary, Sir Eric Mieville, and an Equerry, Wing Commander Townsend. At RAF Witchford the Station Commander was Group Captain J. B. Sims, and the Officer commanding the squadron based there, 115 Squadron, was Wing Commander W. G. Devas. I can find no mention in our records of an Army Officer being present - and, indeed, cannot see one in the two photographs you kindly enclosed.

May I suggest that you also contact the Imperial War Museum, as they have the Forces' official wartime photographs, and should have the captions for these pictures, which may well identify the main characters shown?

Yours sincerely,

Allison Jewett

pp Miss Pamela Clark
Deputy Registrar

Barry Aldridge Esq.,
Ely Museum,
28c High Street,
Ely,
Cambs.
CB7 4HL.

The Royal Collection Trust, Windsor Castle, Berkshire SL4 1NJ. Tel: 0753 868286. Fax: 0753 854910

The Royal Collection Trust is a company limited by guarantee registered in England and Wales.
Registered No. 2713536. Registered Charity No. 1016972.
Registered Office: 66 Lincoln's Inn Fields, London WC2A 3LH

Letter to the author from The Royal Archives in 1995
© Her Majesty Queen Elizabeth II

the city on its short journey to Witchford the occupants were recognised by many people in the streets.

It was a big thrill for a number of Ely High School girls who were standing outside the swimming pool, when a large car approached from the direction of the station and the girls suddenly recognised the occupants. Princess Elizabeth was sitting in front of her parents and delighted the girls by turning to smile and wave to them. The excited girls waved back to receive an answering salute from the King and Queen. Her Royal Highness looked fresh and charming in pale blue and the King was in Royal Airforce uniform.

Because of security, the villagers at Witchford knew nothing of the visit until three quarters of an hour before hand. The School in Witchford was notified and asked if the children could line up on each side of the main entrance to the aerodrome. The Royal family arrived in a Rolls Royce and spent sometime talking to the villagers before entering the airfield, where they were escorted around the RAF Personnel on parade. The formal introductions over, the Airmen were allowed to have photographs taken with the Royal family.

Investiture held – as detailed in operations record book

Assembly in preparation for decorations by His Majesty King George VI 5th July 1944. 115 Squadron, Witchford, Ely, Cambridgeshire.

Above left to right:
Flight Sergeant C.R. McRae, Pilot Officer A.J. Horton, Warrant Officer E.H. Boutilier (RCAF), Pilot Officer E.A. Webb, Pilot Officer R.S. Stewart, Flying Officer R.H. Phillips, Flight Lieutenant A. Howell, Flying Officer R. Birchall, Squadron Leader G. Mackie (A Flight Commander), Flying Officer R. Hulse, Wing Commander F.F. Rainsford (former 115 Commanding Officer June – December 1943), Flight Lieutenant R. Milgate (RAAF), Flight Lieutenant G.D. Seddon (RAAF), Flight Lieutenant G. Hammond (RAAF), Squadron Leader C.H. Baigent (RNZAF B Flight Commander), Wing Commander R.H. Annan (former 115 Commanding Officer December 1943 – June 1944), Squadron Leader Cluefus.

Airmen known to be in background: Flight Lieutenant L.J. Halley (Newfoundland), Warrant Officer J.T. Darby, Flight Lieutenant A.E. Billson (115 Gunnery Leader).

Senior Officers believed to be in background: Wing Commander W.C. Devas (Officer Commanding 115 Squadron), and Group Captain J.B. Sims (former 115 Commanding Officer March 30th 1943 – June 1st 1943) Officer commanding RAF Witchford.

The King presents Flight Lieutenant Seddon with his DFC inside
the Type T2 hangar

The Investiture over, The Royal Party were escorted on a tour of
the airfield in company with senior officers.

Aircrew who were shortly to take off on a daylight raid were
able to be photographed with their Royal Highnesses.

Sadly, only a few days after this photograph was taken, some of these men would lose their lives. Flying Officer S.A. Letts, who can be seen looking over the Princess' left shoulder, was killed along with his crew when his Lancaster LM 616 KO-J crashed at 07.15 hours at Great Offley, Hertfordshire, while returning from an attack on Emieville. The aircraft crashed on to West End Farm, Offley, killing the occupants Mrs. Alice Handley, Miss Mary Handley and Private Elsie Handley of the A.T.S. None of Letts' crew survived. Also seen far right of the photograph is Flight Sergeant Mac McClean Rear Gunner to Colin Campbell's crew.

Above – another photograph of the group in humorous mood. The Queen had just enquired about an Australian airman's trousers. "Why do you wear fur chaps?" she asked. "To keep my knees warm Maam", came the reply.

The tour of the airfield continued with visits to various sections including Flying Control, where the Royal Party were able to stand on the balcony and watch the squadron take off on a daylight raid. The King was also able to inspect the bomb bay of a Lancaster and see how the loading of the bombs was carried out.

Queen Elizabeth and party standing on the balcony (The balcony is visible in the earlier photo of the Control Tower)

The tour in progress as the King and Group Captain Sims walk ahead of the Queen, Princess Elizabeth and escorting officers

2nd left of this group is Wing Commander Peter Townsend DFC, an equerry who would later be linked romantically with Princess Margaret. Far right is the Air Officer commanding 3 Group, Air Vice Marshal Richard Harrison.

In the background can be seen the hangar and behind it the Water Tower. To the right of the hangar is the Squadron Armoury.

The King checks his watch as they leave the parachute section building. The King's Assistant Private Secretary Sir Eric Mieville stands to the left of the doorway as the Princess Elizabeth leaves the building. Also seen in the doorway next to Group Captain Sims, is WAAF Jackie Freeman-Mathews.

The visit ended when they were driven quickly around the domestic sites, messes etc., before leaving the village.

KING AND QUEEN AT ELY

Thrill for Schoolgirls

A number of Ely High School girls were outside the swimming pool on Wednesday morning when they had a thrilling surprise.

A large car approached from the direction of the station and the girls suddenly realised that the occupants were their Majesties the King and Queen and H.R.H. Princess Elizabeth. The Princess was sitting in front of her parents and delighted the girls by turning to smile and wave to them. The excited girls waved back to receive an answering salute from the King and Queen, also. Her Royal Highness looked fresh and charming in pale blue. H.M. The King was in Royal Air Force uniform.

When the Royal party alighted from the Royal Train at Ely station they were received by the station-master, Mr. R. H. Aggas, with whom the King, Queen and the Princess shook hands. H.M. The Queen chatted with Mr. Aggas for some minutes.

As the Royal car drove through the city, the occupants were recognised by many people in the streets.

Ely newspaper cutting 'King and Queen at Ely'

65

Memories of the Royal Visit

One of the Witchford school children that greeted the Royal visitors at the airfield was 13 year old Maud Cooper, now Mrs. Pickford. She remembers that the Rackham School had about 100 pupils at the time and 3 teachers: Headmaster Mr. Dunkling; Mrs. Murfitt and Miss Cranwell. Very little notice of the Royal visit was given and the children were quickly assembled and marched through the village and into the airfield where they lined up in front of one of the hangars, ready to greet the distinguished visitors. Maud has very little memory of what happened when the Royal party arrived as the Headmaster, a strict disciplinarian had made it quite plain what would happen to anyone who misbehaved or stepped out of line. So her concentration was more involved with not doing anything wrong, rather than enjoying seeing the King, Queen and Princess Elizabeth. However, she still remembers how big the Lancasters were close up, having only seen them previously in the distance when travelling along the road between Ely and Witchford. One other memory of Maud's was of Sunday Church services in the village which were attended by Airmen from the drome. "You got to know their faces each week", she said. "Then one Sunday they would not be there, no one would say anything, but you knew they had not returned from a mission. It was such a waste of young handsome men who had everything to live for".

Sylvia Feast, now Mrs. Miller, also remembers the Royal visit as she was one of the Ely High School girls who waved at the Royal Party in Ely`s Station Road.

I was one of the party of 12 to 13 year olds walking from the School in St. Mary`s Street for a swimmimg lesson in the pool at Angel Drove. On the way, the Mistress told us that the King, Queen and Princess Elizabeth were arriving at Ely Railway Station (news had leaked out somehow) and if we liked to forgo our swimming lesson, we could line the pavement and see them. This we did, standing at the bottom of Back Hill where the old Angel Pub and Hotel used to be.

PART 2: The Witchford Intruder Incident

The Witchford Intruder Incident

The intruder incident which took place over Witchford airfield was something that would be repeated many times over airfields in Eastern England, almost always with tragic results. Heavy bombers were always vulnerable when taking off or returning to their bases. The lights of the airfield and the aircraft's own navigation lights made them easy targets for the prowling German night fighters.

The Luftwaffe had employed intruder tactics successfully early in the war, but in 1941 they had been ordered to stop, on what was believed to be a direct order from Hitler, who believed that it was better for the night fighters to shoot down our aircraft over Germany, so that the German people could see the results for themselves, hence boosting morale. This decision did not go down well with the German airmen but it would be late 1943 before some of the Luftwaffe's night intruder force (the Fernnachtjäger) would again fly over Britain.

Photograph of the Messerschmitt Me 410

The ME 410s of II/KG 51 had begun flying intruder sorties in March 1944, although they were mainly intended for bombing.

In April 1944 they were based at Soesterberg in Holland and over the next few months would create havoc over Eastern England with allied aircraft. At the time of the intruder incident at Witchford, II/KG 51 was commanded by Major Puttfarken, who had five kills before he went missing on 23rd April.

A captured ME 410 in RAF markings giving a good view of the Barbette mounted machine guns

The ME 410 was a fast and well armed aircraft that had evolved from the much troubled ME 210. Although similar to our Mosquito in appearance, the ME 410 did not rival it in performance. Powered by two Daimler Benz 603 A V12 engines, the two seater aircraft had a maximum cruising speed of 365 mph and a range at maximum cruising speed of 746 miles. At economical cruising speed it could achieve 1,050 miles. Armament consisted of two 20mm MG 151 Cannon and four7.9mm MG 17 machine guns in the lower fuselage firing forward. It also had two remotely controlled Barbettes on either side of the fuselage, just behind the wings which contained two 13mm MG 131 machine guns. The bomb bay was mounted under the nose and forward of the cockpit. The Barbette mounted guns enabled the fighter to fly under our bombers and perform what the Germans called ` The Schräge Musik Attack`. This meant that, from the safety of a blind spot under the bomber, the fighter could rotate the machine guns upwards and fire into the fuel tanks. Many of our aircraft were lost in this way, never knowing what hit them.

In March 1940 the Headquarters for 3 Group bomber moved from Mildenhall to Exning House, a magnificent mansion, set in acres of land in the small village of Exning, not far from Newmarket, Suffolk. This was not the first time that Exning had been used for military purposes, for back in time Boudica, the female leader of the Icini, had a base here from which she waged war against the Romans.

Exning House situated in the village of Exning near Newmarket, Suffolk. Home to 3 Group Headquarters from March 1940.

When 3 Group arrived, the grounds surrounding Exning House were covered in Nissan Huts to accommodate the personnel that are necessary to organise a Bomber Group within Bomber Command.

It was here in the main house that Air Vice Marshal Richard Harrison C.B., CBE, DFC., AFC., had his office. Harrison was appointed A.O.C. of 3 Group on 27th February 1943. He had taken over the post from Air Chief Marshal the Hon. Sir Ralph A. Cochrane G.B.E., K.C.B., A.F.C., who had been in charge of the group since 1942. Cochrane had himself taken over from Air

Marshal Sir John Baldwin K.B.E., C.B., D.S.O., D.L., who had been appointed as A.O.C. 3 Group in 1939. 3 Group had originally been formed at Andover, Hampshire in May 1936.

Air Vice Marshal Richard Harrison CB, CBE, DFC, AFC. who became A.O.C. of 3 Group on 27th February 1943. Seen here seated at his desk in his office at Exning House.

The Crews:

<u>Lancaster KO-R LL667 MK II</u>
Pilot Officer John (Jock) Birnie
Pilot Officer Arnold Feldman
Sergeant Edwin Kerwin
Sergeant Jack Ferguson
Sergeant William James McMillan
Flight Sergeant David Lloyd Jones
Sergeant George Edward Bailey

<u>Lancaster A4-JLL867 MK I</u>
Flight Lieutenant Charles Eddy MBE
Flying Officer Albert Smith
Flight Sergeant Harold Edward Pugh
Warrant Officer Henry Bennis
Sergeant William Leslie Murphy
Sergeant Alfred Frank Langridge
Flight Sergeant Peter Maddox

Tuesday 18th April 1944

The morning dawned like any other at RAF Witchford, but the night of the 18th/19th would prove to be significant in several ways. This night would see the last German bomber attack on London. One hundred and twenty seven aircraft in total attacked the capital, thirteen of which would not return to their bases. From now on, London would suffer the terrors of the V1 and V2 rockets.

Also on this night the German ME410 long range night fighters of 11/KG/51 would be sent out from their base at Soesterberg in Holland to patrol Eastern England, an act that would prove fatal to fourteen airmen of 115 Squadron based at RAF Witchford and seven airmen of 625 Squadron based at RAF Kelstern in Lincolnshire.

Wing Commander Robert H. Annan Commanding Officer of 115 Squadron received Form B412 from 3 Group Headquarters at Exning near Newmarket. The target for the evening of the 18th/19th would be the Railway Yards at Rouen, one of several targets that would be chosen over the next few weeks to cause disruption to German troop and munition movements before the D Day landings. Twenty seven of 115 Lancasters were detailed for the operation to a target that would be the first on French soil for many of the aircrew.

The villagers of Witchford always knew when an operation was immanent as an old ambulance would make its way through the village up to the airfield followed by the crew transport.

This evening was no exception, with the transport turning off the Main Street into Bedwell Hey Lane where the crews alighted at the briefing room. As they entered the room, some of the crews would probably have already had a rough idea of what area the operation would be in, for as soon as the ground crews received orders that morning for the amount of fuel and bombs to be loaded on to the Lancasters, rumours would start to fly and even a few bets placed as to where the target would be. The door of the briefing room closed behind the last airmen and the guard was placed on the door. With the crews seated and settled, a roll call of crews was called before the curtain covering a large map on the end wall was pulled back to reveal that the target for this evening was to be the Railway Yards at

Rouen – a relief no doubt to the assembled crews, for this would be an operation that meant they would spend a short time over enemy territory, or the like when the targets were in Germany. The various leaders, such as Gunnery and Bombing, gave briefings – as did the Met. Officer on the expected weather. The Commanding Officer, Wing Commander Annan giving the final address.

The briefing room

On leaving the briefing, now with full knowledge of what and where the target would be, the crews would later assemble in the crew rooms further along Bedwell Hey Lane. Here they put on their flying gear and for the superstitious, a check would be made to ensure they were carrying their lucky mascot.

The crews now assembled at the nearby parachute shed, where the transport picked them up to take them out to their various aircraft disposal points around the airfield: Nine crews going to A Flights dispersal; ten to B Flights and eight to C Flights, making up the twenty seven aircraft of 115 Squadron to attack the target.

Drying, locker and crew rooms photographed in 1998
Photo: author

Once at dispersal, various checks were made by crew members before Form 700 was signed and they boarded the aircraft. Some crewmen, like Mac McClean rear gunner to Sergeant Colin Campbell, still had their little superstitious rituals to perform. Mac's was relieving himself on the tail wheel of their Lancaster KO-U before boarding. Pilot Officer Birnie, pilot of B Flight KO-R owned a cross bred greyhound called Sandra. Tonight he had left her with Map Clerk Daphne Valentine, who was already looking after a spaniel for another pilot on the evening's op.

Once inside the aircraft more checks of hatches and instruments were carried out before the engines were started, one by one. Satisfied with his aircraft each pilot signalled for the ground crews to remove the chocks from the wheels. Using the two outer engines for directional movements the pilots moved from their dispersal points to the runway, ready for their signal for their turn to take off. This was a busy time for any airfield with everyone alert including fire and ambulance crews. The night was clear with slight ground haze as Flight Sergeant Ronald Maude waited for the green light to flash from the control caravan, situated on the edge of the airfield. Take off was always carried out in strict radio silience in case the Germans should be listening. Take off and landings were always a nerve wracking time for pilots, for it was then that they were most vulnerable to German intruders.

Before the war Maude was training to be an accountant, having left school in Gloucester in 1939. Now aged 21 years he was about to embark on his 9th operation as Captain of a Lancaster bomber.

At 22.25 the green light flashed and Flight Sergeant Maude opened up the throttles of his Lancaster and roared down the runway into the night. Followed by Sergeant Quinton, Warrant Officer Hemming and the other Lancasters at one or two minute intervals. By 22.55 the last of the Lancasters, that of Flight Lieutenant Hammond of the Royal Australian Air Force was airborne. Twenty six of the twenty seven aircraft detailed for the operation were in the air. One of C Flight's Lancasters failed to take off due to engine failure.

The Lancasters circled until all the aircraft were airborne, then the navigators set their course and 115 Squadron headed for the South Coast en-route for Rouen, as did nine Lancasters of 75 New Zealand Squadron based at nearby Mepal. 75 Squadron were also sending out six Stirlings on a mining operation to Kiel Bay. Some of the other squadrons taking part in this were 625 Squadron based at Kelstern in Lincolnshire and two Pathfinder squadrons, 635 Squadron based at Downham Market in Norfolk, and 156 Squadron from Upwood who were ahead of the main Bombing Force.

In total two hundred and seventy three Lancasters and sixteen Mosquitoes from 1, 3 and 8 Groups were taking part in this operation.

As the engines of all these aircraft faded into the distance their airfields again went quiet as the fire, ambulance and ground crews stood down for a few hours before the bombers returned. Heading south the bombers flew over Newberry before turning to head out over the coast and Selsey Bill. Once over the sea the gunners were able to test their guns before the aircraft crossed the coast at Le Havre. As they crossed the coast they experienced a small amount of flak, but it was considered nothing to worry about by the crews, compared to what they had faced on other operations.

Ahead of the main bomber stream 635 Squadron of 8 Group was nearing the target. Aboard one of these Lancasters was one of the assigned Master Bombers, Wing Commander A.G.S. Cousins D.S.O. DFC who was also Commanding Officer of the Squadron. In 1942 he had commanded 115 Squadron, now based at RAF Witchford and who were in the following Bomber Force. The Master Bomber, or Master of Ceremonies as he was sometimes known, had the unenviable task of staying over the target to direct the main force onto the target indicators dropped by his pathfinders.*

For Pilot Officer Moon and crew of 115 Squadron's A Flight this was their first French target, and the shortest trip they had ever done. For four of the crew it was their 17th Op. Ernie Moon, his Navigator Flight Sergeant Durham, Wireless Operator Pilot Officer McCrae and Rear Gunner Flight Sergeant Frank Kanarens had originally been a Mitchell crew with 180 Squadron before being transferred to 196 Squadron at Witchford as a Stirling crew. Here they completed two mining ops in October 1943 before 196 Squadron left Witchford and Bomber Command.

Moon and his crew remained at Witchford transferring to 115 Squadron. The Rouen op was also another first for the crew. It was the first time they had ever flown a Lancaster I, their regular aircraft MK II Lancaster LL667 KO-E (Easy) had been transferred to B Flight and re-lettered KO-R. It was now being piloted by Pilot Officer Birnie on this trip. Now they were approaching the target in their new Lancaster KO-F (Freddie).

Arriving over the target, Moon and his crew found the Pathfinders had it well lit up with target indicators, but owing to the Met. Report being haywire they had arrived nine minutes late and heard the Master of Ceremonies faintly, only once.

Four nights after this operation Cousins was taking on the roll of M.C. for the third consecutive time on an op to Laon when they were attacked by a Night Fighter. The Lancaster ND508 blew up. Pilot Officer Courtney, the captain of the aircraft, was the only survivor.

The first crew to take off from Witchford on The Rouen op.

Photo P. Maude

Left to Right Back row:
Sergeant Ken Penton Mid Upper Gunner
Sergeant Rob Sutherland Rear Gunner
Flight Sergeant Ron Maude Pilot
Flying Officer Ron Tovey Navigator
Left to Right Front row:
Sergeant Alan Anderson Flight Engineer
Sergeant Harold Foster Bomb Aimer
Sergeant Jack Fyffe Wireless Operator
The Lancaster in the photo above is not the one they flew to Rouen.

The crew of KO-F (Freddie) MKI Lancaster ND 754

<u>Left to Right:</u>
Flight Sergeant H. Durham Navigator, Pilot Officer D. McRae Wireless Operator, Sergeant R. Sharp Flight Engineer, Flight Sergeant W. Fraser Mid Upper Gunner, Pilot Officer E. Moon Pilot, Sergeant W. Swan Bomb Aimer, Flight Sergeant F. Kanarens Rear Gunner.

LL667 was one of 300 Lancaster MK IIs produced with Bristol Hercules engines as an insurance against a possible shortage of Merlins. The aircraft was delivered to 514 Squadron at RAF Waterbeach, Cambridgeshire and almost immediately transferred to 115 Squadron on their arrival at nearby RAF Witchford on the 26th November 1944.

115 Squadron was the first squadron to be completely equipped with the MK II Lancasters.

Identifying the target by the indicators and the river they made their bombing run, Bomb Aimer Sergeant Swan dropping his bombs from 13,500ft. A big explosion was observed by Swan and he noticed that the bombing seemed concentrated.

Flight Sergeant Maude had been the first aircraft to take off from Witchford. He identified the target by the river and the target indicators, and was instructed by the Master of Ceremonies to bomb the concentration of red and green indicators.

A photograph of the target was taken and one good fire was observed.

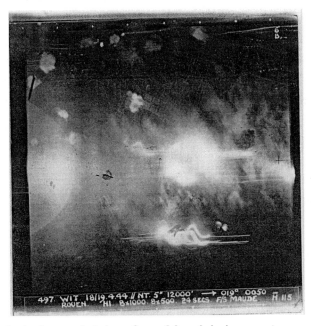

Target photograph taken from Maude's Lancaster over the Marshalling Yards at Rouen. Photo P. Maude

Flight Sergeant Colin Campbell and crew identified the target visually and by the indicators, dropping their bombs from 14,500ft. One 500lb bomb failed to release, leaving them no option but to return to Witchford with it.

Flight Lieutenant Ray Milgate, the Australian Pilot of Lancaster KO-S identified the target by the bend in the river and the indicators dropped by the Pathfinders. With useful directions from the Master of Ceremonies Milgate, Bomb Aimer Flight Sergeant Banks released his bombs at 14,000ft on the concentration of green and reds.

As Squadron Leader Grant, Flight Commander of 115 Squadron's A Flight pulled away from the target he could see aircraft coming in from all directions and was very relieved at how lightly the target was defended. As each aircraft released its cargo of destruction and set course for home, more than one crew was thinking that this operation had been a piece of cake. Light flak and no fighters – if only it was always like this. Soon the 3 ½ to 4 hour round trip would be over and not a single aircraft had been lost.

Bombs released and duty done, the pilots turned for home. Among 115's twenty six pilots were four New Zealanders and four Australians.

Pilot Officer Dick Treasure was one of those New Zealand pilots and captain of KO-W. This was his 19th operation and his second consecutive French target.

Photograph of Pilot Officer G.H.R. Treasure with crew and ground crew. Photo: G.H.R. Treasure.

Back Row Left to Right:

Sergeant Holland Flight Engineer, Sergeant Hollinrake Wireless Operator, Flying Officer Scott Bomb Aimer, Pilot Officer Treasure Pilot, Warrant Officer Gould Navigator, Sergeant Caseley Rear Gunner, Sergeant Dawson M.U.G.

Front Row ground crew Left to Right:

Stan Skinner, Corporal Eddie Brooks, Sergeant Jack Brown, Paddy O'Flarity, Bill Brown.

Flight Lieutenant Eddy and Squadron Leader C.H. Baigent DFC and Bar, Flight Commander of B Flight and Pilot Officer S.W. Holder were the other New Zealand pilots.

Eddy had carried out his first 7½ operations with 75 Squadron, but a crash in a Stirling in July 1943 brought a break in his tour. After recovering from his injuries and converting to Lancasters at Waterbeach, he joined 115 Squadron at Witchford to continue his first tour in March 1944.

Tonight as pilot of KO-R he would clock up 11½ operations.

Squadron Leader Baigent was on his second tour, having completed his first tour of 32 operations with 15 Squadron in November 1942. His second tour with 115 Squadron had begun with six straight trips to Berlin.

Pilot Officer Holder was pilot of C Flight A4-G for George, one of eight MKI Lancasters on this raid.

The four Australian pilots were Flying Officer Clarey, Flight Lieutenant Hammond, Flight Lieutenant Milgate and Pilot Officer Gibson.

Pilot Officer Gibson had started his first tour with 623 Squadron at Downham Market as had Dick Treasure, but 623 who were flying Stirlings had been disbanded. So after converting to Lancasters Gibson joined 115's B Flight at Witchford in December 1943. Tthis was his 20th operation.

Although Rouen had been an easy target for those involved, it had not been the same elsewhere. Twelve aircraft would not return home from targets at Juvisy, Noisy-Le-Sec, Tergnier and three others would not return from mining operations, including one of the Stirlings from RAF Mepal piloted by Flying Officer Murray RNZAF

Ernie Moon's navigator Flight Sergeant Durham plotted the course that would take them over the English Coast near Bognor Regis and from there to Reading where they turned North East and headed back to the safety of Witchford and a mug of hot tea laced with rum.

Back at Witchford the airfield was becoming busy again in preparation for the returning aircraft. Fire and ambulance crews were again in readiness, looking up at the night sky and listening for the distinctive sounds of the Lancaster engines that would indicate their imminent return to base and safety.

Jim Towers was also looking up to the sky as he patrolled the perimeter of the airfield armed with a sten gun. Jim was a fitter, normally working in a hangar on the Eastern side of the airfield where he repaired aircraft damaged on operations. This work usually excused him from other duties including guards, but this month had seen the Germans stepping up intruder sorties and there had been rumours that enemy parachutists may be used against our bomber airfields. So an additional guard was formed, hence Jim was patrolling the airfield. The first guard duty he had ever done.

Seated at his desk at Mepal in 1945 is Wing Commander Cyril Henry Baigent DFC & Bar. Photo via Ken Wooton

Baigent, after completing his tour as B Flight Commander with 115 Squadron at Witchford in November 1944, was posted to 3 Group Headquarters at Exning near Newmarket. In January 1945, newly promoted, he took over the command of 75 Squadron at Mepal after the death in action of Wing Commander Newton, who failed to return from an operation to Vohwinkel on the 1st January.

On the night of the intruder incident at Witchford he was a Squadron Leader and Captain of MKII Lancaster LL716.

In the days that followed the Rouen Raid the German propaganda machine moved into operation, claiming that the attack had not damaged the Railway Yards and that, only civilian targets such as schools and hospitals had been hit. It was not until well after D Day, when the Germans had been pushed from most French towns and cities that an article by War Correspondent George Slocombe appeared in a national newspaper. That article which can be seen below revealed the true story of the Rouen Operation.

Why battered Rouen thought our raid worth while

They saw Germany's crack Army become a fleeing rabble

By GEORGE SLOCOMBE

ROUEN, Saturday.

WHEN the history of our strategy before invasion day can be written it may be found that the most decisive blow struck at the German High Command in France was that of the bombardment of Rouen on April 19 of this year.

All we knew at the time was that the historic city had been terribly battered.

We knew, too, that for some reason the German propaganda Ministry and its satellites in Paris and Vichy had decided to exploit the bombardment of Rouen as an unusually and particularly criminal action.

Now Rouen was in every sense of the word the most important centre of the German High Command in France. Not only had Field-Marshal von Rundstedt his general headquarters here, but the vital centres of the entire Wehrmacht command for northern France—operations, intelligence. Gestapo, communications, supplies, civil affairs—were all distributed throughout the city.

There is still a mystery about the precise objective of the Allied bombing force which struck at Rouen on the night of April 19, and I am not attempting to explain it.

The Germans claimed that we had aimed at the railway network and missed it, and that our bombs fell instead on the civilian population. This French clandestine Press reported at the time that the Germans lighted false flares during our raid to deceive our bomb-aimers.

The same patriotic Press informed us that after the raid the Germans planted delayed action bombs in a number of ancient and historic buildings in Rouen, among them the cathedral, the Palais de Justice, the old Hotel du Bourgtheroulde, which contained a bas-relief on its walls depicting the meeting of Henry the Eighth and Francis the First on the Field of the Cloth of Gold, and a number of other monuments of Anglo-French history. Rouen, therefore, is badly blitzed. But the spirit of the population is magnificent.

'Ringside' seats

They realise what in the haste of our advance across the Seine we did not have time to realise. They had not only seen the disruption of the German High Command as a result of our bombing—the hasty flight of all the German staff officers from their bombed or burning buildings, the loss of their four years' accumulation of intelligence files, the breakdown of communications with the operations units in Northern France.

They had also had ringside seats at the most wonderful circus performance of all time—the flight of the German Seventh Army.

Our British and Canadian soldiers in the Caen-Falaise sector, who had fought stolidly for two months to achieve the rout of the Seventh Army, were denied this spectacle. They were merely the hunters who, after fighting and cornering the game, could at last give chase.

But the people of Rouen, who for four years had been browbeaten, hectored, tortured and killed by the Germans, were by a special providence able to stand on their own bank of the River Seine and watch the broken remnants of the Seventh Army try to cross the broad river.

This is a story that matches that of the retreat of Napoleon's defeated Grand Army across the Beresina.

Our bombing had destroyed all the bridges over the Seine, and our strategy — Montgomery's strategy—had pressed the German Seventh Army back against a broad river with a hostile and derisive population on the other side of it.

Let one of those hostile and derisive Normans tell the story.

First of all let me say that he is one of the Resistance men in Rouen who had reason to know the Germans. His wife had sheltered escaped British prisoners and had helped them to get away. She was caught at last, tortured by them in the cellars of the Palais de Justice, which I today visited, battered and blackened.

"We saw the Germans trying to cross the Seine," he told me. "They were the remnants of the Seventh Army, the best German army that we had seen in France.

"They crossed in ones and twos, in little groups. Some of them swam across. Others tied floating barrels together with string and pushed the barrels in front of them.

"I saw one German officer who pushed a horse across and himself followed, grasping the horse's tail. Others came over on rafts. When they reached this bank of the Seine they were no longer an army. They were a rabble.

"I saw one very tall German officer riding on a donkey. Another German followed him, hobbling on a wounded foot. Most of them had thrown away their arms to cross the river. Not one in 20 carried a rifle.

"They seized everything they could ride on—horses, cows, donkeys, handcarts, bicycles, cars.

Officers obeyed

"The worst humiliation of all was the way the S.S. battalions treated them. If a German officer was riding in a car and an S.S. private saw him, he would order the officer out of the car and take it himself. The officer obeyed meekly. A terrible fall for the pride of the Prussian professional soldier.

"When we saw this happen to the Germans we realised why we had been made to suffer ourselves. We were proud of our city, we were proud of France. We did not know why we had been bombed in April 1944. But we know now. It is something to have seen the might of Germany brought low."

I have never seen a ruined French city that is so proud of its ruins. The old town is very British in spirit, or, to put it more accurately, Britain is very Norman in spirit.

I would like to think that some great British city would do something about lovely ruined Rouen.

A Return Visit on 20th/21st April

Two nights after the ME 410 German Night Fighters had paid their first deadly visit to the skies over Mepal and Witchford airfields, a return visit by a single ME 410 took place on the night of 20th/21st April. Both Witchford and Mepal had dispatched Lancasters to attack Cologne and the ground crews were now awaiting the return of their aircraft.

An air raid warning (White) had been given at 00.50 hours and was still in place at 01.58 hours when an aircraft engine was heard approaching Mepal, followed by bursts of cannon fire as the ME 410 flew low over the airfield. Once it was considered safe, Flight Sergeant Mitchell sent the ground crews out with torches before any of the returning aircraft landed in case any anti personnel bombs had been dropped, as had happened on the night of the 18th/19th.

L.A.C. Vic Smith Ground crew of JN-X and L.A.C. Fred Woolterton Ground crew of JN-M went to check their adjoining dispersals. They did not find any A.P.Bs, but discovered that the ME 410 had been aiming at Lancaster JN-X which had been left on its dispersal with its bomb load, as a defect had been found prior to take off.

Both wheel chocks had been shot away and there was a hole in the Port Wing and another shell punctured the petrol tank without causing an explosion. A spent cannon shell was found under the bomb bay, but fortunately the bomb load had not been hit. It could all have been so different if the arrival of the ME 410 had once again coincided with the returning Lancasters of Mepal and Witchford.

Flight Lieutenant S.W. Holder and crew. Photo taken on completion of their tour of operations in 1944 with Lancaster MKI A4 G-ME 698 of C Flight.

Left to right:

Flight Lieutenant S.W. Holder	Pilot RNZAF
Pilot Officer J. Nicholls	Navigator RNZAF
Flight Sergeant R. Garret	Rear Gunner
Pilot Officer D.W. Francis	Mid Upper Gunner RCAF
Flight Sergeant W. Preece	Wireless Operator
Flying Officer H. Philips	Bomb Aimer
Flight Sergeant A. Stantiall	Flight Engineer

On the night of the Intruder Incident they like many other crews had dropped their bombs at 13,000 feet on the red and green indicators.

Flight Lieutenant Rash with four of his crew and Lancaster KO-J. HK542.

Above Left to Right:
Flight Sergeant S. Rice Rear Gunner, Flight Sergeant W. Kilmurray Wireless Operator, Flight Lieutenant C.D. Rash Pilot. Flight Sergeant C. England Bomb Aimer, Sergeant J. McCabe Flight Engineer.
Not in photo - Sergeant K. Moore* Mid Upper Gunner and Flight Sergeant D. Franklin Navigator.

*Sergeant K. Moore would later lose his life with another crew on 8th June 1944 during an attack on Chevreuse in which 115 Squadron lost seven aircraft.

Flight Lieutenant Rash and crew had landed at 02.00 hrs and were leaving debriefing when the German intruder flew low over their heads.

At debriefing Rash and crew reported that they had identified the target by the red and green target indicators on which they had bombed from 14,000 feet. They had observed a few explosions and the attack had appeared to be going well.

Cameron's crew and Ground crew

Pilot Officer Cameron landed safely back at Witchford at 03.42 hours, three minutes behind Flight Sergeant Maude and leaving only Flight Lieutenant Eddy's aircraft to return to Witchford, as Pilot Officer Gibson had landed at Downham Market and would return to Witchford the next morning.

Lancaster and crew

Lancaster and crew

Australian Pilot Flight Lieutenant Ray Milgate and crew pose in relaxed mood under the port wing of Lancaster KO-S

Left to right:
Sergeant Ron Richardson   Rear Gunner
Flight Sergeant Stan Banks   Bomb Aimer
Flight Sergeant Ron Hulse   Wireless Operator
Sergeant Howard Griffin   Navigator
Sergeant John Zipfel   Flight Engineer
Flight Lieutenant Ray Milgate   Pilot

Missing from the photograph is Sergeant Chapman, Mid Upper Gunner

Corporal Noreen Dunbar seated front right with other Flying
Control staff colleagues during a Christmas party on
22/12/1944

The large rockets being held in the photograph were introduced
after the intruder incident. The rockets would be fired from the
control tower balcony to warn returning aircraft that an enemy
fighter was present in the vicinity.

Others in the photo:
Back row 2nd left Flight Lieutenant Rawlinson Flying Control
Officer.
Middle Corporal Elsie Dean R/T Operator.
5th left Sergeant John Howard,
6th left Flight Lieutenant Finlayson Flying Control Officer,
Front row seated middle Squadron Leader Humphries Senior
Flying Control Officer.

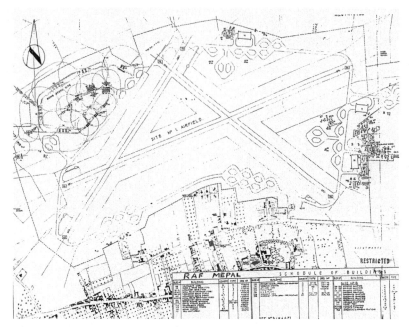

Map of RAF Mepal

WAAF Radio Operator Noreen Dunbar was also waiting and listening as she sat in Witchford's Control Tower: Waiting and listening for the first of the returning aircraft to call in with 115's code name `Blackmass`. Noreen, dressed in Battledress jacket, heavy pullover and trousers, was now doing a job far removed from her civilian job modeling glamorous clothes.

Another person waiting for the returning aircraft was L.A.C. Cook Butcher Tom Bullman, who was preparing the meal of bacon and eggs for the returning crews.

Three miles away in the village of Sutton, Frank Allen was on observer duty when a twin engine German aircraft flew low over their heads. Frank telephoned headquarters to report the sighting but was informed that he could be mistaken as no enemy aircraft had been picked up on radar crossing the coast.

The Lancasters of 75 Squadron were now returning and joining the circuit over Mepal airfield. At 01.57 hours the pilot of JN-M asked for permission to land and was told to follow in JN-V for Victor that was making its approach landing with its navigation lights showing. Just as V for Victor touched down on the 1,950 yard S.W. /N.E. runway several dull thuds were heard, followed by bursts of cannon fire. An enemy ME 410 had dropped anti personnel bombs on the runway and attacked the first three Lancasters attempting to land. None of the Lancasters were hit but the runway lights were immediately extinguished and the remaining aircraft diverted to Tempsford and Newmarket.

Thirty four SD 10A anti personnel bombs had been dropped in two AB250 containers. Only a few of the bombs exploded on impact as they had been dropped from only fifty to seventy five feet. Ground staff marked the positions of the unexploded bombs to be dealt with later by the Armourers. The runways would eventually be cleared and serviceable again by 15.15 hours.

Back at Witchford the Lancasters of 115 Squadron were also returning and Noreen Dunbar received the call she had been waiting for. "Hello Blackmass" This is C -Charlie permission to pancake. Squadron Leader Grant was the first to return and touched down at 01.57 hours. Now the returning aircraft would be stacked ready for their turn to land.

Flight Lieutenant Rash was next to land at 02.00 hours followed by Flight Sergeant Francis two minutes later with Flight Lieutenant Shadforth a further two minutes behind him.

Flight Sergeant Colin Campbell and his crew had just joined the circuit when he saw what he thought was a twin engine fighter pass his starboard wing. Campbell immediately switched off his navigation lights and called up the tower to report his sighting. Informed that no other sighting had been made he was instructed to switch his navigation lights back on.

Warrant Officer Hemming turned his aircraft into the funnels on approach to land. Ahead of him were two other aircraft. The aircraft navigation lights that Hemming could see in the far distance were those of Pilot Officer Birnie and Sergeant Lemoine.

Pilot Officer Rowe-Evans and crew pictured here with their replacement Z Zebra and not the MKII LL726 they flew to Rouen.

Left to Right: Sergeant Len Lewis Flight Engineer, Flying Officer Jack Spruce Wireless Operator, Sergeant Eric Levy Mid Upper Gunner, Pilot Officer B. A. Rowe-Evans Pilot, Flying Officer G. Steer Navigator, Sergeant W. Didcote Bomb Aimer, Sergeant E. Wyatt Rear Gunner.
Photo via Eric Billson

Above Left to Right:

Sergeant W. Young Rear Gunner, (Sergeant W. Andrews was Rear Gunner on 18th /19th April 1944), Sergeant J. Saunders Flight Engineer, Flight Officer E. Maskell Wireless Operator RAAF (Sergeant on 18th /19th `44) Pilot Officer E. Gibson Pilot RAAF Flying Officer. J. Stock Navigator, Sergeant R. Jones Bomb Aimer, Sergeant W. Dawson Mid Upper Gunner. Photo via E. Gibson

Lemoine was just about to touch down as all hell broke loose behind him. Hemming suddenly saw a German Fighter cut in front of him and raked the aircraft in front with cannon fire. Birnie`s aircraft was mortally hit. It immediately caught fire and dived into the ground. As Lemoine's wheels touched the ground the undercarriage collapsed. Lemoine executed a belly landing, the crew escaping without serious injury, but his aircraft now blocked the runway.*

Pilot Officer Moon had also been given permission to land and had F- for Freddie runway lined up and undercarriage down, when they saw an aircraft in front hit by a stream of tracer, catch fire and go straight down.

Frank Kanarens, Moon`s Rear Gunner did not see the action but heard the shock and consternation in the voices of those up front that did. Within seconds over the radio came the call

`Bandits` and the runway lights were extinguished. Ernie Moon upped undercarriage and veered off the approach.

It was now that Frank Kanarens could see the blazing aircraft on the ground not knowing at the time that it was their old Lancaster LL667.

Flight Lieutenant Hammond and crew arrived back over Witchford just as Birnie's aircraft had crashed and the `Bandits` message came over the radio. They saw the runway lights go off and could see the fire from the burning aircraft below. The fire was so intense that it lit up the whole night sky, so much so that they could see men and vehicles on the ground heading for the crash site.

Hammond and all the other pilots left the area for a short cross country and to await further instructions.

On the ground the events had also been witnessed and Witchford's firefighters were already heading for the scene.

Dick Freeman, a farmer in the village of Coveney had got used to the sound of the Lancasters returning to Witchford and Mepal in the early hours, but at 2 O`clock he heard another different sound; the unmistakable sound of a German engine. Suddenly he heard heavy gunfire and saw an aircraft still showing navigation lights going down on fire. It hit the ground with a terrific explosion somewhere in West Fen, at the foot of Coveney hill. Dick set off in the direction of the fire.

The crash report on Lemoine's aircraft states that no fault was found with the aircraft and it was strongly believed that either the pilot or flight engineer had pulled up the undercarriage lever, although both men denied this.

Whether what was going on behind Sergeant Lemoine`s aircraft had any bearing on the incident will probably never be known.

Another witness to the crash was Ernie King who also lived in Coveney. Called to the window by his mother who had heard all the noise, they saw an aircraft going down in a ball of flame. Ernie grabbed his jacket and ran across the fields in the direction of the crash. He arrived at the scene at the same time as another local, Tom Goodjohn, but there was nothing they could do as the heat and flames were so intense. It seemed that the whole field was on fire.

Suddenly bullets started to explode and Ernie and Tom took cover in a ditch until the fire crews arrived.

Soon most of the village was there including Father Beale, the Parson of Coveney church. Most of the villagers had arrived thinking it was a German aircraft that had crashed and were saddened to find otherwise.

The field in which Pilot Officer Birnie's aircraft crashed was known as Ashwell Moor and belonged to Farmer Henry Woodroffe for whom Ernie King worked. The day before the crash they had half planted it with potatoes.

At 02.40 hours, with the runway cleared of Lemoine's aircraft, it was considered the runway lights could now be switched on and the remaining aircraft could now be called in to land.

At 02.45 Flight Sergeant Taylor brought his aircraft in on approach to Witchford, flying over the still burning remains of Birnie's Lancaster and touched down safely on the runway.

Flight Sergeant Burdett landed three minutes later. Pilot Officer Gibson landed at Downham Market and returned to Witchford the next morning.

Gradually at two, three, four, five and six minute intervals more Lancasters returned to touch down safely at base. There was then a nine minute gap before Sergeant Quinton returned at 03.36 hours, followed by Pilot Officer Chantler at 03.38 and Flight Sergeant Maude at 03.42. Three minutes elapsed before Pilot Officer Cameron landed, leaving only one more Lancaster, that of Flight Lieutenant Eddy to return home.

Flight Lieutenant Rash and crew had landed before the intruder attack at 02.00 hours and were now leaving de-briefing when a twin engine German Fighter flew low over the base, low enough for them to see its markings. It was so low that it dislodged soot in one of the chimneys in the kitchen where Tom Bullman was still preparing food for the crews, coating most of the food with a film of soot. Tom had to start again, unaware that some of his food would not be required that morning.

Flight Lieutenant Hammond and crew had landed at 03.13 and were now vacating their aircraft on its dispersal. Just before switching off the radio they heard J-for Johnny given permission to land and Flight Lieutenant Eddy acknowledge.

Now as Hammond's crew stood on the concrete they could see Eddy approaching low across the fields. Suddenly they heard a burst of cannon fire and tracer hit Eddy's aircraft. One wing dropped and hit the ground, cart wheeling the Lancaster which exploded in a ball of fire.

As Witchford's Fire crew were still attending the first incident, Mepal`s tender assisted by attending the second inferno.*

When the attack took place on Eddy's aircraft, two men had run to man the gun on the roof of the control tower. One was Flight Lieutenant Eric Billson Gunnery Leader at Witchford and the other was the Commanding Officer Squadron Leader Annan. On reaching the gun they found there was no ammunition. When the full impact and details of what had happened filtered through, Squadron Leader Annan was devastated to find out that it was Eddy's aircraft that had been the second victim to fall to an intruder, for the six men that made up Flight Lieutenant Eddy's crew had previously been his crew until his appointment as Commanding Officer at Witchford.

Witchford was not alone in receiving a visit from II/KG/51 for, as 625 Squadron also returning from Rouen at 02.30 hours arrived over their base at Kelstern in Lincolnshire, a Lancaster was seen to go down in flames.

Pilot Officer J.P. Cosgrove RCAF Captain of ME734 and his crew of Sergeant Bennett, Flight Sergeant Mercer, Sergeant Jeeves, Sergeant Williams, Sergeant Page and Sergeant Beechey were all killed.

Flight Lieutenant Eric Billson, Gunnery Leader seated at his desk. Photo Eric Billson

*Mepal`s fire crew attending the Witchford Lancaster's crash site caused some confusion for several airforce personnel, who to this very day thought that 75 Squadron had lost a Stirling to the intruder and it was this crash that the Mepal fire crew were attending. 75 Squadron did lose a Stirling on this night but this was lost on a mining operation and crashed in Denmark.

At Witchford, guards were sent out to cordon off the two crash sites. Among these men was Jim Towers who had been patrolling the airfield perimeter. It would be daylight before the full story of Witchford's losses would filter through to all personnel.

Ron Ball, a ground crew NCO was devastated when he heard the news, especially as he had got to know Birnie and his crew. He remembered how they had turned up at dispersal one day, smart, keen and ready to take over a Lancaster in Ron's charge.

Many years later in a letter written to `The Tiller`, the 115 Squadron Association newsletter, Noreen King (formerly Dunbar) who was the WAAF Radio Operator the evening of the attack recalled the events.

"That night is embedded in my mind. I was terrified but prayed it did not show. It was a sad terrible night, how awful to be shot down anywhere, but especially when one is home. Bullets were flying everywhere with noise and flames. The sky was brilliant with the blaze".

Sergeant Harry Durham, Pilot Officer Moon`s navigator wrote in his diary the next day.

<u>Op No. 17. Rouen.</u>
This was our first French target and the shortest trip we have ever done.
The trip itself was a piece of cake. We bombed the T.I.s` which should have been on the Marshalling Yard, whether they were or not, I do not know.
On return to home was when the trouble started. We had twenty seven kites on and everyone got back around the same time. A Gerry intruder must have followed us back and the first we knew of it was when Pilot Officer Birnie in our old E-Easy was shot down making his approach. Over the R.T. came the word `Bandits`, and everyone made a dash to get miles away, we went to the Wash.
After a while we came back and landed ok. Then Flight Lieutenant Eddy got shot down. None of those two crews got away with it. Old Jones`y was with Birnie, worse luck.
What a time was had by all, fourteen kites were missing on the night. The Gerry also shot down two from Mepal and one from Waterbeach. He also dropped a stick of bombs down the runway at Mepal and shot up the Watch Office.

Sergeant Durham's entry in his diary, that fourteen aircraft were lost on the night was correct for main operations, but for some reason the three aircraft shot down over their bases on return from Rouen are not counted as operational losses and are not included in the figure of fourteen aircraft lost on various operations that night. Counting these three aircraft plus one Halifax lost on a minor operation, eighteen aircraft were lost that night.

Below is a list of targets and losses for 18/19th April 1944.

Rouen
> *273 Lancaster and 16 Mosquitoes took part.*
> *Losses: 3 Lancasters shot down over their bases on return.*

Cologne
> *26 Lancasters took part.*
> *Losses: 0.*

Juvisy
> *202 Lancasters and 7 Mosquitoes took part.*
> *Losses: 1 Lancaster.*

Noisy-Le-Sec
> *112 Halifaxes, 61 Lancasters and 8 Mosquitoes took part.*
> *Losses: 4 Halifaxes.*

Tengier
> *139 Halifaxes, 21 Lancasters and 8 Mosquitoes took part.*
> *(The 8 Mosquitoes also operated on the Noisy-Le-Sec op.)*
> *Losses: 6 Halifaxes.*

Minelaying Operations

Kiel Bay, Swinemund and the Danish Coast.
> *88 Halifaxes, 44 Stirlings and 36 Lancasters took part.*
> *Losses: 2 Stirlings and 1 Halifax.*

In attendance to main operations several minor attacks were also taking place in which one Halifax was lost.

On 6th March 1944, 75 N.Z. Squadron at Mepal received its first Lancaster which would herald the start of the Squadron's conversion to the Merlin engine bomber. The Stirling would now be used mainly on mining operations, with the Lancasters taking over the role of main bombing targets.

On the night of the 18th/19th April, Mepal's Lancasters were involved in bombing the Railway Yards at Rouen, while the remaining Stirlings carried out mining duties in Kiel Bay.

Stirling EH 955 AA-K took off from Mepal at 20.41 hours and was attacked by a Night Fighter over Denmark and crashed at

Jenning, a small hamlet 3km South of Gram. Flight Sergeant Hill and Irwin, New Zealanders and Sergeants Kahler, Mulligan and Woollam were laid to rest in the local Churchyard.

It was probably the news of the loss of this Stirling that gave rise to the rumours that 75 Squadron had also lost two aircraft to the Night Fighters of 11/KG51.

One other Stirling was also lost on the mining operation. No trace of the Lakenheath based aircraft or its 149 Squadron crew were ever found.

The Aircraft Movement card for Lancaster MK I LL667: One of 100 Lancaster MK IIs delivered between October 1943 and March 1944 by Armstrong Whitworth.

LL667 was one of 300 Lancaster MK IIs produced with Bristol Hercules engines as an insurance against possible shortage of Merlins. The aircraft was delivered to 514 Squadron at RAF Waterbeach, Cambridgeshire and almost immediately transferred to 115 Squadron on their arrival at nearby RAF Witchford on the 26th November 1943. 115 Squadron was the first squadron to be completely equipped with the MK IIs Lancasters.

The ME 410s of 11/KG/51 would return to their base at Soesterberg well pleased with their night's work, but their efforts on this night would be nothing to their achievements later in the month, when on the night of the 22nd/23rd led by their Commander, Major Puttfarken, they would shadow the returning B-24s of the 2nd Bomb Division back to their bases.

Nine B-24s and one Albemarle would fall victim to the guns of the deadly Messerschmitts.

11/KG/51 did not escape unscathed. Two of their aircraft did not return, one of which was Major Puttfarken's. Dietrich Puttfarken had taken his total of kills to five on this night of the 22nd/23rd April, but his aircraft was believed to have been damaged by return fire from one of his victims and it is thought that both he and his crewman Ofw Willi Lux were lost without trace when they crashed into the North Sea. The second ME 410 was shot down and crashed at Ashby St. Mary in Suffolk, killing Pilot Oblt Klaus Kruger and Fw Michael Reichart.

Post Mortem

So who did shoot down the two Lancasters from Witchford and the Lancaster from Kelstern on the night of the 18th/19th April 1944?

A new book published in 2004 titled `Luftwaffe Night Fighter Combat Claims 1939-1945` by joint authors John Foreman, Johannes Matthews and Simon Parry, gives us the clues we need. The book contains a definitive list of claims submitted by Luftwaffe Night Fighter pilots for Allied aircraft shot down in W.W.II.

We know that only three Allied aircraft were shot down on British soil on the night in question, and luckily there are only three claims made, all by ME 410 pilots.

Oblt Claus Breissner claimed to have shot down a Lancaster near Cambridge at 02.25 hours. Hptm Dietrich Puttfarken claimed to have shot down a Lancaster in England at 02.25 hours, and Lieutenant Wolfgang Wenning made a claim for downing a Halifax North West of Hull at 03.47 hours.

Birnie`s Lancaster was recorded as being shot down at 02.10 hours, so bearing in mind that these times could be approximate and Witchford not being that far from Cambridge, it is a good chance that it was Hptm Puttfarken who shot down Birnie`s aircraft at 02.10 hours.

I also believe that Oblt Claus Breissner who claimed shooting down a Lancaster at Cambridge, did in fact shoot down Flight Lieutenant Eddy`s Lancaster at 03.47 hours over Witchford.

That leaves Lieutenant Wolfgang Wenning Technical Officer of MKII KG51 as being responsible for shooting down Pilot Officer Cosgrove's Lancaster over Kelstern airfield. Although his claim was for a Halifax, none of which were lost on British soil that night.

Wenning was killed when he collided with an Airspeed Oxford at Rugby on 27th April 1944.

A further complication is that Witchford's 115 Squadron Gunnery Leader Squadron Leader Eric Billson has always maintained that one of the attacking aircraft was a JU88 and that it came down the runway at low level firing its cannons at a Lancaster attempting to land.

Noreen Dunbar who was the Radio Operator in the Tower that evening also recalled bullets flying everywhere substantiating that an attack took place not only in the landing circuit, but on the airfield itself. It is my belief from evidence I have, that it was a single aircraft that made the first attack on Mepal airfield and then went on to shoot down Birnies Lancaster in the circuit at Witchford.

My reasoning is that no bombs were dropped on Witchford airfield and why, if there had been more than one ME 410 in the Witchford/Mepal area, were there no further attacks on Witchford based Lancasters who were sitting ducks in the landing circuit area.

Therefore, if it was a single Night Fighter that made the attacks on both airfields, all its bombs would have been deposited at Mepal. Also, having shot up the runway at Mepal and attempting to down the two 75 Squadron Lancasters, followed by shooting down Birnies aircraft at Witchford, he would have probably used up all his ammunition, so could not make any further attacks.

Ten ME 410s had taken off from their base at Soesterberg in Holland and were well dispersed on East Anglia and Lincolnshire. JU 88s, an aircraft of similar appearance to an ME 410 especially in the dark, were also operating that night, and could have been involved in the second attack on Witchford 1 hour and 38 minutes after the first incident.

However, the claims for shooting down the three Lancasters are all made by ME 410 pilots. So, were Flight Lieutenant Eddy and his crew unlucky enough to have arrived back over Witchford at exactly the same time as further enemy aircraft arrived over their base?

Other airfields that came under attack were Tuddenham near Bury St. Edmunds where another ME 410 dropped thirty four 5D 10As in a field North East of the village at 02.45 hours. At 02.10 hours Little Snoring also had a visitor with eight 5D 10s exploding near the main runway. Other areas attacked were Sheringham, Westleton and Hockwood in Norfolk. Mickfield and Stoneham in Suffolk.

A varied mixture of bombs had been dropped including anti personnel and phosphor in attacks over East Anglia.

The Luftwaffe fighters did not return entirely unscathed, as one JU 88 hit by anti aircraft fire was so badly damaged that it crashed landed in Bradwell Bay. This must have been the aircraft that was reported to relatives of the victims of the intruder attacks, as being responsible for that terrible night in the skies over Witchford and Kelstern.

On the 3rd September 1944 the home base of the ME 410s of 11/KG/51 would receive some of their own medicine when Bomber Command paid a visit to six airfields in Southern Holland. 348 Lancasters, 315 Halifaxes and 12 Mosquitoes took part. 2 Halifaxes failed to return.

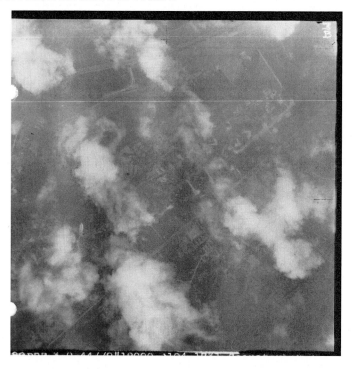

Soesterberg airfield under attack. Photo taken from Flying Officer McNulty's 466 Australian Squadron Lancaster based at Driffield.

Hauptman Dietrich Puttfarken

The Commanding Officer of II/KG 51 who was responsible for shooting down at least one of the Witchford Lancasters.

In March 1944 V/KG2 formed the Nucleus of II/KG 51, the Gruppekomandeur of which was 23 year old Major Dietrich Puttfarken from Hamberg.

Puttfarken was originally a Bomber Pilot and had completed many operations. He was awarded the Ritterkreuz on October 7th 1942. In March 1944 II/KG 51 moved from its base in

Hildesheim to Soesterberg in Holland, from where they began a new phase of devastating intruder operations. One favourite tactic was for the ME 410s to follow our bombers returning home from a bombing operation and attack them at their most vulnerable time while circling over their bases or when approaching to land. Another tactic was for the squadron to split up after crossing the Coast and seek out individual targets which they either bombed or strafed.

The night of the 18th/19th April 1944 was a busy night for both Allied and German Airmen. The Americans had started the day by sending 775 Bombers to attack various targets including the Heinkel works. Bomber Command sent their aircraft to bomb communication targets in France on which they dropped 4,000 tons of high explosives. Other smaller attacks were also taking place including Mosquito attacks on Berlin.

The Luftwaffe was also active and preparing to follow our bombers back to their bases. Among them were Puttfarken's ME 410s.

The action did not go entirely all one way, as one JU88, seriously damaged by anti aircraft fire, was forced to land in Bradwell Bay. It is highly possible that this aircraft was the aircraft that was blamed (probably wrongly) for shooting down at least one of the three Lancasters lost over their bases that night. It may also have been the one that Ernie Beer was instructed to inform Mrs. Maddox had shot down the Lancaster on board which was her son.

Puttfarken's squadron of ME 410s was again in action on 22nd April when they attacked American aircraft returning from a mission.

The American losses were heavy, but the Germans suffered a great loss also when Hauptman Puttfarken and his crewmen failed to return to their base at Soesterberg in Holland.

At Soesterberg, II/KG 51 waited for their aircraft to return. The crews recounted the night successes and waited for the return of others. As daylight broke, it began to be realised that two crews were not coming back. 9K and HP the mount of Oberleutnant Kruger was now a smoldering heap of twisted metal in a Norfolk field. The big shock was that the Gruppekomandeur was missing. Major Dietrich Puttfarken

Ritterkreuz Holder with five aircraft already destroyed to his credit was missing.

His loss remains a mystery to this day, and it must be assumed that he and his Beobachter, Oberfeldwebel Willi Lux had fallen victim to the North Sea.

PART 3: The Exhibition & Excavation

My second encounter with Witchford airfield

Research and Exhibition

For many years I had thought it sad that no visual record of what happened at RAF Witchford and its near neighbour RAF Mepal during World War II was available locally for future generations to see.

It was a telephone call one Sunday in June 1994 from my wife Sue who was on duty in Ely Museum, which started this whole story. She informed me that a gentleman had just called in and asked if the Museum had anything about Witchford airfield, as he was stationed there during the war. Informed that there was not, he was saddened and somewhat dismayed, especially as his Squadron 115 had suffered the heaviest losses in the whole of Bomber Command. My wife had said to this man, Charlie Wernham as I now know him, that I had two or three photographs of Witchford at home. Charlie was very interested and asked her if he could meet me. Sue was phoning to tell me she had given him directions to our home and he was on his way.

Charlie and I spent most of Sunday afternoon talking about the airfield and his time there as a Rear Gunner, and I agreed with him that it was sad that there was no mention of either Witchford or Mepal in the Museum. It was probably this meeting with Charlie that caused me, two months later, to accompany my wife to Ely Museum's Annual General Meeting and (unlike me) to stand up, when the meeting reached the point of any other business and ask what the Museum had planned for 1995, the 50th Commemoration year of the end of hostilities in World War II.

The Chairman said that nothing was planned and had I any ideas as to what could be done. I suggested that, in view that the Ely area had been surrounded by airfields, and that the Cambridgeshires had suffered greatly at the hands of the Japanese, with a little research, an exhibition to relate the parts that they had played in World War II, could be put together as a tribute to them and the many local people who had also played their part. The Chairman was impressed and said that as I seemed to have the bright ideas, would I like to organise such an exhibition for the Museum. I had painted myself into a corner, so I accepted the challenge. It was not until I arrived home that I began to think, "Where the hell do I start?"

I began with the local Library and, as my wife also worked there as a part-time Library Assistant, I was soon able to find the right books. The very first book I decided to read was `Action Stations: Military Airfields of East Anglia', by Michael J.F. Bowyer. This excellent book gives a run down on all East Anglian airfields. I quickly looked up Witchford and Mepal, which were two and six miles from Ely respectively. It was here that I came across the mention of an intruder incident at Witchford on 19th April 1944, in which 115 Squadron lost two aircraft.

Having lived in Ely all my life, I was amazed that I had not heard any mention of this before. Little did I realise what reading those few lines would involve me in, over the next few years. I visited the library again and checked the old newspapers for 1944, but there was no mention of the crashes I was looking for. It did not take me long to realise and I suppose it was obvious, that reporting of such incidents would not be allowed, not only from the security point of view but also that of moral. The next step was a trip to the Public Records Office at Shire Hall, Cambridge; one of many such visits which would take place over the next few years.

The preparation for the War Years exhibition began to gather pace with offers of help coming in from all directions. Amongst the volunteers were the Royal Naval Association, the Royal Air Force Association and the members of the Cambridgeshire Regiment, who were survivors of the Japanese Prison Camps. Many of these men have now become good friends of mine. Also volunteering help were two men who are probably more responsible for me writing this book than anyone. Giuseppe Lombardi (Joe to his friends) and Ken Wooton. Joe and Ken both live in Cambridgeshire. Joe is a mine of information on the Stirling Bomber and Ken is a walking history book on Mepal airfield, the wartime base of 75 N.Z. Squadron.

Joe offered to loan his collection of aircraft memorabilia to the exhibition and Ken part of his extensive photographic collection on Mepal and 75 Squadron.

One day I was given the name of a man who had seen one of the two Lancasters shot down. I immediately phoned retired farmer Dick Freeman and made an appointment to go and see him. Evidently during the war he lived in the village of Coveney which is about three miles from Ely, but now he lived in a 1960's built farmhouse at the foot of Coveney Hill. When I called to see him he related his story to me of what he had seen on that tragic night back in April 1944.

On leaving Dick's house he accompanied me along his drive back to my car, which was parked on the wide grass verge on a sharp corner on the road back to Ely. As we reached my car Dick pointed to a spot in the field behind my car, about a hundred yards away and said "Well, a lot of that Lancaster is still buried there you know. When are you going to dig it up?" I assured Dick I was not involved with aircraft recovery, thanked him and made my way home. It was during another meeting with Joe, Ken and Graham Austin another volunteer to help with the exhibition, that I mentioned my meeting with Dick Freeman.

Joe was aware of the crash but was interested that Dick knew the exact spot and that he knew that some wreckage still remained. Joe asked me to find out who owned the field and see if we could get permission to run a special metal detector over the field. I made contact with the landowner, Nigel Fyffe, who expressed interest in finding out what was buried in his field and he immediately gave his permission.

It was January 1995 when Joe and his friend Colin Pratley brought the special detector to the field and did a preliminary investigation. This investigation showed three very strong readings, at distances where engines would have been if still attached to the aircraft, and one weak reading where the fourth engine would have been. During these checks, small pieces of aircraft were found including a piece of plastic looking material which Colin said proved that the aircraft was a MKII Lancaster. Colin explained that this plastic material, which I was later to find out was called Rotaloyd, was the covering to the aircraft's wooden propellers. I was amazed at this and I must admit that until the day in August that the excavation took place and proved him right, I still doubted that any Lancaster had wooden propellers.

From the readings of the metal detector, Joe decided that it was well worth applying for an MOD licence to excavate the site and Nigel Fyffe gave permission for an excavation to take place after his crop had been harvested in August. The MOD licence was to eventually come through at the beginning of August.

The opening date for the War Years exhibition was mid May, originally planned for only one month. It had grown to such an extent that war related memorabilia had virtually taken over the entire Museum. A decision was made by the Museum Trustees, led by Chairman Dennis Adams, to extend the exhibition through to November, to incorporate Remembrance Sunday.

From left to right: Barry Aldridge, Sue Aldridge, Ken Wootton, Graham Austin in Ely Museum during the War Years Exhibition 1995

The exhibition proved to be a great success probably because of the year and possibly because it was history within living memory.

It was the display on Witchford airfield that attracted the Directors of Grovemere Holdings to the exhibition and for David Brand, the Managing Director, whose father had purchased a large area of the old airfield after the war, to ask what was to happen to the Witchford memorabilia after the War Years exhibition had finished. When I said, I did not know, he suggested that I set up a display in his office foyer, which was on the old airfield and part of the aptly named Lancaster Way Business Park, which his company Grovemere Holdings owned.

When I informed David Brand of the forthcoming Lancaster excavation, he showed a great interest in becoming involved along with his co-directors. Their involvement was to prove invaluable, for they not only organised transport for moving recovered wreckage but contacted a Mr. Amory of Amory Construction, who provided a Hi-Mac digger and driver for the two day excavation, free of charge.

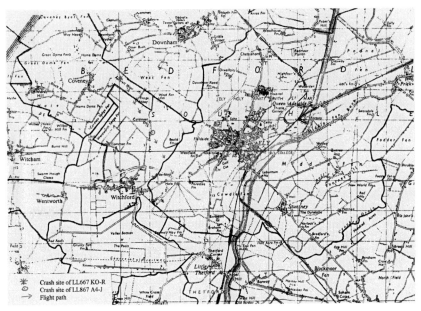

Flight path and crash site on map

The Recovery of the Wreckage

The stubble stretched across the field like a giant yellow carpet. It was 7.30am on August 19th 1995, V.J. Day. We were having one of our hottest summers on record and already the temperature was climbing. I pulled off the fen road into a field known to locals as Ashwell Moor. There, in the middle of this

119

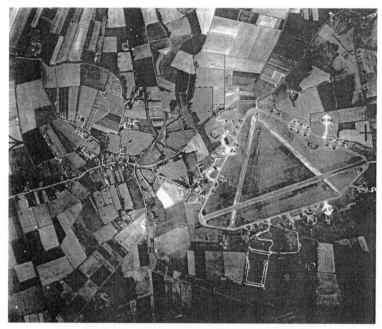
Arial view of Witchford Airfield

sea of yellow was a small white caravan and a giant Hay-Mac excavator. The owner of the caravan was Ken Wooton.

He and the excavator driver, Ian Scott were already on their second pot of tea, sitting around a small table, in a couple of collapsible chairs. I declined a cup of tea and looked across the flat fen, back towards Ely, two miles away. I could see the flag fluttering in the light breeze on the distant ship of the fens (Ely Cathedral). Glancing back to the road I could see more vehicles approaching, all heading for Ken's caravan which was acting as a location point, as well as a tea hut.

Soon the field held dozens of cars, trucks, trailers and their occupants, and what an assortment: Builders, farmers, accountants, directors, engineer, artist and archaeologist. We all hung around chatting, Ken greeting everyone with the offer of a cup of his brew. We were all waiting for Giuseppe Lombardi and his friend Colin Pratley, who would be bringing the equipment, with which, earlier in the year, we had pin-pointed the object that had brought this unlikely gathering together on this warm August morning. Giuseppe, or Joe as we call him for obvious reasons, was late but on arrival wasted no time in relocating the site and instructed Ian the Hay-Mac driver to remove the top soil over a large area. The excavator roared into life, its tracks vibrating the ground as it moved into position. I glanced back towards the Cathedral and followed the skyline until I could just see the top of a large apex roof. It was the sole remaining hangar of the old wartime airfield, RAF Witchford.

Excavator driver Ian Scott takes off the top soil as the dig begins

Just in front of the digger's cab you can just see the silhouette of Ely Cathedral. To the right and just off the picture on the horizon is the sole remaining hangar of RAF Witchford

My mind drifted back to the stories which had brought us all here today, when over fifty one years ago a wartime tragedy happened which was to account for the largest loss of life in the Ely area in World War II. When on the night of the 18/19th of April 1944, 115 Squadron would lose one of its aircraft, shot down by a night fighter in a ball of flame and ninety eight minutes later would lose a second in an identical way, which crashed into another field at Beald Farm only a short distance away.

Looking back to the Cathedral and its fluttering flag, I decided in this year of commemoration (1995) of 50 years since the end of the war against Germany and Japan, to investigate and research the incident that cost the lives of fourteen brave men whose names along with thousands of others should never be forgotten.

A Report on the excavation of Lancaster LL667 by Team Leader Giuseppe Lombardi

For many years I had known of the two Lancasters which were shot down by enemy aircraft and had crashed near Witchford, but it was while myself and close friend Ken Wooton were helping Barry Aldridge in 1994 with the preparation for Ely Museum's very successful War Years exhibition for 1995 which was to mark the commemoration of both V.E. and V.J. Days that the subject came up. While Barry was researching RAF Witchford of the two crashed Lancaster we decided to find the crash site of the Lancasters as we had heard that at least one of them had dived into the ground. Barry sought permission from the landowners Nigel Fyffe and in early 1995 we arrived at the field one Sunday morning to try to locate the impact point of Lancaster LL667. Wheat had just been planted in the field and any digging would have to wait until the harvest in August.

I had bought along Colin Pratley, a long standing colleague, both of us experienced in locating recovering wreckage from crash sites. Also present in the hunt was our friend Ken Wooton who was to be heavily involved in the recovery and later presentation of the display items.

We had with us the necessary equipment to locate the impact point. I was mildly amused to find that when we arrived at the field, it seemed that every Tom, Dick and Harry from the village that were around at the time of the crash, was there to `advise` us on where to look. Another aviation group had previously looked at the site some years before, but did not find the impact point. There was much heated discussion amongst the old men who all claimed it crashed in different parts of the field. As the field was quite large, Colin and I quietly went about our usual routine for searching based on our experiences. After only about fifteen minutes, we found what we were looking for, set up the equipment and obtained a large reading. To us, it could only mean one thing, remains of one of the Bristol Hercules engines. Assuming it was an engine, and just guessing that it was the port outer, I then walked in a direction based upon the information we had been given as to the orientation in which the Lancaster was flying before it crashed. I had previously made a mental note of the distances between all engines, and with this knowledge I stood over the inner engine, and sure enough we got the expected readings. I then walked across what I guessed to be the cockpit area. As luck would have it I had gone in the right direction and I was now standing over the remains of the starboard inner engine. We continued and located the other outer engine. We marked the site with a pole and the old men who stood watching seemed very impressed with the speed in which we located the site.

They did not know about the methods we used, but we could guess the conversation in the local pub that night. We had gone home very happy too.

My next job was to obtain a MOD license to dig on the crash site and this arrived several months later. This was going to be a large job, so we required a mechanical digger to excavate the site, along with other equipment. Barry had made contact with David Brand, of Grovemere Holdings who seemed keen that a display of memorabilia goes on display at Witchford airfield which he owned. They very kindly arranged for a 360 tracked digger, with driver, and all the necessary buckets which I had requested. They also provided the transport to remove the wreckage from the site.

We finally arranged for the dig to take place over the weekend of 19/20th of August, just after the crop was taken off.

On arrival at the field at about 8.30am, Colin and I were somewhat surprised at the turn out of people on the field. We were hoping for a quiet dig, but we knew that there would be a lot of people milling around on this one, because of the publicity it had received. In the past this has caused us problems and this occasion was to be no exception. The others in our small team arrived soon after.

I started by briefing those who were to take part in the dig and then got the driver to remove the top soil and put it to one side so it could be replaced last of all. We then started to erect the red plastic fencing which would keep people well away from the hole we were to dig. Unfortunately, when we started to unroll the fencing I soon realised that we had not got what I had asked for, and it was nowhere near enough for the job. I then took the decision that we would use the earth removed from the hole to build two earth berms at each of the long sides of the hole as we progressed to each engine. We then used the fencing to block off either end. In this way, I hoped to keep the onlookers away from the hole and out of danger.

We then relocated the port outer engine and started to dig for this. The digger made light work of removing the soil and soon reached the clay underneath. We had found some remains just under the topsoil, but these were just much corroded pieces of aluminum. At a depth around 18 feet we uncovered the propeller reduction gear from the port outer engine. Lots of other pieces from the engine were found, but there was no engine. We were not put off by this as we knew the next reading was stronger and were sure the rest of the engines were buried.

Moving over to the port inner engine, we dug down about 15 feet and came to the back of the engine which was laying face down, in the direction of the dive in which the aircraft was in, as it struck the ground. We carefully cleaned off some of the heavy mud which encased the back of the engine to examine the various pumps, motors and other accessories which were still attached to it. By this time I was down in the hole along with Colin and a few others to guide the driver on where to put the bucket. It was most important that any damage to the wreckage which could be easily caused by the buckets teeth was reduced to a minimum. It was a hot day and very tiring work down the hole. There was a constant stench of aviation fuel as well as the sticky mud to contend with.

After careful maneuvering of the diggers` position, and with the aid of our hand spades, we started to uncover the rest of the engine. As more of the mud was removed we discovered that the propeller reduction gear was amazingly still attached to the engine (this usually breaks off on impact on this type of engine). The next job was to right the engine and fix a lifting chain. Once this was achieved, the digger gave a heave as the unit, weighing in at around a ton, was hoisted to ground level for the first time in over 50 years. Further inspection revealed that it was in remarkable condition, with some of the cylinders still attached, and all the brittle alloy aluminum casings were largely intact, even the propeller gear partially turned on its bearings! The unit was then hoisted on the trailer and finally arrived back at Witchford airfield - over 50 years late!

Next we moved over to the cockpit area. Once the soil was removed, it was down to sifting with our spades to find the small items which are now on display at Witchford.

By now a sizeable crowd had gathered to watch the operation, but not all heeded our warnings to stay behind the fence, or at the top of the earth berms on to which most had climbed. One or two took no notice of our repeated requests to move back, and on one occasion I had to ask the driver to switch off the engine while I persuaded them to leave the edge of the hole. We also had a visit from the Press who took a few photos for the Cambridge Evening News which went out that evening. At one time there were 50 cars parked in the field and people were coming and going all day.

Time was moving on and we decided to pack up for the day at around 7.00pm and return early the next morning to continue.

The next day was similar to the first and we recovered the two starboard engines, along with many other smaller pieces of interest, including an undercarriage oleo strut. These were recovered from a depth of around six feet. The engines, although still in very good condition, were without their propeller reduction gear which was retrieved separately. Late in the day, two friends of mine arrived by air in their microlights and landed in the same field, close by. I took the opportunity to borrow one of the machines and took up one of our team as passenger to get an aerial view of the site. I was amazed at the size of the hole, even from the air, which showed the scale of the work undertaken.

Later in the day we started to back fill the hole. When we were nearly finished I repaired the land drain, which we had broken through earlier, before the digger leveled the ground and replaced the top soil.

We were all pleased with the results but the job did not stop there, for many more hours of work were needed. Steam cleaning, followed by hours of hard work was undertaken to make the display at Witchford presentable.

Giuseppe Lombardi
19th January 97

Working on the excavation

The author holds one of the early finds, A Graviner fire
extinguisher. Photo Roy Kent

Nigel Fyffe the land owner seated on shooting stick looks on as the hole in his field gets deeper. Without his co-operation and help, the recovery of the wreckage would not have been possible.

In the background, Ken Wooton's caravan/come tea hut, in the foreground the Press arrive to take pictures.

An engine has just been lifted clear of the hole and is being inspected by Team Leader Giuseppe (Joe) Lombardi. In the background a large amount of earth is being raked through to find small objects. It was here that a crucifix was found by Ray Woodbine. (See later in this book).
Photo: Cambridge Newspapers Ltd.

The photograph above shows the Bristol Hercules starboard inner engine of Lancaster LL667 having just been lifted from where it has laid buried for over 50 years. One of the three engines recovered but the most complete. It was decided to clean this engine so that it could be displayed.

Hours and hours were spent on this task, especially by Bryan Lely who spent much of his spare time pressure washing the engine in sometimes freezing temperatures. On the day of the dig David Brand and Grovemere's other Directors had been in the thick of the dust and muck, armed with shovels and spades and now, after the recovery of the wreckage, David Brand provided the use of his workshop for cleaning and final preparation. It was over a year before oil stopped dripping from the engine and the smell of burning disappeared. The engine is now the centre piece of the display in the foyer of Grovemere's offices.

The engines of the MK II Lancaster have caused much argument and fuss, especially when the story of the shooting down of the two Lancasters was told on BBC Look East on 20th April 2005. The next morning their switchboard was jammed with irate callers stating that any fool knows Lancasters were only powered by Merlin engines and not Bristol Hercules. I received a phone call from the BBC the next morning and was able to convince them that the facts they had been given were true. That night BBC Look East took pleasure in pointing out that the press often get it wrong but on this occasion, they were right. 301 Lancasters were built using the Bristol Hercules engine.

115 Squadron were the first squadron to be completely equipped with these MK II Lancasters while based at East Wretham, Norfolk, moving to RAF Witchford in November 1943. The MK IIs were gradually phased out and replaced by MK Is and IIIs by the end of April 1944.

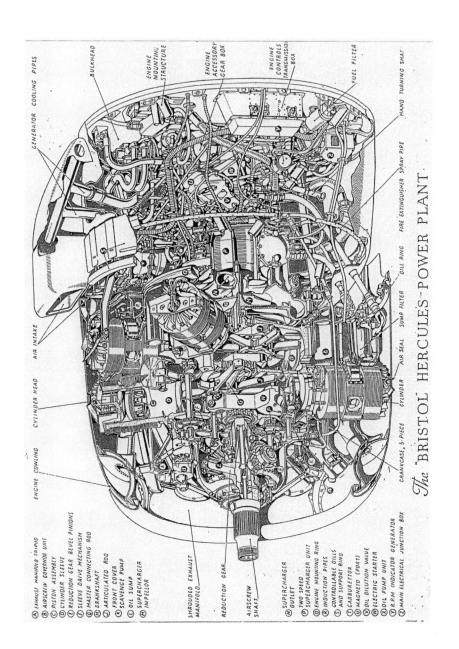

The "BRISTOL HERCULES" POWER PLANT.

GENERATOR COOLING PIPES
BULKHEAD
ENGINE MOUNTING STRUCTURE
ENGINE ACCESSORY GEAR BOX
ENGINE CONTROLS TRANSMISSION BOX
FUEL FILTER
HAND TURNING SHAFT
FIRE EXTINGUISHER SPRAY PIPE
GILL RING
SUMP FILTER
CYLINDER
AIR SEAL
CRANKCASE, 3-PIECE

AIR INTAKE
CYLINDER HEAD
ENGINE COWLING

(A) EXHAUST MANIFOLD TRIPOD
(B) AIRSCREW GOVERNOR UNIT
(C) PISTON ASSEMBLY
(D) CYLINDER SLEEVE
(E) REDUCTION GEAR BEVEL PINIONS
(F) SLEEVE DRIVE MECHANISM
(G) MASTER CONNECTING ROD
(H) CRANKSHAFT
(J) ARTICULATED ROD
(K) FRONT COVER
(L) SCAVENGE PUMP
(M) OIL SUMP
(N) SUPERCHARGER IMPELLOR

SHROUDED EXHAUST MANIFOLD
REDUCTION GEAR
AIRSCREW SHAFT

(O) SUPERCHARGER OUTLET
(P) TWO SPEED SUPERCHARGER UNIT
(Q) ENGINE MOUNTING RING
(R) INDUCTION PIPES
(S) CONTROLLABLE GILLS AND SUPPORT RING
(T) CARBURETTOR
(U) MAGNETO (PORT)
(V) OIL DILUTION VALVE
(W) ELECTRIC STARTER
(X) OIL PUMP UNIT
(Y) R.P.M. INDICATOR GENERATOR
(Z) MAIN ELECTRICAL JUNCTION BOX

Plan of the Bristol Hercules Power Plant

130

Bryan Lely pressure washing the engine in September 1995. Bryan was to spend many wet, cold weekends repeating this process before the engine could be moved to the workshop for its final preparation.

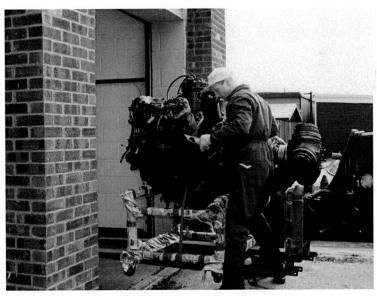

The engine cleaned and prepared for display is checked by Bryan Lely for its short trip from David Brand's workshop to the Grovemere House foyer.

Graham Austin and the author with Directors Howard Whetstone, Christopher Tooth and Managing Director David Brand, as the engine arrives at the company's office block.

The starboard inner engine of LL667 in its final position as centre piece of the RAF Witchford Display of Memorabilia in the office foyer of Grovemere House, on the Lancaster Way Business Park, formerly RAF Witchford.

Graham Austin, one of the first to offer help with the War Years exhibition is also an amateur artist. I asked him to paint me a picture from Dick Freeman's eyewitness account of the intruder incident. The painting had to contain a certain amount of artist's licence to show the three aircraft involved in one picture.

The end result can be seen below.

Photo via David Muncey

The excavation was over and now began the long job of trying to piece together the story of what happened on that tragic night in April 1944.

I had no idea how long my research would take and would never have believed I would still be trying to finish the story in 2009.

My original intention was to write a book solely about the intruder incident but during the research, I have made contact with many men and women who served at RAF Witchford, all of whom have shown great patience with my many questions, and on being asked, related to me other stories of RAF Witchford, so I decided to include some of these stories and memories in Part 4 of this book.

PART 4: Personal stories

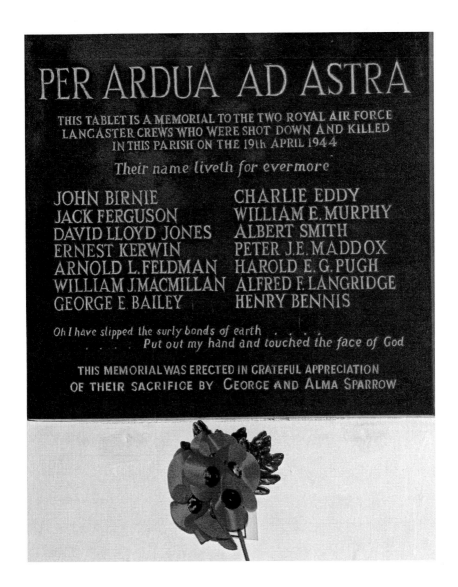

Memorial Tablet

Personal Tales and Memories on and around RAF Witchford

I would like to thank all those who contributed stories and memories of their time at Witchford; many sadly, are no longer with us.

Fate and Sergeant Donald's Crew

Bennis, Maddox, Pugh and Langridge first met during training at RAF Wing in Buckinghamshire in June 1943, when they formed Sergeant Dickie Donald's six man Wellington crew along with Navigator Sergeant Gibson.

By July Sergeant Gibson's place in the crew had been taken over by Flying Officer Smith.

In September the crew was posted to RAF Little Snoring in Norfolk to No. 1678 Conversion Flight converting to the Bristol Hercules powered Lancaster MK II. As the Lancaster required a Flight Engineer they were now joined by Sergeant Brotherton. On 4th September Donald and his crew were accompanied by Pilot Officer Rogers instructing Donald with familiarisation of the Lancaster and carrying out dual circuits and landings. Later in the day Flight Lieutenant Farquason took over as instructor and more circuits and landings were practiced. The following day Pilot Officer Rogers was again instructing but that evening, the 5th September, Donald was to join another experienced second pilot for his first operation. Flying as second pilot or second Dicky as it was more commonly known was general practice in Bomber Command and was intended to give an uninitiated pilot the opportunities to fly his first operation over enemy territory with an experienced crew before commencing operations with his own crew.

Crew photo taken during training at RAF Wing,
Buckinghamshire

Back row Left to Right: Bennis, Donald, Smith.
Front row Left to Right: Maddox, Langridge, Pugh.
Photo via Anne Mathews

Sergeant Donald

The crew that Donald was to fly with that evening was Squadron Leader J.B. Starky's, target Mannheim. Six aircraft were detailed to attack the target; the first taking off from Little Snoring at 20.10 hrs and the last at 20.15 hrs. The combined bomb load for the six MKII Lancasters was 6 x 4,000lb HCs, *96 x 30lb incendries and 2,160 x 4lb incendries.*

Squadron Leader Starky was flying Lancaster DS 682 KO-Y * and was accompanied on this op by five other B Flight aircraft captained by:

Sergeant D. Pirie and crew flying	DS 773 KO-T
Flight Sergeant E. Bradford	DS 721 KO-S
Flying Officer R. C. Newcomb	DS 683 KO-R
Sergeant L. Halley	DS 664 KO-X
Pilot Officer K. Harris	DS 631 KO-Z

* DS 682 KO-Y was usually flown by Pilot Officer Howell and crew who were on leave at the time of the Mannheim op. See `The Wise Owl`s' later in this book.

Sergeant Halley had to abandon the sortie as the oxygen supply to his rear gunner was faulty so returned early after jettisoning his bombs safely.

The five remaining aircraft continued towards their objective until, 20 miles from the target, Squadron Leader Starky`s aircraft was attacked head on by a JU 88 and again from astern. The Lancaster was riddled by bullets in the attack which destroyed the starboard elevator. Starky gave the order to abandon the aircraft which was carried out by Navigator Sergeant Irwin and the Wireless Operator Sergeant Farrell. Immediately after Sergeant Farrell left the aircraft the Lancaster became more stable and air-worthy enabling Squadron Leader Starky to fly the aircraft back to England and make a crash landing at RAF Ford at 01.45 hrs.

Flight Engineer Sergeant Moll and Dicky Donald both received wounds in the JU 88 attack but Rear Gunner Sergeant Willis and Mid Upper Gunner Sergeant Tugwell claimed to have shot the German aircraft down. Due to his injuries Sergeant Donald was now unable to continue flying with his own crew. The four other aircraft were able to reach the target which they identified by means of green target indicator markers on which they dropped their bombs from heights ranging from 19,500 feet and 21,000 feet before returning safely to base.

On 9th September Squadron Leader Robert Annan took over as Captain of Donald's crew and training on the conversion course continued throughout the month, the latter part of which was at RAF Foulsham.

October arrived and Annan and crew were now back at Little Snoring as an Operational crew with 115 Squadron's A Flight. They did not have to wait long for their first operation when, on 2nd October, they took part in a gardening operation (mining) to the Friesian Isles where they dropped six vegetables. (Mines). On their second operation to Hanover on 13th October they received a hot reception being attacked by fighters four times; three times by JU 88s and once by an ME 109.

The 18th saw a return to Hanover and again they managed to evade the attentions of an ME 109.

On 18th November Annan and crew took part in their first operation to Berlin.

On 26th/27th November, 115 Squadron moved to RAF Witchford, Cambridgeshire. The crew took part in ops to Berlin and Leipzig during January, the former from which they returned early due to severe icing problems. At the end of December the crew was again without a Captain as Squadron Leader Annan was promoted to the rank of Wing Commander and took over as Commanding Officer of 115 Squadron.

Smith, Maddox, Brotherton, Langridge, Bennis and Pugh were now spare crew, and flew individually with other crews who were short of a crewman through illness or leave etc. On the 14th January Flight Sergeant Pugh flew with Flight Sergeant Fogaty on an operation to Brunswick in Lancaster DS 629 KO-H. After leaving the target area at a height of 22,000 feet, Fogaty's aircraft was attacked from below by a JU 88. The enemy aircraft not being seen till after it broke away from the attack. The starboard inner engine was hit by canon shells which caused a violent shuddering of the aircraft. Flight Engineer Sergeant Life was wounded in the hand and leg and the Mid Upper and front turrets were put out of action. Hydraulic oil and smoke filled the aircraft as the JU 88 made a second attack, in which the starboard wing received more damage. A third attack took place but the Lancaster was not hit, but had lost height to 12,000 feet. It was at this point that it was realised that the starboard inner engine had been shot away.

Flight Sergeant Fogaty was determined to take his aircraft and crew home rather than abandon the aircraft over enemy territory or ditch in the sea.

Navigator Flying Officer Paddon set a course for home and Fogaty, through skillful airmanship, brought the Lancaster home at a height of only 5,000 feet to execute a successful landing with a burst tyre at the emergency landing airfield at Woodbridge in Suffolk - and without further damage to aircraft or crew.

Flight Sergeant Fogaty was awarded the DFM for his masterly handling of a difficult situation and with fine crew co-operation saved both crew and aircraft.

Sergeant S.R. Life was admitted to East Suffolk and Ipswich Hospital with machine gun wounds. Tragically after recovering from his injuries Sergeant Life was drowned at Denver Sluice near Kings Lynn during Dinghy drill on the 11th July 1944. He was 19 years old.

Promoted to Flying Officer, Fogaty's war ended on 31st March 1944 when his aircraft was hit by flak during an operation to Nuremburg. Finished off by a Night Fighter the crew baled out apart from their Captain who made an emergency landing at Neckartenzlingen.

Captain and crew were taken as POWs.

Pilot Officer Paddon, Sergeant Lomas and Pilot Officer Simpson had flown with Fogaty on the Brunswick operation.

While flying as a spare bomb aimer Flight Sergeant Pugh also flew two operations on 27th and 30th January with Flight Sergeant Whyte to Berlin. On the 15th of February on another op to Berlin Alan Charles Whyte now a Pilot Officer failed to return to Witchford. His aircraft LL 651 A4-A crashed near Newruppin. Navigator J. Ellis was the only survivor.

Robert Brotherton newly promoted to Flight Sergeant also stood in for the regular engineer of Pilot Officer Canning and crew on the 20th of January, target Berlin, but was destined not to return. Their aircraft LL 650 KO-J was attacked over the target and crashed 16km from the centre of Berlin. Only Rear Gunner Sergeant Hocking survived and was taken as a POW.

On February 2nd Smith, Maddox, Pugh, Langridge and Bennis accompanied their old Skipper Wing Commander Annan on an Airtest of Lancaster MKII KO-M. They were joined by a new Flight Engineer Sergeant William Leslie Murphy who took the place of the late Flight Sergeant Brotherton. Shortly after this airtest they were posted the short distance to RAF Waterbeach to join a new Skipper, Flying Officer Charles Eddy RNZAF who was completing his conversion from Stirlings to Lancasters with 1678 Conversion Flight.

Moon and crew flew the MK II Lancaster on a regular basis from early January to the 30th March `44. LL667 was at that time lettered KO-E (Easy) of A-Flight. During January, Moon and crew took LL667 to Berlin five times.

By the time Pilot Officer Birnie had taken over the aircraft on 11th April, it had been transferred to B-Flight and re-lettered KO-R (Roger) probably to fill the gap left by the loss of B-Flight's Lancaster DS 766 KO-R, which was hit by flak during an attack on Frankfurt on the 22nd/23rd March `44. The Lancaster was badly damaged and its Pilot Flight Sergeant Pope attempted to land at Woodbridge (the emergency landing airfield), but crashed nearby.

Flight Sergeant Pope, Sergeant Grady, Sergeant Haugh and Sergeant Bretscher were killed.

Sergeants Holman, Hatfield and Mabey were injured. Sergeant Hatfield died three days later.

MKII 667 – The only known photo of this aircraft

This photograph of Pilot Officer Ernie Moon`s crew and Ground crew was taken under the aircraft's starboard inner engine in February 1944.

From left to right - Unknown (ground crew), Pilot Officer Dallas McRae, Sergeant W. Swan, Flight Sergeant Frank Kanarens (Rear Gunner), Pilot Officer Ernie Moon (Pilot),

Flight Sergeant W. Fraser, Sergeant R. Sharp, Unknown (ground crew).

The Recovery of wreckage from Lancaster Bomber KO-R LL 667

Among the more personal items found during the excavation of Jock Birnie's MK II Lancaster were a silver cigarette case and a Spanish-made baby Colt automatic. The gun was of a very low caliber and was definitely not a service issue. Also found was a back from an Air Ministry issue watch. As the digger driver emptied his bucket to the side of what was becoming a large hole, a team of four would rake through each bucketful in the hope of finding any small items of interest. During one of these rake throughs Ray Woodbine, one of the team, gave a shout that he had uncovered something interesting. The item turned out to be a Crucifix, slightly bent by the heat of the fire which had engulfed the aircraft.

Some weeks later I took the cross to a local jeweller to find out what it was made of. Upon examination he was able to tell me that the cross was made of brass which was originally silver plated as traces of it could still be seen, with the figure of Christ in gold. The cross would have been inlaid with Mother of Pearl and the jeweller's opinion was that it was probably one hundred years old. The jeweller had also noticed that the heat of the fire had caused a misalignment between the back and front of the cross, which led him to believe that the cross was probably made to open, leaving a recess inside, in which a photo or item of personal value may have been kept. Both I and the jeweller were keen to find out if the cross did open and if anything was contained inside. After applying fine penetrating oil the jeweller turned the bulbous top and ring at the top of the cross to which a chain may have been attached. After three or four turns the cross opened like a pair of scissors, and inside the uncovered recess was a blackened, small, rolled tube. Sadly, in an attempt to remove the tube it fell into fine dust and gone (I thought) was any chance of ever finding out which member of the crew the cross belonged to. How wrong I would be proved to be, when a chain of events began to fold. Three months later I was asked to give a talk in Sleaford in Lincolnshire to the Fenland Branch of the Bomber Command Association about how I become involved in excavating a Lancaster Bomber and what we found.

This was the first time I had given a talk about anything, so I was very nervous about talking to a group who knew more than I would probably ever know about the subject. All went well and after the talk everyone came and inspected a selection of small parts and items of interest that I had taken along. Among these items was the cross.

A lady approached the table on which the items were displayed and asked if she could pick up the cross to which I replied, "Yes". On picking up the cross she immediately dropped it, claiming it had burned her fingers. I must have given her a funny look for she said, "I am deadly serious. You should take this to a clairvoyant as it has a story to tell", to which I replied that I did not believe in such things.

A few weeks later I arrived home on a Monday evening from work and my wife informed me that she had read in our local paper that a clairvoyant evening was being held in the Lamb Hotel, only half mile from our house in Ely, and she thought it would be a good idea to go and get an opinion on the cross and to find out what story it had to tell. The clairvoyant evening was to be on Friday and every day my wife pestered me to take the cross in for an opinion. I finally gave in and on Friday we took the cross to the Lamb Hotel wrapped in tissue and placed inside an envelope. On arrival we were introduced to one of two lady clairvoyants to whom I gave the envelope and said "Please could you tell us something about the contents of this envelope". The clairvoyant removed the tissue and immediately said that the cross was generating heat which meant it had been in a terrible fire. I was thinking that you would not have to be a brain surgeon to work out that heat had bent the cross and not impact. But, from this point on I was surprised by what she said. She told us that the cross did not originate from this country but came from overseas. The cross originally belonged to a lady who, as a young woman had almost decided to be a nun. She did not become a nun and eventually married and had two sons. She was a devout Catholic and her husband died early in the marriage and she had a hard time bringing up her family on her own. She gave the cross to one of her sons when he came to this country. He never wore the cross around his neck but carried it in his pocket. The cross was in his pocket when he was killed in a most terrible fire, not two miles from this spot that had lit the sky like daylight. The clairvoyant told us that she could not tell us more because there were too many people in the room which would cause distractions, but she could tell us that the man's surname began with the letter M.

I must admit that I was somewhat taken aback by what the clairvoyant told us, for the facts that I had already researched were that the Mid Upper Gunner of LL 667 was Flight Sergeant William James McMillan, a Canadian from Gananoque and he was the only Catholic on the aircraft. The coincidences did not stop there, for a few weeks later I received a letter from Frank Kanarens, a former 115 Squadron Rear Gunner who informed me that he and his crew had flown LL 667 from early January to the 30th March 1944 before handing it over to Birnie's crew. Frank had read all about our excavation of LL 667 in the Squadron Newsletter. Accompanying his letter was a photograph of his crew standing under the starboard inner engine of LL 667, the very engine that we had decided to clean and display. The photograph is the only known picture of the ill-fated aircraft.

Frank had emigrated to Canada after the war and was now living in Gananoque, the home town of Flight Sergeant McMillan.

A few days after Frank received his Squadron Newsletter, he went for a haircut. While waiting he picked up a magazine and was surprised to see a photograph inside of William James McMillan in an article about locals who had lost their lives in World War II.

Wreckage of LL 667

Frank decided to try and contact the family, but sadly the only surviving members were second cousins. However, they were able to confirm that Mrs. McMillan had been a devout Catholic, had been widowed early in her marriage and giving her son a Crucifix when he left for England would have been just the thing she would have done, but they had no definite proof that she had done so.

Frank Kanarens comes back to his former RAF base

In 1997, fifty three years on and minus his wellies, Frank Kanarens – former 115 Squadron Rear Gunner (front) – again poses with the starboard inner Bristol Hercules engine of LL667.

Frank visiting England from his home in Canada called in at his former base at Witchford, to look at the display of memorabilia. Also in the picture are Frank's brother-in-law and sister-in-law and in front of them, Frank's wife Ivy.

The following pages from Frank Kanarens' log book show part of LL667's flying history and a tough period for air crews through which Moon's crew thankfully survived.

JANUARY 1944.

Time carried forward — 216·00 85·20

Date	Hour	Aircraft Type and No.	Pilot	Duty	Remarks (including results of bombing, gunnery, exercises, etc.)	Flying Times Day	Night
		LANCASTER			(1 x 4,000 Lb 8 cans)		
2/1/44	00·40	LL 667	F/SGT MOON	REAR GUNNER	OPERATIONS :— BERLIN. M/U TURRET U/S AFTER LEAVING ENGLISH COAST ON OUTWARD JOURNEY. D.C.O		7·05
3/1/44	00·30	JS 678	F/SGT MOON	REAR GUNNER	(1 x 4,000 x 10 cans) OPERATIONS :— BERLIN FIRED SHORT BURST AT JU.88 ATTACKING PORT QUARTER. NO HITS CLAIMED OWING TO EVASIVE ACTION TAKEN. E/A DID NOT OPEN FIRE.		6·30
4/1/44	11·40	LL 667	F/SGT. MOON	REAR GUNNER	AIR TEST	·40	
5/1/44	11·55	LL 667	" "	" "	AIR TEST	·20	
14/1/44	10·35	LL 701	"	" "	AIR TEST	·30	
14/1/44	17·10	LL 667	F/SGT MOON	REAR GUNNER	(1 x 4,000 Lb 8 cans) OPERATIONS :— BRUNSWICK		5·10
20/1/44	16·45	LL 667	F/SGT MOON	REAR GUNNER	OPERATIONS :— BERLIN		7·10
25/1/44	14·15	LL 667	"	"	LOCAL FLYING	1·25	
25/1/44	10·55	LL 667	"	"	AIR TEST.	·25	
26/1/44	11·40	LL 667	"	"	LOCAL FLYING	·45	
27/1/44	18·00	LL 667	F/SGT MOON	REAR GUNNER	OPERATIONS :— BERLIN (1 x 4,000 10 cans)		8·10
29/1/44	00·20	LL 667	F/SGT MOON	REAR GUNNER	OPERATIONS :— BERLIN (1 x 4,000 Lb 10 cans)		8·00
31/1/44	14·15	LL 667			AIR TEST.	·35	

Total Time — 220·40 127·25

Time carried forward — 220·40 127·25

Date	Hour	Aircraft Type and No.	Pilot	Duty	Remarks (including results of bombing, gunnery, exercises, etc.)	Flying Times Day	Night
			SUMMARY FOR	MONTH JANUARY			
			sergeant S/LDR		TOTAL HOURS DAY. 4·40		
			COMMANDING "A" FLIGHT No. 83 ION.		TOTAL HOURS NIGHT. 42·05 TOTAL HOURS 46·45		
			FEBRUARY	1944.			
		LANCASTER					
5/2/44	11·50	LL 667	F/SGT. MOON	REAR GUNNER	BOMBING. 3,000 FT.	1·05	
5/2/44	11·15	DS 661	" "	" "	LOCAL FLYING	1·10	
9/2/44	10·20	LL 667	" "	" "	LOCAL FLYING	1·30	
10/2/44	11·00	LL 667	" "	" "	FIGHTER AFFIL.	·45	
15/2/44	14·50	LL 667	"	"	FIGHTER AFFIL. D.N.C.O.	1·05	
15/2/44	11·00	LL 667	"	"	AIR TEST.	·40	
16/2/44	17·25	LL 667	F/SGT. MOON	REAR GUNNER	OPERATIONS :— BERLIN (1 x 8,000 Lb)		7·35
19/2/44	10·45	LL 667			AIR TEST	1·00	
19/2/44	23·55	LL 667	F/SGT MOON	REAR GUNNER	OPERATIONS :— LEIPZIG. TURNED BACK DUTCH COAST. OXYGEN IN M/U U/S. (1 x 4,000 Lb cans) JETTISONED COOKIE RETAINED INCENDIARIES. LANDED WATERBEACH. D.N.C.O.		3·10

Total Time — 227·55 138·10

Excerpts from Frank Kanarens' Log Book

Date	Hour	Aircraft Type and No.	Pilot	Duty	Remarks (including results of bombing, gunnery, exercises, etc.)	Flying Times Day	Flying Times Night
		LANCASTER					
20/2/44	00·10	LL 667	F/SGT. MOON	REAR GUNNER	OPERATIONS :— "STUTTGART" M/U FIRED TWO SHORT BURSTS AT ATTACKING ME. 109. NO CLAIMS. E/A DID NOT OPEN FIRE. (1 X 4,000LB 13 CANS.)		7·00
24/2/44	18·50	DS. 728	S/LDR CRANT	REAR GUNNER	OPERATIONS :— "SCHWEINFURT" (1 X 2000LB. 13 CANS)		7·10
25/2/44	21·30	DS. 728	F/SGT. MOON	REAR GUNNER	OPERATIONS :— "AUGSBURG" HIT BY A/A INC. IN STARB. INNER TANK, ALSO DAMAGE TO LEADING EDGE OF PORT WING BY FALLING "COOKIE" (1 X 4000LB 1 X 500LB, 14, CANS)		7·15
					SUMMARY FOR MONTH FEBRUARY		
					TOTAL HOURS DAY 7·15. TOTAL HOURS NIGHT 32·10 TOTAL HOURS. 39·25		
			thelgnant.. S/LDR				
		COMMANDING "A" FLIGHT. No. 115 SQUADRON.					
						TOTAL TIME ...227·55/59·35	

Date	Hour	Aircraft Type and No.	Pilot	Duty	Remarks (including results of bombing, gunnery, exercises, etc.)	Flying Times Day	Flying Times Night
		LANCASTER					
1/3/44	14·20	LL 667	F/SGT. MOON	REAR GUNNER	AIR TEST & LOCAL FLYING	2·00	
4/3/44	11·05	LL 692	" "	" "	FIGHTER AFFIL.	40	
18/3/44	12·25	DS. 826	P/O MOON		AIR TEST	·30	
18/3/44	19·50	DS 826	P/O MOON	REAR GUNNER	OPERATIONS :— "FRANKFURT" (1 X 4000LBS, 12 CANS)		4·50
22/3/44	18·55	DS 826	P/O MOON	REAR GUNNER	OPERATIONS :— FRANKFURT CAME BACK FROM TARGET ON 3 ENGINES, PORT OUTER FEATHERED. (1 X 4000LBS. 17 CANS)		6·20
24/3/44	18·35	DS 826	P/O MOON	REAR GUNNER	OPERATIONS :— "BERLIN" AGAIN CAME BACK FROM TARGET ON 3 ENGINES STBD. OUTER FEATHERED. (1 X 4000LBS. 12 CANS)		8·10
29/3/44	12·40	DS 826	SGT. FRANCIS	REAR GUNNER	AIR TEST	·35	
30/3/44	12·00	LL 667	P/O MOON	" "	AIR TEST	·30	
30/3/44	22·30	DS 826	P/O MOON	REAR GUNNER	OPERATIONS :— "NÜRNBERG" (1 X 4000LBS. 16 CANS)		7·30
					SUMMARY FOR MONTH MARCH		
		COMMANDING A FLIGHT. No. 115 SQUADRON.	M.Radcliffe... S/LDR		TOTAL HOURS DAY 4·15. TOTAL HOURS NIGHT 26·50 TOTAL HOURS 31·05		
						TOTAL TIME 232·10/86·25	

Excerpts from Frank Kanarens' Log Book

Many strange things have happened concerning the cross, especially since it has been on display in a glass cabinet in the RAF Witchford Display of Memorabilia. I still look for logical reasons for things that cannot be explained, but I have moved from being a complete doubter to having an open mind.

The cross that probably belonged to William James McMillan

You can see in the photograph how the cross pivots on its base to reveal a recessed section, which on opening contained a rolled up tube – probably a photo which disintegrated immediately when it was touched. There was no chain on the cross which may have been lost, but remember the words of the clairvoyant. "He never wore it round his neck, but carried it in his pocket".

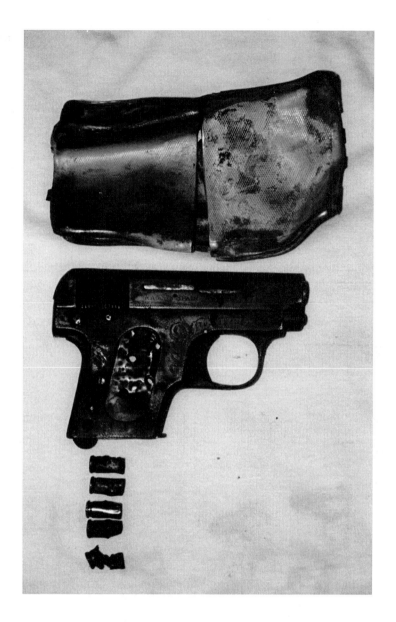

Silver cigarette case and gun

Above can be seen the silver cigarette case and gun. The silver cigarette case, despite its battered state, could still be carefully opened. Inside were traces of tobacco from the cigarettes possibly preserved by the fact that the case was embedded in clay. The case bore the hallmarks of the Birmingham Mint.

Also preserved due to the clay, were many items from the Dinghy, including Malted Milk tablets.

The gun as mentioned before was a Spanish made baby Colt automatic. The lead from the bullets had melted in the terrible fire, but why the gun did not explode with heat is another mystery. You can see where the plastic grips on the gun have melted away.

One theory put forward was that the gun may have been the personal weapon of Arnold Feldman, the only Jewish member of the crew. Being a member of a Bomber crew and being Jewish would not have brought him much favour with the Germans if he had been captured.

Lancaster LL667 MKII KO-R

Pilot Officer John Birnie	Age	26
Pilot		
Sergeant Jack Ferguson		19
Flight Engineer		
Flight Sergeant David Lloyd Jones		30
Navigator		
Pilot Officer Arnold Lepine Feldman RCAF	27	Bomb
Aimer		
Sergeant Ernest Kerwin		30
Wireless Operator		
Sergeant William James McMillan		19
Mid Upper Gunner		
Sergeant George Edward Bailey		23
Rear Gunner		

Ernest Kerwin (married) from Western Wakefield.
George Edward Bailey from Rainham in Kent.

Lancaster LL867 A4-J

Flight Lieutenant Charles Eddy RNZAF	Age	29
Pilot		
Sergeant William Leslie Murphy		
Flight Engineer		
Flying Officer Albert Smith		
Navigator		

Flight Sergeant Harold Edward George Pugh   *24*
Bomb Aimer
Flight Sergeant Peter John Edward Maddox 22   *Wireless*
Operator
Sergeant Alfred Frank Langridge   *32*
Mid Upper Gunner
Warrant Officer Henry Bennis RCAF   *22*   *Rear*
Gunner

Flight Lieutenant Eddy MBE
     Buried in Cambridge City Cemetery.
Warrant Officer Henry Bennis
Sergeant Ernest Kerwin
Pilot Officer Arnold Feldman

Pilot Officer John (Jock) Birnie

Pilot Officer Birnie

Pilot Officer John (Jock) Birnie was educated at Whitehaven County Secondary School, and lived at Spout House, Gosforth, and Seascale, Cumbria with parents Walter and Bessie and Sister Lorna.

After leaving school he worked as a Clerk for the Hermatite Steel Company at Barrow. In his spare time he was a member of the Whitehaven A.T.C. where he gained his enthusiasm for flying. Aged 17 ½ years Jock enlisted on the 2nd March 1941 and his service commenced on the 26th March 1941. After basic training he was recommended for Pilot training on 26th June 1942 arriving in Canada on the 8th August 1942 to commence training.

He was awarded his Pilot's wings on 2nd April 1943 and promoted to Flight Sergeant. It was here in Canada where he met up with some of his future crew. Jock returned to England to continue training at No. 17 Operational Training Unit, moving on to No. 1678 Conversion Flight at Waterbeach to convert to Lancasters. Having completed his course he arrived at RAF Witchford on 29th January 1944, being promoted to Pilot Officer on 2nd February 1944.

Pilot Officer Birnie's first war operation with 115 Squadron was on 15th February target Berlin, when he flew as Second Pilot to Pilot Officer C.G.Hammond in Lancaster KO-V DS641. This was to be a record breaking night for Bomber Command, sending out the most Lancasters, Halifaxes and dropping the highest tonnage of bombs.

On the night of the 20/21 February 1944 Birnie, as Captain of Lancaster MKII KO-W DS781, took off with nineteen other Lancasters from Witchford target Stuttgart.

His crew were the men with whom he would eventually lose his life:

Pilot Officer A. Feldman	Bomb Aimer
Sergeant E. Kerwin	Wireless Op/Air Gunner
Sergeant J. Ferguson	Flight Engineer
Sergeant W.J. McMillan	Mid Upper Gunner
Flight Sergeant D. Lloyd-Jones	Navigator
Sergeant G.E. Bailey	Rear Gunner

Birnie and crew continued with raids on Schweinfurt on 24th February 1944, Stuttgart with KO-U LL666 on 1st March 1944, and Stuttgart again on 15th March 1944 with KO-V DS620, Frankfurt with the same aircraft on 22nd March 1944.

On 11th April 1944 Pilot Officer Birnie took charge of KO-R LL667 for the first time, returning to Aachen the following evening again with KO-R.

His next operation to Rouen on 19th April 1944 sadly would be the last he and his crew would carry out.

The final entry on his records states, 'Casualty to flying battle damage'. He was twenty years old.

When news of John (Jock's) death arrived at the village of Gosforth, his parents and his sister Lorna were devastated. Also devastated was his old Headmaster Mr. Wilson who had so inspired the young John Birnie with his stories of flying in World War I.   Every year on Remembrance Sunday, after John's body was buried in the little church opposite the family home, Mr. Wilson would place a single poppy on the grave: A tribute from one airman to another.

War-time bomber to be dug up

A BOMBER, shot down during the Second World War while being flown by a Gosforth pilot, is to be dug up in Cambridgeshire.

Pilot Officer John 'Jock' Birnie, aged 20, died in the crash and was buried at St Mary's Church, Gosforth. His sister, Lorna Sloan, pictured with a photograph of her brother, has been told of the excavation by the RAF.

Mrs Sloan, of Wasdale

Exclusive report by Sian Davies

Road, Gosforth, said: "He was well liked, and very bright. He failed his eleven plus, but my parents managed to pay for him to go to grammar school and he passed eight subjects, four with credit."

Mrs Sloan said Jock's love of flying was fuelled by a former headmaster of Gosforth primary school, Will Wilson, who had flown in the first World War.

Mr Wilson was devastated by Jock's death and would put a single poppy on his grave every year.

Mrs Sloan said she did not want to see the plane, but was not upset that it was being dug up. She said she was mystified about how its remains had been found.

A German ME410 had followed the squadron back to Witchford Airfield, Ely, in 1944.

When the planes' landing gear was down, they were defenceless, and the fighter shot down two bombers.

Jock, whose plane was hit first in the attack, only had three missions left to complete his tour of duty.

The crash was in boggy land and was followed by two days of rain.

Barry Aldridge, a member of the excavation team, said: "Rather than recover the bomber, the RAF covered it with earth.

Gosforth newspaper cutting

158

Sergeant Jack Ferguson RAF – Flight Engineer of KO-R LL667R LL667

Sergeant Jack Ferguson

Jack Ferguson photographed above during his RAF training was born on November 26th 1924 at his grandparent's home in Park Avenue, Kendal, Westmoreland (now Cumbria). The only son of John and Mary Ferguson, Jack had two sisters Mary, three years his senior and Alvis, eight years younger. He learned to play the violin and would often be accompanied by Sister Mary on the piano. On leaving school he started work with Farrers, tea and coffee merchants in Kendal, where coffee was roasted over a gas flame. Jack had an easy going nature and a ready smile and was well liked by his employers and all who knew him.

At the outbreak of war, Jack's father was posted abroad leaving Jack to do his best in looking after the family.

Jack became a Police Runner and also joined the Army Cadets in which he was promoted to Lance Corporal. On reaching the age of eighteen he volunteered for Aircrew, being accepted for training in February 1943. His interest in flying had been generated after a ten shilling (50p) flight over Blackpool before the war. Having no educational qualifications he had to work and study hard to obtain his ambition to become a Flight Engineer. After basic training he joined course 69, twenty four weeks of intensive instruction at a Technical Training School at St. Athan in Wales. This course also included time spent at the Austin Motor Company. On completing the course, Jack was posted on 20th November 1943 to Wratting Common, a Cambridgeshire airfield close to the Suffolk boundary, to join 1651 Heavy Conversion Unit. Wratting Common was a sub-station of No. 31 Base at Stradishall in Suffolk, which was under the control of 3 Group. 1651 Conversion Unit had just arrived here from Waterbeach with their Stirlings. Jack, promoted to Sergeant would now embark on a five week course and become Flight Engineer for Flight Sergeant Birnie of A Flight. The course would include one week at a Ground Station followed by forty hours of flying which included training in Fighter Affiliation, Navigation, Air Firing and Radar training.

On completion of the course, Jack and his crew moved to RAF Waterbeach, Cambridgeshire and 1678 Conversion Flight to convert from the Stirling to the Lancaster MKII.

On the 28th January 1944 they moved a short distance from Waterbeach to RAF Witchford to join 115 Squadron as an Operational crew.

Sergeant Ferguson's grave in Parkside Cemetery, Kendal, Cumbria. Photo: Alvis Davidson (Sergeant Ferguson's sister)

Sadly the crew were embarking on what would prove to be a very short operational life span, as proved to be the case with many others.

Below, the envelope no family wished to see on their door mat, but sadly thousands did throughout World War II.

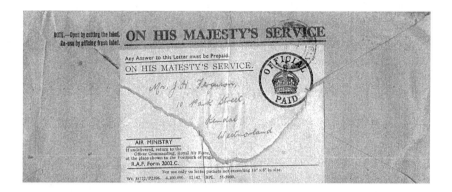

This brown envelope posted at Witchford and bearing the Ely postmark arrived at the Ferguson family home in Kendal, containing the news of Jack's death.

115S/C.1700/2/P.1.   28th. April, 1944.

Dear Mr. Ferguson,

It is with deep regret that I have to confirm the death of your son 1591340 Sergeant Jack Ferguson.

He left this Squadron on the night of the 18th. April 1944 to attack an important target in enemy occupied territory, unfortunately on return to this country his aircraft crashed due to enemy action. It is poor consolation but he was instantaneously killed and you will be relieved to know that he did not suffer.

Your son had served with this Squadron for only a short time, but proved himself a very capable Flight Engineer, and had become a popular member of the Squadron; his loss will be keenly felt by all.

His personal effects have been carefully collected and forwarded to the Royal Air Force Central Depository, Colnbrook, who will communicate with you in due course. For your information I enclose the names and addresses of the next of kin of other members of the crew.

Please accept the most sincere sympathy of myself and all personnel of the Squadron in your tragic bereavement.

Yours very sincerely,

Robert Annan

Wing Commander.

Mr. J.H. Ferguson,
10 Park Street,
Kendal
WESTMORLAND.

The contents of the envelope

The letter signed by the Commanding Officer Wing Commander Robert Annan explaining the circumstances of Sergeant Ferguson's death. (One of the fourteen letters he had to write due to the tragic events of the 19th April 1944)

He had signed many such letters since taking over Command of the Squadron and it would be a task he would have to perform many more times in the future.

Farrer's tea and coffee shop in Kendal, 1995

A plaque on the wall inside Farrer's in memory of Jack
Ferguson.

Flight Sergeant David Lloyd Jones RAFVR Navigator of LL667

Flight Sergeant David Lloyd Jones

David Lloyd Jones was the only son of Mr. & Mrs. J.W. Jones of Davey Cottage in Aberystwyth, Wales. He had one sister Gwendoline who was married to Rea Yates, also in the RAF and stationed at RAF Waterbeach, not far from where David was stationed at Witchford. On leaving school David joined the staff of the National Library where his kind disposition and upright character earned him general respect. He was also a talented musician and excellent pianist whose talents were often sought after and appreciated. He became a member of The Evened Daines Dance Band, playing double bass. The band was to make many broadcasts on Welsh radio.

David had volunteered for the RAF in 1939. Later he was called up and after basic training was posted to No. 41 Air School, East London, South Africa to begin his training as a Navigator. It was here in South Africa that David met a WAAF called Gwen. Gwen's father had brought David and a couple of his friends home for a meal. David and Gwen were immediately attracted to each other, and began going out to dances and the movies. They fell deeply in love and after three months decided to get married.

David was 28 years old and Gwen was 21. They got married on a Saturday and on the following Monday David was posted back to England to continue his training. Two years later, Gwen while attending her brother's wedding was to receive the news of David's death.

Flight Sergeant David Lloyd Jones's funeral took place on Monday 24th April with full Military honours. After the service his body was laid to rest in Aberystwyth cemetery. Owing to time and distance Gwen was unable to make the journey from South Africa to attend her husbands` funeral.

The Evened Daines Dance Band taken in 1935

Photo: Violet Daines.

David is standing back right.

Front left is Ralph Daines, Alto Sax player, son of the Band's leader, who is seated in the centre of the group.

David Lloyd Jones during RAF training (first left bottom row)

Author's note

In 1996 I made contact with David Lloyd Jones' wife Gwen, now Mrs. Naude who still lives in South Africa. In reply to my letter she recalled the short but happy time they spent together.

David was a wonderful person. When we went out to dances he would always join the band for he was a very talented musician. We only knew each other a short time before we got married, but in those days with the war, you tended to live for each day. It was such a shock when I received the news of his death. After the war I came over to England and stayed with David's family in Wales. They were such a lovely family but it was so sad that David was not there. I spent many hours sitting by his grave. After two years I became home sick and returned to South Africa. Later I re-married and had two lovely daughters. My second husband died when we were both fifty. I am now seventy five and have two son-in-laws and five grandchildren. I still keep busy with church work and go out to the Ballet etc. I thank you for all you are doing in keeping the memory of David and his Comrades alive.

Flight Sergeant Arnold Feldman

Flight Sergeant Arnold Feldman was born on the 21st November 1916 in Montreal, Quebec, Canada to parents Samuel and Beatrice Feldman. Arnold grew up to become a keen Model Aircraft builder, loved all sports and enjoyed reading. In May 1937 Arnold applied to join the Royal Canadian Air Force, giving his trade as an electrician. His medical report stated that he was 5 feet 6¼ inches tall, weighed 129 lbs, had grey eyes and brown hair.

When war broke out Arnold trained as an Observer, receiving his badge on 5th February 1943. On 23rd June he embarked ship at Halifax bound for England, arriving on 1st July. In England he trained as a Bomb Aimer before moving on to No. 17 Operational Training Unit at Turweston in Buckinghamshire on 10th August 1943.

Photograph of Birnie, Feldman and McMillan

Arnold was now part of a trained crew and with them moved to RAF Waterbeach, Cambridgeshire to join No. 1651 Conversion Unit to convert to the Lancaster Bomber. On completion of their course, Arnold and his crew captained by Pilot Officer John Birnie were posted to 115 Squadron based at RAF Witchford, only a few miles away from Waterbeach.

Flight Sergeant William James McMillan

Flight Sergeant William James McMillan was born in Gananoque on 24th March 1925, the son of James and Janet Catherine (nee McCartney) of Gananoque E. Toronto, Ontario. William's father James Rutherford McMillan was originally from Ireland and was a devout Catholic, as was his wife Janet. William also had a younger brother of which little information is available. William, a student, enlisted in the Royal Canadian Air Force on the 24th November 1942 at the age of 17 years. Earlier in the war the minimum age to enlist was 18, but had now been lowered by 6 months. William's father, a salesman, had died when his sons were quite young, leaving his wife to bring up her sons on her own. After training at several establishments in Canada, William set sail from Halifax, Nova Scotia for England on the 13th September 1943, arriving in England on the 19th. A trained Air Gunner, William joined No. 17 Operational Training Unit at Turweston Buckinghamshire. This is where he met Arnold Feldman and John Birnie who he would eventually crew up with and become Mid Upper Gunner.

Flight Sergeant William James McMillan

Warrant Officer Henry Bennis

Warrant Officer Henry Bennis – Rear Gunner

Henry Bennis was born on 15th February 1922 to parents Jacob and Nellie Bennis of Medicine Hat, Alta.

Both Henry's parents were born in Holland; his mother's surname being Owerkleeft.

Henry enlisted in the Royal Canadian Air Force on 24th July 1942. Henry's father, a glass cutter by trade, was now deceased.

Before enlisting, Henry had worked for a florist in Medicine Hat for nearly three years. He enjoyed playing hockey and skating. Training as an Air Gunner he received his badge on 4th December 1942.

Henry left Canada for England on 4th January 1943. On 23rd February he was posted to No. 26 O.T.U. at RAF Wing Buckinghamshire, leaving for 1678 Operational Training Unit at Waterbeach Cambridgeshire on 26th August.

A move to No. 1488 Bombing and Gunnery Flight took place on 6th September followed by a return to Waterbeach and 1678 Conversion Flight on the 22nd.

Flight Lieutenant Charles Eddy MBE RNZAF

Flight Lieutenant Charles Eddy MBE RNZAF

Charles Eddy was born in Bree Road, Hamilton, Victoria, Australia on 31st July 1914. He was one of five children, three boys and two girls, born to parents Matthew and Isabella Eddy. After leaving school Charles worked as an agricultural salesman for D. Laidlaw and Co. agricultural engineers. In early 1939 the company developed a new farm product and Charles was sent in June of that year to New Zealand to promote this new invention with farmers at a yearly convention. For some reason the convention was delayed and Charles had to spend longer in New Zealand than expected.

Meanwhile in Europe war clouds were gathering. In March Hitler had broken the Munich agreement and marched into Prague, taking Czechoslovakia. Next he turned towards Poland. Britain's Prime Minister, Neville Chamberlain, declared support for Poland but on the 1st September 1939 Germany invaded, two days later Britain declared war on Germany. The commonwealth countries immediately began to recruit servicemen and Charles Eddy instead of returning to Australia enlisted in the Royal New Zealand Airforce. After initial training Charlie, as he liked to be known, moved to No. 1 Elementary Flying Training School at Taieri. It was here that he began his Pilot's course with the D.H. 82 Tiger Moth. In December 1941 he moved to No. 1 Flying Training School at Wigram to continue his training with the twin engined Airspeed Oxford.

On the 22nd April 1942 Charlie completed his training in New Zealand and shortly after left for the long sea voyage to England.

In August 1942 Pilot Officer Charles Eddy arrived at No. 3 A.F.U. at South Cerney in Gloucestershire to continue his association with the Airspeed Oxford. October brought a move to Hampstead Norris in Berkshire and No. 15 Operational Training Unit, where he was to have his first experience of flying the Pegasus powered two engined Wellington I.C. As at all O.T.U.s , here at Hampstead Norris training intensified with circuits, landings and bombing being practiced to perfection throughout the following months and into the New Year. Three Sergeants, Lucas, Rodgers and Franklin who had become regular crew members of Eddy's at Hampstead Norris, moved with him to 1657 Conversion Unit at Stradishall in Suffolk, to convert to the Stirling MK I. The other Sergeants that joined the crew were Warring, Horton and Holderness.

The conversion was completed by the 20th of the month, mostly under the instruction of Warrant Officer Eby.

Training and conversion complete, Charles Eddy was posted to an Operational Squadron, 75 New Zealand Squadron based at Newmarket. Promoted to Flying Officer, his first experience of war came on the 5th March when he accompanied Pilot Officer Lowe and crew as Second Pilot on a raid to Essen. Flying Officer Eddy was to fly with Lowe again two nights later when the target was Nuremberg. After dropping their bombs they turned for home and were attacked by a night fighter, cannon shells and tracer slashed through the cockpit wounding Eddy.

Lowe (later to become Air Chief Marshal Sir Douglas Lowe) also received cuts to his face but put the bomber into a corkscrew, lost their attacker and managed to bring their Stirling BF 337 safely home.

After recovering from his injuries Flying Officer Eddy returned to the squadron in April. It was the 23rd May before he was back on operations, flying his third operation as Second Pilot with his A Flight Commander Squadron Leader Laud, target Dortmund. Eddy's next operation with his own crew was a mining op to the Friesian Islands which took place on the 1st June when they dropped five mines, discovering on return that they had thirty nine flak holes in the fuselage of their Stirling. Another mining trip to the Friesians on the 5th June was followed by a raid on Dusseldorf on the 11th. A Flight's Commander Squadron Leader Laud did not return from this operation, his Stirling BK 817 was shot down by a Night Fighter, only one crew member Sergeant Mathews survived. On the 20th June 75 Squadron moved to RAF Mepal, a brand new airfield in Cambridgeshire. It was here at Mepal on the 13th July that Flying Officer Eddy, accompanied by a Second Pilot Sergeant Hartstien and his now regular crew of Pilot Officer Lane, Flight Sergeant Hurt, and Sergeants Bourgeois, Warring, Vicars and Lucas took off on an op to Aachen. This target would clock up seven and a half operations for Charles Eddy, the half op coming from involvement in an Air Sea rescue. Over the target they received some flak damage which resulted in Pilot Officer Eddy having to land the Stirling EE866 at RAF Oakington near Cambridge. On touching down the starboard undercarriage collapsed owing to a burst tyre and the Stirling turned over coming to rest upside down and on fire. Eddy despite having received injuries to his spine and scalp remained in the aircraft to assist the Bomb Aimer Flight Sergeant Hurt from the overturned second pilots seat. Once clear of the aircraft Flight Lieutenant Eddy, on being informed that one member of his crew was missing, returned to the blazing aircraft in a vain attempt to extricate the mid upper gunner Sergeant Vicars from his turret. It was not until heat and flames made it impossible to continue rescue work that he was persuaded to leave the aircraft. His face was scorched and he collapsed immediately and was taken to hospital.

The sad sight of Flying Officer Eddy's Stirling in which Sergeant
Vicars lost his life

After nearly two months recovering from his injuries, Charles
Eddy returned to his squadron at RAF Mepal, taking part in
practice bombing over the Wash on the 14th September. His
next flight with the squadron and his last before being posted,
did not take place until the 13th December when formation
flying was practiced.

December 23rd saw Flying Officer Eddy at the controls of a
1483 bomber gunnery flight Wellington at Newmarket. During
his stay at Newmarket Charles would fly Wellingtons and
Martinets carrying out fighter affiliation and target towing for
various squadrons including 622, 192 and 15. A move to 1678
Conversion Unit based at RAF Waterbeach took place during
the second week of February 1944 and on the 15th his
conversion to the MK II Lancaster began when he was joined by
his new crew of Flying Officer Smith, Flight Sergeant Pugh,
Flight Sergeant Maddox, Sergeant Langridge, Flight Sergeant
Bennis and Sergeant Murphy. This experienced crew had been
posted from RAF Witchford to join Eddy after they had become
a spare crew owing to their pilots` promotion to Commanding
Officer of 115 Squadron. On this first flight together they were
accompanied by Flying Officer Coles who instructed and

demonstrated the aircraft's handling during circuits and landings.

Three days later Flying Officer Coles again accompanied them for more circuits and landings with Lancaster DS828, later that day Eddy took sole control of the aircraft. Halfway down the runway a tyre burst and DS828 slued off the runway. All crew escaped injury and the aircraft was repairable.

The conversion course continued throughout February and into March when, on the 10th, during a cross country flight in DS619, a small electrical fire broke out causing damage to the radio and other equipment; Wireless Operator Flight Sergeant Maddox receiving slight burns to his hands while putting out the fire. March 20th Flying Officer Eddy and his crew moved the short distance from Waterbeach to Witchford. Henry Bennis was now promoted to Warrant Officer. They did not have to wait long to continue their tour of operations for, on the 24th, 115 Squadron were detailed to attack Berlin. This would be operation eight and a half for Eddy and his crew, who returned safely in their Lancaster LL676 KO-G, but four other Lancasters did not return to Witchford, twenty two of the twenty eight crew on board did not survive.

115 Squadron was a 2 Flight Squadron, but on the 25th March C Flight was formed at Witchford. Flying Officer Eddy and crew were one of several crews moved from A or B Flights to make up the new C Flight.

On 30th March Eddy, an ex 75 Squadron pilot, took the controls of Lancaster MKI LL867 A4-J, a Lancaster transferred from 75 Squadron at Mepal to 115 Squadron to make up the new flights aircraft. Taking off from Witchford they took the aircraft up to 26,000 feet before carrying out air firing over the Wash. On return they landed at Feltwell before returning to base.

LL867 became Eddy's` regular aircraft and on the 9th April, accompanied by his Commanding Officer Wing Commander Annan, his crew's ex skipper, he took the aircraft to bomb Paris Ville Neuve. All the Squadrons aircraft returned safely.

The following selection of pages from Flight Lieutenant Eddy's log book show some of his movements from his enlistment in New Zealand in 1939 to the final entry in his log book made by his Flight Commander Squadron Leader G.Y. Mackie (Now Lord Mackie).

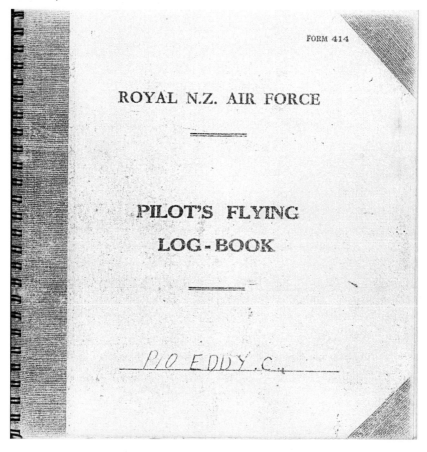

FORM 414

ROYAL N.Z. AIR FORCE

PILOT'S FLYING
LOG-BOOK

P/O EDDY. C.

Pilot Officer Eddy's Log Book

The 12th November 1941 and Leading Aircraftsman Charles Eddy takes his first steps towards becoming a pilot at the Elementary Flying School at Taieri, New Zealand.

YEAR:		AIRCRAFT.		PILOT, OR 1ST PILOT.	2ND PILOT, PUPIL, OR PASSENGER.	DUTY (INCLUDING RESULTS AND REMARKS).
		Type.	No.			
MTH.	DATE					
—	—	—	—	—	—	— TOTALS BROUGHT FORWARD

SEQUENCE OF INSTRUCTION.

1.	Air experience.
1A.	Familiarity with cockpit layout.
2.	Effect of controls.
3.	Taxying.
4.	Straight and level flight.
5.	Climbing, gliding, and stalling.
6.	Medium turns.
7.	Taking off into wind.
8.	Powered approach and landing.
9.	Gliding approach and landing.
10.	Spinning.
11.	First solo.
12.	Sideslipping.
13.	Precautionary landing.
14.	Low flying (with instructor only).
15.	Steep turns.
16.	Climbing turns.
17.	Forced landing.
18.	Action in the event of fire (with instructor only).
18A	Abandoning an aircraft.
19.	Instrument flying.
20.	Taking off and landing out of wind.
21.	Restarting the engine in flight (with instructor only)
22.	Aerobatics.

I hereby certify that I understand the petrol system and cockpit layout of the D.H. 82 aircraft. action in the event of fire and the method of parachute descent.

Signed...*G. Eddy*......

DATE *12.11.41*

Rank. *L.A.C.*....

GRAND TOTAL [cols. (1) — (10)]

_____Hrs. _____Mins.

TOTALS CARRIED FORWARD

Sequence of Instruction

Instruction continues with training on how to start and run up the engine of the DH 82 Tiger Moth.

Instruction continues with training on how to start and run up the engine of the DH 82 Tiger Moth.

Single-Engine Aircraft.				Multi-Engine Aircraft.						Passen-ger	Instr./Clou. Flying (Incl. in Cols. (1) to (10)).	
Day.		Night.		Day.			Night.					
Dual.	Pilot.	Dual.	Pilot.	Dual.	1st Pilot.	2nd Pilot.	Dual.	1st Pilot.	2nd Pilot.		Dual.	Pilot.
(1)	(2)	(3)	(4)	(5)	(6)	(7)	(8)	(9)	(10)	(11)	(12)	(13)

I,....*C. Eddy*.......... certify that I have received Instruction, and fully understand, fuelling procedure, engine starting and running up, and Airscrew starting of the D.H. 82 Tiger Moth.

INSTRUMENT FLYING

DEFINITION OF PRACTICES.

I. Straight and Level.

II. Climbing and Gliding.

III. Turns.

IV. Changing Course.

V. Recovery from Spin.

VI. Taking Off.

NOTE: The ROMAN NUMERALS indicated above will ALWAYS be used.

NO.1.E.F.T.S.TAIERI

SPINNING RECOVERY DRILL

1. Apply FULL OPPOSITE rudder:

THEN

2. Move the control column FORWARD UNTIL THE SPINNING STOPS.

3. Centralise the rudder.

4. EASE the aeroplane out of the dive.

(1)	(2)	(3)	(4)	(5)	(6)	(7)	(8)	(9)	(10)	(11)	(12)	(13)

Instrument Flying

The first few hours of flight begin.

1941 MONTH. DATE.		Type.	No.	PILOT, OR 1ST PILOT.	2ND PILOT, PUPIL, OR PASSENGER.	DUTY (INCLUDING RESULTS AND REMARKS).
—	—	—	—	—	—	— TOTALS BROUGHT FORWARD
Nov	10	DH82	761	F/O Mc KENZIE	SELF	1 AIR EXPERIENCE. 1A FAMILIARITY WITH COCKPIT LAYOUT.
NOV	10	DH82	716	F/O Mc KENZIE	SELF	1A FAMILIARITY WITH COCKPIT LAYOUT. 2 EFFECT OF CONTROLS 3 TAXYING.
NOV	11					
NOV	11	DH82	761	F/O Mc KENZIE	SELF	1A FAMILIARITY WITH COCKPIT LAYOUT. 4 STRAIGHT AND LEVEL FLIGHT. 5 CLIMBING, GLIDING AND STALLING.
NOV	11	DH82	761	F/O Mc KENZIE	SELF	1A FAMILIARITY WITH COCKPIT LAYOUT 5 CLIMBING GLIDING AND STALLING 6 MEDIUM TURNS
NOV	12	DH82	719	F/O Mc KENZIE	SELF	6 MEDIUM TURNS 7 TAKING OFF INTO WIND

GRAND TOTAL [Cols. (1) to (10)].
2 Hrs. 30 Mins.

TOTALS CARRIED FORWARD

1941 The first few hours of flight begin

1942, Charles Eddy moves to the Flying Training School at Wigram to continue his training with the Airspeed Oxford.

1942, Charles Eddy moves to the Flying Training School at Wigram to continue his training with the Airspeed Oxford.

YEAR:	AIRCRAFT.		PILOT, OR 1ST PILOT.	2ND PILOT, PUPIL, OR PASSENGER.	DUTY (INCLUDING RESULTS AND REMARKS).
	Type.	No.			
␣TH. ␣DATE.	___	___		___	___ TOTALS BROUGHT FORWARD

PILOTS' FLYING LOG BOOKS - STANDARD ENTRIES:

FLYING TRAINING SCHOOLS

SEQUENCE OF INSTRUCTION.

1. Air experience.
1A. Familiarity with cockpit layout.
2. Effect of controls.
3. Taxying.
4. Straight and level flight.
4A. Single-engined flying.
5. Climbing, gliding, and stalling.
6. Medium turns.
7. Taking off into wind.
8. Powered approach and landing.
9. Gliding approach and landing.
10. Spinning.
11. First solo.
12. Sideslipping.
13. Precautionary landing.
14. Low flying (with instructor only).
15. Steep turns.
16. Climbing turns.
17. Forced landing.
18. Action in the event of fire (with instructor only).
18A. Abandoning an aircraft.
19. Instrument flying.
20. Taking off and landing out of wind.
20A. Night flying.
20B. Formation flying.
21. Restarting the engine in flight (with instructor only).
22. Acrobatics.

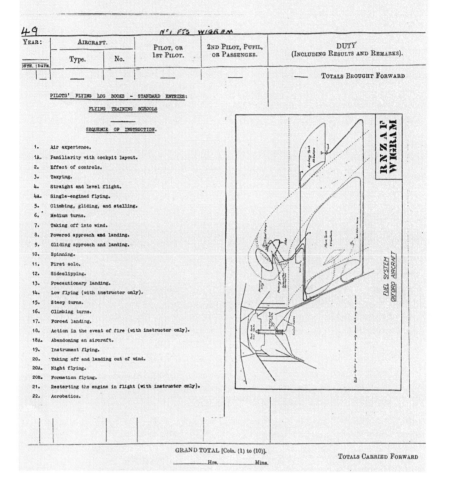

RNZAF WIGRAM

FUEL SYSTEM OXFORD AIRCRAFT

GRAND TOTAL [Cols. (1) to (10)].

_____ Hrs. _____ Mins.

TOTALS CARRIED FORWARD

RNZAF Wigram (1)

YEAR: 1942		AIRCRAFT.		PILOT, OR 1ST PILOT.	2ND PILOT, PUPIL, OR PASSENGER.	DUTY (INCLUDING RESULTS AND REMARKS).
MONTH.	DATE.	Type.	No.			
—	—	—	—	—	—	— TOTALS BROUGHT FORWARD
MARCH	14	AIRSPEED OXFORD	1284	F/O COOKE	SELF	PILOT NAV. WIGRAM - POSITION X. TIM
					L.A.C. HUGHES	OAMARU - TIMARU - WIGRAM OBS
	14		1284	F/O COOKE	SELF	WIGRAM TO
					LAC HUGHES	BIRDLINGS FLAT
			1241	L.A.C. HUGHES	SELF	18 W.S.4 D 3 COURSE
			1241	SELF	LAC. HUGHES	18 W.S. 4 D 3 COURSE
	16		1331	F/O SMITH	SELF	WIGRAM TO
					L.A.C. HUGHES	BIRDLINGS FLAT
			1331	SELF	LAC. HUGHES	18 W.S. 4 D 3 COURSE
			1331	L.A.C. HUGHES	SELF	18 W.S. 4 D. 3 COURSE
			1268	SELF	~	HEIGHT TEST 15,000'
			1268	P/O ELLIS	SELF	BIRDLINGS FLAT TO WIGRAM
	17		283	F/O WORSP	SELF	31 AIR TO AIR CAMERA GUN (BEAM)
					L.A.C. HUGHES	31 AIR TO AIR CAMERA GUN (BEAM)
			283	SELF	LAC. HUGHES	31 AIR TO AIR CAMERA GUN (BEAM)
			283	L.A.C. HUGHES	SELF	31 AIR TO AIR CAMERA GUN (BEAM)
			1271	F/O COOKE	SELF	INSTRUMENT FLYING 1 TAKE OFF
			1271	F/LT BRABYN	SELF	BIRDLINGS FLAT
					LAC. HUGHES	TO WIGRAM
	19		1241	SELF	L.A.C. HUGHES	866 PHOTO LINE OVERLAPS + STEREO FAIR

GRAND TOTAL [Cols. (1) to (10)].

138 Hrs. 05 Mins.

TOTALS CARRIED FORWARD

RNZAF Wigram (2)

The long sea journey to England over training continued with the Airspeed Oxford at South Cerney, Gloustershire.

YEAR: 1942		AIRCRAFT		PILOT, OR 1ST PILOT.	2ND PILOT, PUPIL, OR PASSENGER.	DUTY (INCLUDING RESULTS AND REMARKS).
MTH.	DATE	Type.	No.			
—	—	—	—	—	—	— TOTALS BROUGHT FORWARD
AUG	21	AIRSPEED OXFORD	BM 844	P/O SPEARS	SELF	N/F 4 LANDINGS 1.OSA.
			BM 844	SELF	—	N/F 1 LANDING
			BG 158	SGT STEELE	SELF	X.C. 5000' L.P. S.E. TURNS + COURSE
			ED 120	SGT STEELE	SELF	N/F 1. LANDING 2.O.S.A.
			ED 120	SELF	—	N/F 3 LANDINGS
	22		3937	SGT TURNER	SELF	X.C. 5000' L.P. S.E
			ED 234	F/SGT BRANCH	SELF	N/F 1 LANDING
			ED 234	SELF	—	N/F 4 LANDINGS
	23		V 3754	P/O HILDITCH	SELF	X.C. 5000' L.P. SE TURNS + COURSES
			ED 234	F/SGT BRANCH	SELF	N/F 2 LANDINGS
			ED 234	SELF	—	N/F 4 LANDINGS
	26		ED 234	P/O HILDITCH	SELF	N/F 2 LANDINGS
			ED 234	SELF	—	N/F 2 LANDINGS
			HP 391	F/O COKE - KERR	SELF	N/F 2 LANDINGS
	27		BR 481	SGT STEELE	SELF	X.C. 5000' L.P. S.E. TURNS + COURS.
			X7 247	SGT STEELE	SELF	N/F 1LANDINGS 1.OSA.
			X7247	SELF	—	N/F 4 LANDINGS 1. OSA.
	28		ED 234	SELF	—	PRECISION FLYING 2000'
			HP 391	SELF	—	N/F 7 LANDINGS

GRAND TOTAL [Cols. (1) to (10)].
232 Hrs. 10 Mins.   TOTALS CARRIED FORWARD

South Cerney: The long sea journey to England over, training continued with the Airspeed Oxford at South Cerney, Gloucestershire

184

December 1942, Charles Eddy moved on to an Operational Training Unit at Hampstead Norris in Berkshire to begin flying with the four engined Wellington bomber.

103   HAMPSTEAD NORRIS 15 O.T.U.

Year: 1942-3		Aircraft.		Pilot, or 1st Pilot.	2nd Pilot, Pupil, or Passenger.	Duty (Including Results and Remarks).
Month	Date	Type.	No.			
—	—	—	—	—	—	— Totals Brought Forward
DEC	9	WELLINGTON.iF	914	F/LT WHITTET	SGT LUCAS SELF	LOCAL FLYING 2 LANDINGS
	11		9103	F/SGT HOBB	CREW SELF	AIR TEST
	14		557	SELF	CREW	X COUNTRY
			557	SELF	CREW	X COUNTRY
	15		694	F/LT WHITTET	CREW SGT LUCAS ROGERS	CHECK DUAL
	15		694	F/LT WHITTET	SELF	CIRCUITS & LANDINGS
			694	SELF	SGT LUCAS SGT ROGERS	..
	17		694	SELF	SGT. LUCAS SGT. ROGERS	CIRCUITS & LANDINGS
			694	SELF	SGT LUCAS ROGERS	.. ..
	19		2755	SELF	SGT LUCAS SGT ROGERS	" "
	19		8871	F/LT WHITTET	SELF & CREW	DUAL BOMBING
	19		8871	SELF	CREW	SOLO CIRCUITS & LANDINGS
	22		1090	P/O. MATTOCK F/LT WHITTET	SELF & CREW	DUAL X/C & BOMBING
	23		2755	SELF	CREW	SOLO X/C + BOMBING
	24		1090	SELF	CREW	SOLO X/C + BOMBING
	27		1660	SELF	CREW	SOLO X/C + BOMBING
	27		1090	SELF	CREW	FROM CHIPPING MORTON
	30		8871	SELF	CREW	SOLO X/C + BOMBING
	31		698	SELF	CREW	SOLO X/C + BOMBING
JAN.	2		8871	SELF.	CREW.	SOLO X.C. LIVE BOMBING + AIR F
	3		1647	SELF.	CREW.	SOLO X.C.
	3		8871	SELF.	CREW.	SOLO X.C.

GRAND TOTAL [Cols. (1) to (10)].
321 Hrs. 30 Mins.   Totals Carried Forward

In December 1942, Charles Eddy moved on to an Operational Training Unit at Hampstead Norris in Berkshire to begin flying with the two engined Wellington bomber

185

February 1943, conversion to the Stirling bomber with 1657 Conversion Unit at Stadishall.

1657 C.U STRADISHALL

YEAR: 1943		AIRCRAFT.		PILOT, OR 1ST PILOT.	2ND PILOT, PUPIL, OR PASSENGER.	DUTY (INCLUDING RESULTS AND REMARKS).
MTH.	DATE	Type.	No.			
—	—	—	—	—	—	— Totals Brought Forward
FEB	10	STIRLING 1	N3700	S/Ldr BUTTERFIELD	SELF CREW	FAMILIARIZATION, C+L
	11	"	N3708	" "	SELF SGT. FRANKLIN " ROGERS " LUCAS " WARING " HORTON " HOLDERNESS } CREW	CIRCUITS & LANDINGS
	12	"	N3670	W/O HINWOOD	SELF CREW	CIRCUITS + LANDINGS 1 OVERSH
	13	"	N3..6	W/O EBY	SELF CREW	CIRCUITS + LANDINGS
	14		W7447	W/O EBY	SELF CREW	C + L?
			W7447	SELF	CREW	C+ L?
			W7447	W/O EBY	SELF CREW	— — —
	15		W7447	SELF	CREW	CIRCUITS & LANDINGS
	16		D=321	SELF	CREW	CIRCUITS & LANDINGS
	18		N3708	SELF	CREW	LOADED CLIMB 15,000. 9 × 500Lb
	18		N7570	W/O EBY	SELF + CREW	CIRCUITS & LANDINGS
			N3708	W/O EBY	SELF + CREW	C + L?
			N3700	W/O EBY	SELF + CREW	C + L?
	19		BF342	W/O EBY	SELF + CREW	C + LS
			BF342	SELF	CREW	CIRCUITS & LANDINGS
	20		BF613	SELF	CREW	CIRCUITS & LANDINGS

TOTAL FLYING TIMES IN 1657 C.U.

W. R. Butterfield S/Ldr.

GRAND TOTAL [Cols. (1) to (10)]. 350 Hrs. 25 Mins.   TOTALS CARRIED FORWARD

In February 1943, conversion to the Stirling bomber with 1657 Conversion Unit at Stradishall

A posting to RAF Newmarket and 75 New Zealand Squadron brought the first operational experience for Flying Officer Eddy.

YEAR: 1943		AIRCRAFT.		PILOT, OR 1ST PILOT.	2ND PILOT, PUPIL, OR PASSENGER.		DUTY (INCLUDING RESULTS AND REMARKS).
MTH.	DATE	Type.	No.				
		—	—	—	—	—	— TOTALS BROUGHT FORWARD
					SELF		
MARCH	5	STIRLING I	BK646	P/O LOWE	SGT CARSWELL " BODLEY " WILMER " WEBB F/S ELLIS	1	ESSEN . 1170×416 + 32 A.... INCENDIARS LDRD. 1×2000lb 2×1000lb (1) (WOU 425)
	7	"	FF327	SELF	CREW SELF		LOCAL FLYING
	8	"		P/O LOWE	SGT CARSWELL " BODLEY " WILMER " WEBB F/S ELLIS	2	NÜREMBERG (2) ✓
APRIL	28	BRISTOL BEAUFIGHTER	D	SGT ROBINS	SELF		LOCAL FLYING A.I.
	29	"	J	" HUGHES F/LT ANDREWS	SELF		AIR FIRING G.C.I
MAY	17	STIRLING 3		SELF	CREW		AIR TEST LANDED OAKINGTON
		"	BN617	SELF	CREW		BOMBING + SEA FIRING WASH
	23	"	III BK817	S/LDR LAUD	SELF	3	DORTMUND. (3)
	25			SELF	SGT LUCAS		CIRCUITS + LANDINGS 3
	25		R9240	S/LDR LAUD	SGT WARING " HURT " OWENS		1 OVERSHOOT
			R9240	SELF SELF	CREW		CIRCUITS + BUMPS 4 1 OVERSH.
			R9240	S/LDR LAUD	CREW SGT LUCAS " WARING " HURT " OWENS " BOORGOIS		" " "
	27		BP377	SELF			LOCAL FLYING CIRCUITS + BUMPS
	28		R9240	SELF			" " " " "
	29		III EN880	F/O JOLL SELF	CREW SGT LUCAS " STOKES " WARING " BOORGOIS PN LANE		NFT PHOTOGRAPHY
	31			SELF SGT DALZEL			N.F.T

SUMMARY FOR MAY 75(NZ) SQUADRON

A. FLIGHT

DATE 1. 6. 43

GRAND TOTAL [Cols. (1) to (10)].

380 Hrs. 25 Mins.

TOTALS CARRIED FORWARD

A posting to RAF Newmarket and 75 New Zealand Squadron brought the first operational experience for Flying Officer Eddy.

By July 1943, 75 Squadron had moved to RAF Mepal, Cambridgeshire.
On returning from an operation on 13th July Flying Officer Eddy crash landed
at RAF Oakington near Cambridge.

75 ('N.Z.) SQUADRON

YEAR:		AIRCRAFT.		PILOT, OR 1ST PILOT.	2ND PILOT, PUPIL, OR PASSENGER.	DUTY (INCLUDING RESULTS AND REMARKS).
MONTH.	DATE.	Type.	No.			
—	—	—	—	—	—	TOTALS BROUGHT FORWARD
JULY	5	STIRLING III	EF585	SELF	CREW	TEST & COMPASS SWING
	7	" "	EE586	SELF	CREW	TEST & AIR SEA FIRING
	8	" "	EE948	SGT HARTSTEIN	CREWS	N.F.T MILDENHALL
	"	" "	EE879	SELF	CREW	U/C TROUBLE BOMBS & PETROL JETISON
	9	I	R9243	SELF	CREW	MOSAIC OF DROME
	10	III	EE886	SELF	CREW	BOMBING WASH N.F.T
	12	III	R9243	F/LT JOLL SELF	CREWS	TO NEW MARKET
	12	III	BK465	SELF	CREW SGT HARTSTEIN	FROM NEWMARKET TO MEPAL TEST
	13	III	EE886	SELF	P/O LANE F/S HORT SGT BOURGEOIS SGT WARING SGT VICARS SGT LUCAS	WAR OPERATIONS (7½) AACHEN CRASHED DUE TO BURST WHEEL B/C BURNT OUT SGT VICARS KILLED ON RETURN AT OAKINGTON O
SEPT	14	III	EE897	SELF P/O WILLIAMS	CREW	BOMBING WASH
DEC	13	III	EF152	SELF W/O HUMPHRIES	CREW	FORMATION FLYING

SUMMARY FOR 75 (N 2) SQUADRON

A. FLIGHT

GRAND TOTAL [Cols. (1) to (10)].
426 Hrs. 55 Mins.

TOTALS CARRIED FORWA

By July 1943, 75 Squadron had moved to RAF Mepal,
Cambridgeshire. On returning from an operation on 13th July
Flying Officer Eddy crash landed at RAF Oakington near
Cambridge

188

January 1944, Flying Officer Eddy had returned to RAF Newmarket to join 1483 Bomber Gunnery Flight.

115   1483 BOMBER GUNNERY FLIGHT

YEAR: 1944 MONTH. DATE	AIRCRAFT.		PILOT, OR 1ST PILOT.	2ND PILOT, PUPIL, OR PASSENGER.	DUTY (INCLUDING RESULTS AND REMARKS).
	Type.	No.			
	—	—	—	—	—— TOTALS BROUGHT FORWARD
JAN					
11	WELLINGTON X	LN.456	F/C HELFER SELF F/O MOULDEN	F/S HOLLOWOOD WARTON . FINCHAM W/COO . GORDON W/O EGLI	LOCAL
"	STIRLING III	EF. 465	SELF F/O M.G.FPR	F/S HOLLOWOOD	C.C.G HORRICANE 16 MAG
12	WELLINGTON	HE987	SELF	SGT HASTINGS	AIR TEST
"	" "	" "	SELF	W/O WEEKS	LOCAL
24	MARTINET	B747	SELF	—	LOCAL
25	" "	K974	SELF F/S CARTLAND	—	LOCAL
"	" "	K974	SELF	—	TOWING 15 SQUAD AIR TO A.
26	" "	T353	SELF	—	C.C.G
27	" "	JN553	SELF	—	FIGHTER AFFILIATION
"	" "	P967	SELF	—	" "
28	" "	A697	SELF	SGT FAIRIE	AIR TEST . WEST- RAYNHAM
30	" "	B747	SELF	—	FIGHTER AFFIL
"	" "	N967	SELF	—	TOWING 622 SQUADRON
31	" "	L975	SELF	—	FIGHTER AFFILIATION

SUMMARY FOR JAN 1944

[signature] O/C 1483

MARTINET FLIGHT

EB	2	MARTINET	P967	SELF	—	FIGHTER AFFIL
	"	" "	M974	SELF	—	TOWING 192 SQUADRON
	3	"	V354	SELF	—	" 15 SQUADRON
	4	"	T353	SELF	—	C.C.G.

GRAND TOTAL [Cols. (1) to (10)].
464 Hrs. 15 Mins.   TOTALS CARRIED FORW

By January 1944, Flying Officer Eddy had returned to RAF Newmarket to join 1483 Bomber Gunnery Flight

189

February 1944, Flying Officer Eddy is posted to RAF Waterbeach,
Cambridgeshire to convert to the Lancaster MKII bomber. It is here that he is
joined by Flying Officer Smith, Flight Sergeants Pugh, Maddox, Bennis and
Sergeants Langridge and Murphy.

YEAR: 1944		AIRCRAFT		PILOT, OR 1ST PILOT.	2ND PILOT, PUPIL, OR PASSENGER.	DUTY (INCLUDING RESULTS AND REMARKS).
MONTH	DATE	Type.	No.			
		—	—	—	—	TOTALS BROUGHT FORWARD
FEB	15	LANCASTER II	DS728	F/O COLES	SELF CREW	CIRCUITS & LANDINGS
	15		DS 728	F/O COLES	SELF CREW	
	18		DS 528	SELF	CREW	BURST WHEEL ON TAKE OFF (PRANG)
	20		DS 617	SELF F/O FINNERY	CREW SGT CUNNINGHAM	C & L's
	21		LL 690	SELF	CREW	FIGHTER AFFILIATION
	21		DS 633	SELF	CREW	X COUNTRY
	22		DS 619	SELF	CREW	X COUNTRY
	24		DS 631	SELF	CREW	X COUNTRY
	24		DS 757	F/O RHYS	SELF	C & L's
	25		DS 623	F/O COLES	SELF	C & L's
MARCH	9		DS 619	F/O RHYS	SELF	C & L's
	9		DS 619	SELF	F/O SMITH F/S PUGH F/S MADDOX SGT HILL	C & L's
	10		DS 618		SGT LANGRIDGE W/OP F/O FINNERY F/O SMITH F/S PUGH F/S MADDOX SGT BENNIS	SMALL CIRCUITS AND C/T's WITH R/T IN USE u/s
	10		DS 619		F/O SMITH SGT LANGRIDGE F/S MOLL F/S BENNIS F/S MADDOX	X COUNTRY BULLSEYE

SUMMARY FOR 16 ... ...
... ... O/C
LANCASTER FLIGHT.

GRAND TOTAL [Cols. (1) to (10)].
491 Hrs. 26 Mins.
TOTALS CARRIED FORWARD

In February 1944, Flying Officer Eddy is posted to RAF
Waterbeach, Cambridgeshire to convert to the Lancaster MKII
bomber. It is here that he is joined by Flying Officer Smith,
Flight Sergeants Pugh, Maddox, Bennis and Sergeants
Langridge and Murphy

On the 20th March 1944 Eddy and his crew moved to RAF Witchford and 115 Squadron to continue their first tour of operations.

		Aircraft		Pilot, or 1st Pilot	2nd Pilot, Pupil, or Passenger	Duty (Including Results and Remarks)
Year:		Type	No.			
Month.	Date					Totals Brought Forward
MARCH	20					
	··	LANCASTER II	N 694	(F/O) SELF	CREW	WATERBEACH + RETURN
	22	·· ··	N ··	SELF + SELF	··	LOCAL AIR TEST
	23	·· ··	G	F/R HALLEY F/LT SEDDON	··	AIRTEST + CORN SCREW
	24	·· ··	LL 676	SELF	SULLIVAN, SWEETING CHABOT, ONDERSMA	WAR OPERATIONS (8½) BERLIN
	26		LL 676	SELF	F/SGT MUGH F/O SMITH MURPHY + 40 OTHERS	1 x 4000 LB (75 MILES) H.L. BOMBING 16½
	27	LANC	I	G	W/CDR ANNAN SELF	CREW	BASE-ASHBOURNE-BASE (C+LS)
	29	··	··	B	F/O HOWELL SELF	F/O SMITH, W/O BENNIE F/LT BENNIS, PORE LANCERIDGE, MARSH	LOCAL FLYING C+LS
	30	··	··	J	SELF	CREW + HOWOOD	LT CLIMB (26,200') FIRING, WASH LANDED FELTWELL - BASE
						SUMMARY FOR MONTH MARCH.
						signature S/o o/c
						115 SQUD LANC FLIGHT.
APRIL	4	LANC	I	3	SELF FIEMOLER	CREW	AIR FIRING
			III	G	SELF	CREW	C + LS
	5		I	A	SELF	CREW	LOCAL
	6		I	J	SELF W/C ANNAN	··	H₂ .S.
	7		I	LL 867	SELF	CREW	H₂ .S.
	8		I	LL 867	SELF SELF	CREW F/O SMITH, PEAN McDON, BENNIE MURPHY, LANCSHORE	1-CO NTRY BOMB LOAD
	9		I	·· ··	W/O ANNAN		WAR OPS PARIS VILLE NEUVE (9½) 10 .10CO LBS 4x 500 LBS
					GRAND TOTAL [Cols. (1) to (10)]. ___ Hrs. ___ Mins.		TOTALS CARRIED FORWARD

On the 20th March 1944 Eddy and his crew moved to RAF Witchford and 115 Squadron to continue their first tour of operations

April 10th and the Squadron was in action again, this time taking part in an op to the Railway Yards at Laon. Of the 148 Lancasters and 15 Mosquitoes taking part from 3, 6 and 8 Groups, only one aircraft, a 622 Squadron Lancaster from Mildenhall failed to return.

On return from this operation Eddy received the news of his promotion to Flight Lieutenant, but sadly this would be the last time he and his crew would safely return to Witchford to enter another completed operation in their log books. The final entry in Flight Lieutenant Charles Eddy's log book would be made by his C Flight Commander.

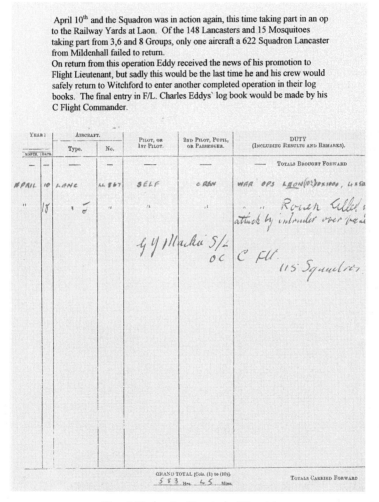

April 10th and the Squadron was in action again, this time taking part in an op to the Railway Yards at Laon. Of the 148 Lancasters and 15 Mosquitoes taking part from 3,6 and 8 Groups, only one aircraft a 622 Squadron Lancaster from Mildenhall failed to return.

On return from this operation Eddy received the news of his promotion to Flight Lieutenant, but sadly this would be the last time he and his crew would safely return to Witchford to enter another completed operation in their log books. The final entry in F/L. Charles Eddys' log book would be made by his C Flight Commander.

Final Entry in the Log Book

HAMILTON AIRMAN AWARDED THE M.B.E.

Mr. M. E. Eddy, of Bree road, Hamilton, father of the late Flight Lieutenant Charlie Eddy, of the New Zealand Air Force, has received from the Air Ministry the following letter— Further to the information passed on to you by the New Zealand Liaison Officer, Melbourne, with reference to the award of the M.B.E. to your son, Flight-Lieutenant Charlie Eddy, the following reference has been received from Air Ministry—"One night in July 1943; Flight-Lieutenant Eddy was pilot and captain of an aircraft which crashed when attempting an emergency landing and burst into flames immediately. He received concussion and injuries to his scalp and spine. Despite his injuries Flight-Lieutenant Eddy remained in his aircraft and assisted the bomb aimer from the overturned second pilot's seat. After getting clear of the aircraft, Flight-Lieutenant Eddy, on learning that one member of the crew was absent, re-entered the blazing wreckage, and, assisted by a medical officer, in vain attempted to extricate the mid-upper gunner, who was trapped in his turret. It was not until heat, flames and smoke made a continuance of rescue work impossible, that Flight-Lieutenant Eddy was persuaded to abandon his efforts. His face was scorched whilst he was attempting to rescue the gunner, and he collapsed immediately after finally leaving his aircraft. Flight-Lieutenant Eddy showed gallantry in dangerous circumstances and his unselfishness was instrumental in saving the bomb aimer's life. On behalf of the Air Board, I desire to express my sincere congratulations on your son's fine achievement. —T. A. Barrow, Air Secretary." Flight-Lieutenant Eddy was for some time after his courageous exploit prevented by his injuries from further flights on service, but his death occurred on an early subsequent flight.

Left
The report that appeared in a Hamilton, Australia newspaper in June 1944.

Below
The New Zealand memorial cross awarded to Charlie Eddys' mother.
The cross was instituted by The New Zealand Government in December 1946 for award to widows and mothers of New Zealand soldiers, sailors and airmen who were killed on active service during World War II.

The New Zealand memorial cross awarded to Charlie Eddy's mother. The report appeared in a Hamilton, Victoria, Australia newspaper in June 1944

The cross was instituted by the New Zealand Government in December 1946 for award to widows and mothers of New Zealand soldiers, sailors and airmen who were killed on active service during World War II.

193

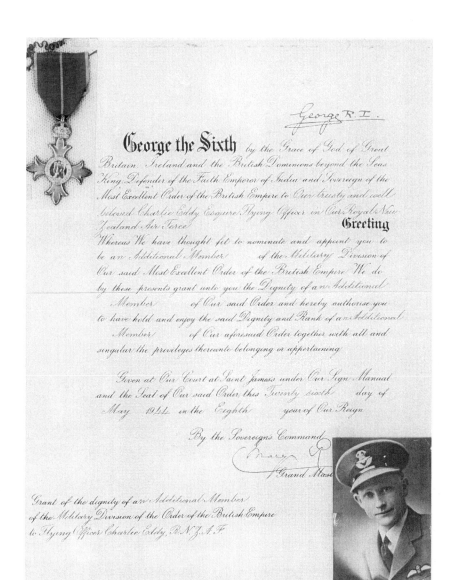

George R.I.

George the Sixth by the Grace of God of Great Britain Ireland and the British Dominions beyond the Seas King Defender of the Faith Emperor of India and Sovereign of the Most Excellent Order of the British Empire to Our trusty and well beloved Charlie Eddy Esquire Flying Officer in Our Royal New Zealand Air Force **Greeting**

Whereas We have thought fit to nominate and appoint you to be an Additional Member of the Military Division of Our said Most Excellent Order of the British Empire We do by these presents grant unto you the Dignity of an Additional Member of Our said Order and hereby authorise you to have hold and enjoy the said Dignity and Rank of an Additional Member of Our aforesaid Order together with all and singular the privileges thereunto belonging or appertaining

Given at Our Court at Saint James's under Our Sign Manual and the Seal of Our said Order this Twenty sixth day of May 1944 in the Eighth year of Our Reign

By the Sovereign's Command

Mary R
Grand Master

Grant of the dignity of an Additional Member of the Military Division of the Order of the British Empire to Flying Officer Charlie Eddy, R.N.Z.A.F.

George VI Certificate

Type of Aircraft		Mark	R.A.F. Number
LANCASTER		1	LL867

Contractor	Contract No.	Engine installed :—
Armstrong Whit.	A/C239	Merlin 24
		Maker's airframe No. :—

Unit or Cat'y/Cause	Station or Contractor	Date	Authority	41 or 43 Gp. Allot.
	75 Sqn	16.3.44	163 7/3	
	115 Sqn	28.3.44	151 30/3	
Cat E.2		19.4.44	FB/Pgn/52	
	S.O.C.	27.11.44	623/209	

A.M. Form 78

The Aircraft Movement card for Lancaster MK I LL867

Powered by the British built Rolls Royce Merlin 24 engines, LL867 was one of 350 MK Is, built by Armstrong Whitworth and delivered between November 1943 and August 1944.

LL867 was delivered new to 75 Squadron at RAF Mepal, Cambridgeshire on the 16th March 1944 and transferred to 115 Squadron four miles away at RAF Witchford on the 28th.

Painted with 115's C Flight code letters of A4 and the Call sign J, it was first flown by Flying Officer Eddy on the 30th March.

A4-J LL867 completed only two operations before being shot down over Witchford by the intruder on the 19th April. The first to the Marshalling Yards at Villeneure St. George, Paris on the 9th April 1944 and the second to the Marshalling Yards at Laon on the 11th April.

LL867 had completed only 31 hours flying time.

Sergeant Alfred Frank Langridge

Sergeant Langridge

Sergeant Langridge was 32 years of age, which was considered
quite old compared to the age of most aircrew.

Flying Officer Albert Smith

Flying Officer Albert Smith was Navigator of Flight Lieutenant
Eddy's crew

Flight Sergeant Peter John Edward Maddox RAFVR

Peter Maddox. Wireless Operator of A4J LL867. Peter was the only son of Mrs. and the late Herbert W. Maddox of Stathleven, Cowes, and Isle of Wight.

A former pupil of the Newport Grammar School, he joined the RAF in 1941. Before enlistment he was employed by Messrs

Rowe & Son and S.F. Burchell Clothiers and Outfitters before becoming a salesman in the sports department of the Army and Navy Stores, London. In his leisure time he played cricket for the Northwood Cricket club.

After basic training Peter Maddox trained as a Wireless Operator/Air Gunner. In May 1943 he joined an Operational Training Unit at RAF Little Horwood.

Flight Sergeant Maddox had a sister Anne. She remembers the last time she saw him on leave in the Isle of Wight. Peter was walking with Anne and her husband when he said it was time for him to go back. They watched as he walked back along the path and disappeared. Anne had a feeling she would not see him again. At the time of his death Flight Sergeant Peter Maddox was 22 years old.

Ernie Beer & Terry Brunt

Terry Brunt was a Ground Crew member of 115 Squadron and was a friend of Ernie Beer who was the Wireless Operator of Flight Lieutenant Hammond's crew. Terry married and settled in Ely after the war. Terry and his wife Dorothy always kept in touch with Ernie and notified him that the wreckage of Pilot Officer Birnie's aircraft was to be recovered in 1995. Terry sent Ernie a print of the incident, the original of which is seen earlier in this book.

The following is a letter sent to Terry and Dorothy by Ernie Beer in reply:

Dear Terry and Dorothy   *23/10/95*
First I must apologies for typing a personal letter and second also for taking so long in writing. I have been plagued with arthritis which not only affected my back and neck also decided to attack my legs, wrists and fingers. Despite this, I actually wrote a long letter on the 4th October but with fingers alternately 'seizing up' and grinding to a halt, then deciding to go forward and up at the same time and, as a variation, to take a dive. The result although interesting was not legible. Made a Doctor's prescription look almost clear. Mind you, having said

all that, I am sure that as you read on it will become abundantly clear that my typing leaves much to be desired. But here goes.

I was lost for words at the sight of the picture which had arrived in time for my birthday. The letter enclosed was also very welcome. I can understand Dorothy's reluctance to send it but I can assure her it is very much appreciated. At the moment it is being framed by an expert and I can assure you both that it is another way of remembering those unlucky lads. That is all they were – lads.

In answer to your question, Yes, I was on the squadron at the time. Not only that I was on the operation with those lads and actually witnessed the shooting down of the second aircraft. (J for Johnny). It is a long story so I will be as brief as I can as I feel you might like a first-hand account.

My aircraft was V for Victor (a MKII Lancaster) and we had raided Rouen and were circling the airfield at Witchford. All were waiting to land all at different heights to avoid risk of collision. Those nearest the ground, of course, would get first permission.

Over the radio telephone (R/T) came the message for the first aircraft in the circuit to `Pancake` (land). It touched down on to the runway and was part way along when its undercarriage collapsed, no one was hurt and the aircrew got out safely. It would take some time to clear the runway and all airborne aircraft were warned to remain at the same height and await further instructions. In the event with the ground crews working like fury, it took an hour to clear the runway and the next aircraft was told to pancake.

Apparently, it was about to touch down when all hell was let loose. Bright flashes lit up the surrounding countryside and the two criss cross searchlights which guided us to the airfield were put out and all airfield lights were extinguished. An urgent cry `Bandits, Bandits` came over the radio (enemy aircraft attacking) and we dutifully turned off our navigational lights. One bright light was flickering from below. It was Birnie and crew. All killed. Fire tenders, ambulances and other vehicles could be seen by fire to be dashing about, many airmen dashing about too. The aircraft had crashed in a field clear of the runway. Air gunners re-manned their turrets and we were all on our toes. It was very eerie as we could see no sign of an enemy aircraft.

One pilot in the circuit, a New Zealander, called out over the R/T, "Sod this for a lark, we are off on a short cross country run, be back later". They were never seen again.

A further wait and the airfield lights came on, the searchlights lit up the sky once again and the signal came over the air "All clear". V for Victor, received instructions to put flaps and wheels down and to pancake. With trepidation we touched down and taxied to the end of the runway and gave our signal `Clear of runway` and heard J for Johnny given permission to land and heard the acknowledgement. We busied ourselves preparing to disembark. Gathering up our bits and pieces, maps, codes, logs and parachutes, making sure that everything was switched off etc and thankfully climbed out onto the ground.

We could hear the hum of aircraft above and could see the navigation lights of J for Johnny as it approached to touch down, when there were blinding flashes of cannon fire which lit up the Lancaster and seemed to strike it between the shoulder blades (the wings). The aircraft staggered. The pilot, Flight Lieutenant Eddie, endeavoured to bring it under control. The starboard wing dropped; touched the ground and the whole aircraft appeared to perform cart wheels. It exploded with terrible noise and came to rest near some living quarters. The flames were horrific and the rescue teams were helpless as they tried to get near enough to put out the flames.

My crew was detailed to take charge of the crew of J for Johnny funerals. The pilot of V for Victor to be in charge of Flight Lieutenant Eddies. Bob Hawkins my navigator in charge Smithies (the navigator). Myself to attend Flight Sergeant Maddox (Wireless Operator) in the Isle of Wight – his home. We were detailed to attend a briefing at the Adjutants office. When I arrived there the Vicar of Witchford was sitting there. He was asking for permission to, for the names of the Men who had died that night to be read out in Church on Sunday.

I was allowed to make my way to the Isle of Wight a day early. I stopped over in London for the night and called into my home to see Marjory. I walked into our house to be greeted by my Mother-in-law who turned to Marjory and said, "You see, I told you he would come. We are expecting you". I then saw a number of Birthday cards on the mantel shelf. The only time I have ever forgotten her birthday.

At the Isle of Wight, after the funeral service, Mrs. Maddox, a little grey haired lady asked me to her house for tea. She wanted to know her son had lived in the RAF and how he had died. I informed her that a German aircraft that crashed into the sea at Bradwell Bay was possibly responsible for shooting down her son's Lancaster. The lad was the last of five local lads, all friends; four had died in the Air Force and one in the Navy.

Mrs. Maddox burst into tears sobbing 'Good, good', then she stopped and said "I do not mean it, for after all, that is someone else's son." After tea she excused herself and she went off to work in a munitions factory.

On the way back to Witchford I had time to reflect on the day and thought with women like Mrs. Maddox we will win this war. I salute her and all women like her.

A squad of RAF Air Sea rescue men and sergeant, who acted as poll bearers, made a very smart turnout and did well right up to the last salute.

I hope I have not bored you- I am sure you will understand what a lasting effect the whole thing had upon me and the others like me.

Again, thank you both for the picture which I shall treasure to the end of my days.

See what I meant when I said, I am no typist!

God bless you both with good health. Take care of each other and I hope to see you again one day.

Yours sincerely

Ernie Beer.

Sadly, Terry and Dorothy are no longer with us.

- There is no evidence that the German Aircraft that crash landed in Bradwell Bay shot down the two Witchford Lancasters. The story may have been related to relatives of the deceased in the hope it would make them feel better about the tragic events.

- The German aircraft was a JU 88 badly damaged by anti aircraft fire, the crew deciding that they would not make it back to base.

Sister's trip to honour war victim

FLIGHT Sgt Peter Maddox, killed when two Lancaster bombers returning from a wartime mission were shot down over Ely, was remembered by his sister at Witchford on Sunday.

Anne Mathews, 82, had travelled from her home on the Isle of Wight to lay a wreath in memory of her 22-year-old brother.

Accompanied by her daughter, Cecily, she joined Barry Aldridge, Curator of the RAF Witchford Display of Memorabilia, to pay tribute to Peter at the 115 Squadron Memorial at Lancaster Way Business Park.

Earlier, she had attended the Remembrance Service at St Andrew's Church, Witchford.

The site, formerly RAF Witchford, was where Peter and 13 fellow airmen died when a German night fighter ambushed the squadron as they returned from an operation to the Marshalling Yards at Rouen in France on April 19, 1944.

Mr Aldridge has researched the incident since being involved in recovering wreckage of both aircraft in 1995.

He contacted Anne the following year and has laid a wreath in memory of her brother on her behalf since then. However, this year Anne wanted to lay her own tribute to Peter.

He had joined the RAF in 1941 and trained as a wireless operator and air gunner. Two years later, he joined the Operational Training Unit at RAF Little Horwood.

Anne remembered the last time she saw him on leave in the Isle of Wight. He was walking with Anne and her husband when he said it was time for him to go back.

They watched as he walked

POIGNANT MEMORIES: Barry Aldridge with Anne Mathews and daughter Cecily beside the Lancaster Way memorial. Right: Peter Maddox.

back along the path and disappeared.

Anne had a feeling she would not see him again.

The loss of the two Lancasters accounted for the largest loss of life in Ely during the war.

After six years of research into the tragedy, Barry hopes to publish a book, *The Witchford Intruder Incident*, telling the story.

Newspaper cutting of Maddox's sister (Ely Standard)

Anne Matthews standing near the Lancaster engine with her daughter Cecily. Photo via Anne Matthews

Anne believes the following poem by Patience Strong is appropriate for her brother and all other young men who gave their lives for their country.

The Mark of Destiny by Patience Strong

He was made for love and laughter, useful work and happy life.
Not for hate and violence, the battle and the bitter strife.
He was made to play good cricket, and to walk the countryside.
Free to take the morning road with merry heart and swinging stride.
Yet he did not live to reap the harvest of the fields of time.
Not for him the fruit of manhood ripening to golden prime.

Fate upon that clear young brow had drawn the Mark of Destiny.
He was of the generation born to save humanity.

Flight Sergeant Peter Maddox. Photo via Anne Matthews

Flight Sergeant Harold Edward Pugh. RAF

Flight Sergeant Pugh

Harold Pugh was born on 9th May 1920 to parents Harold George and Elsie Pugh of Hindringham in Norfolk. On leaving school in 1937 he went to work as a Costing Clerk but with hopes of becoming an engineer in future years. Engineering was his greatest hobby. He belonged to a model engineering club and with his father built two working locomotives. In December 1941 Harold married his girlfriend Olive. Not long after their marriage Harold joined the RAF being first posted to America and then to 31 Bomber and Gunnery School at Picton, Ontario, Canada. His course (No. 62) ran from 31st August 1942 until 23rd October that year. Leading Aircraftsman Pugh went on to qualify as an Air Bomber (Navigator), flying on Avro Ansons at 33 Air Navigation School at Mount Hope.

On returning to England in March 1943 Harold was posted to RAF Wing in Buckinghamshire to continue training on Ansons with No. 26 Operational Training Unit on course No. 19. A move to RAF Little Horwood in May gave him his first experience of being a Bomb Aimer on a Wellington III. June 14th saw a return to Wing where he continued to train with the Wellington and Pilot Sergeant Donald, who Harold had flown with on several occasions at Little Horwood.

Harold was now part of a regular crew in training which would eventually take them to RAF Witchford as an Operational crew.

Flight Sergeant Pugh was buried in Hindringham Churchyard, Norfolk, with full military honours.

Shortly after his death his wife Olive gave birth to their daughter Carolyn.

H.E.G. Pugh,
Course 62.
31 B&G School. Picton.

R.C.A.F. R.96
(R.A.F. 1767)
25M-4-42 (2048)
H.Q. 885-R-96

Certificates of Qualification

(To be filled in as appropriate)

1. This is to certify that *658462* ... *P.211 H.E.G.*
   has qualified as *Air Bomber [Navigator]*
   with effect from ... Sgd ...
   Date ... Unit ...

2. This is to certify that **658462 LAC PUGH H.E.**
   has qualified as **AIR BOMBER [NAVIGATOR]**
   with effect from **4/12/42** Sgd ... **S/L**
   Date **9/12/42** Unit **33 A.N.S.**

3. This is to certify that ...
   has qualified as ...
   with effect from ... Sgd ...
   Date ... Unit ...

4. This is to certify that ...
   has qualified as ...
   with effect from ... Sgd ...
   Date ... Unit ...

Light vision Test H.... 14/1/43. 21/32.

Certificate of Qualification

209

All four airmen are buried adjacent to one another in Cambridge Newmarket Road Cemetery (War graves section).

Flight Lieutenant Charles Eddy MBE

Wireless Operator Henry Bennis

Pilot Officer Arnold Feldman

Sergeant Edwin Kerwin

Date	Aircraft Type & Number	Crew	Duty	Time Up	Time Down	Details of Sortie or Flight	References
1944. 18/19th APRIL.	Lancaster Mark III. (KO)A.IM.510	W/O. HEMMING, L.	Captain.	22.27	02.56	27 aircraft (9 from 'A' Flight - 10 from 'B' Flight and 8 from 'C' Flight) were detailed to attack ROUEN in accordance with FORM B. 42 received from Headquarters, No.3 Group. 1 aircraft failed to take-off.	
		F/S. GROOM, W.	Navigator.			A/C A.IM 510 W/O HEMMING.L. and crew	
		SGT. STONEMAN, A.	A/B.			A/C.G.ND.809 S/L. J.R.GRANT. do.	
		SGT. HOWIE, H.	WOP/AIR.			A/C.F.ND.794 P/O.E. MOON do.	
		SGT. CARTER, J.	R/G.				
		SGT. BUCKLEY, N.	MU/AG.				
		SGT. HARDOW, E.	F/ENG.				
	Lancaster Mark III. (KO)G.ND.809	S/L. J. R. GRANT.	Captain.	22.45	01.57	A/C.C.ME.718 F/S. BURDETT, M. do.	
		F/S. WALLERS. S.	Navigator.			A/C.D.LL.880 F/S. FRANCIS,S. do.	
		P/O. J. RODGERSON	A/B.			A/C.H.ND.790 F/S. TAYLOR, H. do.	
		SGT. PARRY. W.	WOP/AIR.			A/C.J.HK.542 F/L. C.D.RASH do.	
		T/S. KOSS. C.	R/G.			A/C.E.HK.545 F/B. W.G.SHADFORTH. do.	
		16601590 - USAAF				A/C.B.ND.631 SGT. LEMOINE, M. do.	
		SGT. TABNER, E.	MU/AG.			A/C.H.LL.715 S/L. C.H.BAIGENT DFC-Bar. do. (NZ.411988)	
		SGT. CLARKE,R.	F/ENG.			A/C.Y.DS.620 F/L. G.G.HAMMOND. do. (AUS.415240 - RAAF)	
	Lancaster Mark III. (KO)F.DN.794	P/O. E. MOON	Captain.	22.32	02.52	A/C.Q.DS.542 P/O. E. GIBSON. do. (AUS.410049 - RAAF)	
		F/S. DURHAM, H.	Navigator.			A/C.E.LL.667 P/O. I. BIRNIE. do.	
		SGT. SWAN, J.	A/B.			A/C.S.LL.641 F/L. R. MILGATE. do.	
		P/O. McRAE	WOP/AIR.			(AUS.409952 - RAAF)	
		F/S. KANARENS,F.	R/G.			A/C.U.LL.666 F/S. CAMPBELL, G. do.	
		SGT. FRASER,W.	MU/AG.			A/C.N.DS.781 P/O. G.H.R. TREASURE do.	
		SGT. SHARPE, G.	F/ENG.			(NZ.414699 - RNZAF)	
	Lancaster Mark I. (KO)G.ME.718	F/S. BURDETT.M.	Captain.	22.37	02.48	A/C.Y.DS.734 F/S. CAGIENARD, R. do.	
		F/S. MANSFIELD, E.	Navigator.			A/C.L.LL.726 P/O. R.A.HOWE-EVANS do.	
		SGT. CROCKER,G.	A/B.			A/C.F.ND.760 F/S. STEWART, R. do.	
		F/S. BUTLER,D.	WOP/AIR.			A/C.J.LL.667 F/L. G. HOUT. do.	
		W/O. TAILLANCOURT,A.	R/G. (R.195285 - RCAF)			(NZ.239003 - RNZAF)	
		SGT. MOSEY, F.	MU/AG. (R.167371 - RCAF)			A/C.G.ME.698 P/O. S.W.HOLDER do. (NZ.421054 - RNZAF)	
		SGT. DEAVILLE,A.	F/ENG.			A/C.C.LL.684 P/O. D. CAMERON. do.	
	Lancaster Mark I. (KO)D.LL.880	F/S. FRANCIS, S.	Captain.	22.33	02.02	A/C.K.LL.684 F/S. MAUDE, R. do.	
		F/O. FOUNTAIN,W.	Navigator.			A/C.K.ND.753 P/O. R. CHANTLER. do.	
		SGT. HITCHCOCK, A.	A/B. (R.149998-RCAF)			A/C.D.ND.745 F/O. C. CLAREY. do. (AUS.426312 - RAAF)	
		SGT. WHARTON, A.	R/G.			A/C.A.ND.756 SGT. QUINTON, C. do.	
		SGT. LANE, A.	R/G.				
		SGT. MULLEN, H.	MU/AG. (R.187036 - RCAF)			BOMB LOAD.	
		SGT. SKELLION, A.	F/ENG.			The above aircraft carried 72 x 1,000 lb. G.P. 136 x 1,000 lb. M.C. and 208 x 500 lb. M.C. Bombs.	

Date	Aircraft Type & Number	Crew	Duty	Time Up	Time Down	Details of Sortie or Flight	References
1944. 18/19th APRIL.	Lancaster Mark I. (A4)G.ME.698	P/O. S.W.HOLDER	Captain. (NZ.421054 - RNZAF)	22.31	03.22		
		F/S. NICHOLLS,I.	Navigator. NZ. 421085 - RNZAF				
		F/O. H. PHILLIPS	A/B.				
		SGT. FRECCK, W.	WOP/AIR.				
		SGT. GARRETT, E.	R/G.				
		P/O. D.W.FRANCIS	MU/AG. (J.85090 - RCAF)				
		SGT. STANTIALL,A.	F/ENG.				
	Lancaster Mark III. (A4)C.ND.809	P/O. D. CAMERON	Captain.	22.29	03.45		
		SGT. TOWNSEND,R.	Navigator.				
		SGT. ATTWOOD, G.	A/B.				
		SGT. RODY, G.	WOP/AIR.				
		SGT. McDONALD, G.	R/G. (R.182759 - RCAF)				
		SGT. GALLIMORE,R.	MU/AG.				
		SGT. JONES, H.	F/ENG.				
	Lancaster Mark I. (A4)H.LL.884	F/S. MAUDE, R.	Captain.	22.25	03.42		
		F/O. R.N.TOVEY	Navigator.				
		SGT. FOSTER,H.	SGT A/B.				
		SGT. FYFFE, J.	WOP/AIR.				
		SGT. SUTHERLAND,R.	R/G.				
		SGT. PERTON, K.	MU/AG.				
		SGT. ANDERSON, A.	F/ENG.				
	Lancaster Mark III. (A4)K.ND.753	P/O. R. CHANTLER	Captain.	22.38	03.38		
		SGT. SWEENEY,A.	2nd Pilot.				
		P/O. D. DEEM	Navigator.				
		F/S. FRANCIS, R.	A/B. (R.162542 - RCAF)				
		SGT. NASH, D.	WOP/AIR.				
		SGT. FARMER, K.	R/G.				
		SGT. BROWN, W.	MU/AG. (AUS.17786 - RAAF)				
		SGT. TWEEDIE, J.	F/ENG.				
	Lancaster Mark III. (A4)D.ND.745	F/O. C. CLAREY	Captain. (AUS.426312 - RAAF)	22.28	03.27		
		SGT. LINK, R.	Navigator.				
		SGT. KIRKLAND, A.	A/B.				
		SGT. HANCOCK, D.	WOP/AIR.				
		F/S. BARLOW	R/G. (AUS.427790 - RAAF)				
		SGT. MIDDLETON	MU/AG.				
		SGT. LUTON,	F/ENG.				

DETAIL OF WORK CARRIED OUT
By No.11½ Squadron.
For the Month of APRIL 19__

77

Date	Aircraft Type & Number	Crew	Duty	Time Up	Time Down	Details of Sortie or Flight	References
1944. 18/19th APRIL.	Lancaster Mark II. [KO] Q.DS.787	P/O E.GIBSON (AUS.414D049 - RAAF) P/O. J. STOCK SGT. JONES, H. F/S. MASKELL, E. (AUS.410612 - RAAF) SGT. ANDREWS, W. SGT. DAWSON, N. (R:84010 - RCAF) SGT. SAUNDERS, J.	Captain Navigator. A/B. WOP/AIR. R/G. MU/AG. F/ENG.	22.46	02.50	A/C. N.LL.716 (Captain S/L.C.H.BAIGENT DFC-Bar) Target identified by PFF. Bombed red and green target indicators from 14,000 feet. PFF well concentrated. Photo expected. / A/C. Q.DS.787 (Captain P/O. E. GIBSON) Target identified by red and green target indicators on which bombed from 14,000 feet. Instructed by M.C. to some concentration of reds to S.W.	
	Lancaster Mark II. [KO]R.LL.667	P/O. J. BIRNIE F/S. JONES, D. F/S. FELDMAN, A. (R.8244 - RCAF) SGT. KERWIN, E. SGT. BAILEY, G. SGT. McMILLAN.W. (R.209012 - RCAF) SGT. FERGUSON,J.	Captain. Navigator. A/B. WOP/AIR. R/G. MU/AG. F/ENG	22.52	02.10.	A/C.R.LL.667 (Captain P/O. J. BIRNIE) Results of bombing unknown. Shot down by enemy aircraft over base at 02.10 hours. No survivors. / A/C. S.LL.641 (Captain F/L. R. MILGATE) Target identified by bend in River and PFF. Bombed on good concentration of red and green target indicators from 14,000 feet. Slight fires seen. Master of Ceremonies very useful.	
	Lancaster. Mark II. [KO]S.LL.641	F/L. R. MILGATE (AUS.409952 - RAAF) SGT GRIFFIN.H. F/S BANKS.S. F/S HULSE.R. SGT RICHARDSON. SGT CHAPMAN.R. SGT ZIPPEL,J.	Captain Navigator A/B WOP/AIR R/G MU/AG F/ENG	22.54	03.08	A/C. U.LL.666 (Captain F/S. CAMPBELL,C.) Target identified both visually and by indicators. Bombed red target indicators from 14,500 feet. Target indicators very scattered. 1x500 lb. failed to release and brought back. Photo taken. / A/C. V.DS.620 (Captain F/L. G.G.HAMMOND) Target identified visually and by target indicators. Bombed southern end of red target indicators under instructions of Master of ceremonies. Bombing seemed concentrated. Photo taken.	
	Lancaster Mark II [KO]U.LL 666	F/S. CAMPBELL.C. SGT GUYER.S. W/O CAMPBELL.J. (R. 156965 - RCAF) SGT BURNS.K. SGT McLEAN.F. SGT STEPHANIAN.P. SGT TWEEDIE.T.	Captain Navigator A/B WOP/AIR R/G MU/AG F/ENG	22.40	03.11	A/C. W.DS.781 (Captain P/O.G.H.R.TREASURE) Target identified by river bend lit up by photo flash and red target indicators. Results of bombing not observed through haze. Photo taken. / A C. Y.DS.734 (Captain F/S. CAGIENARD,R.) Target identified by river and target indicators. Bombed green target on instructions, from 14,000 feet. A few bomb explosions seen. Photo taken.	
	Lancaster Mark II [KO]V.DS 620	F/L.G.G. HAMMOND (AUS.416249 - RAAF) F/O. R. HARKINS F/O. F. BAGGALEY F/O. E. REEE. P/O. R. CHAPLIN. SGT. KENNEDY,T. SGT. COOK, D.	Captain Navigator. A.B. WOP/AIR. R/G. MU/AG. F/ENG.	22.55	03.13.	A/C. Z.LL.725 (Captain P/O. B.A. ROWE-EVANS) Target identified by river bend and lights from street in built-up area. Bombed target indicators from 13,000 feet. PFF scattered. Photo taken. / A/C. F.ND.760 (Captain F/S. STEWART,R.) Target identified by red and green target indicators on which bombed from 14,000 feet. B mb burst seen.	

Date	Aircraft Type & Number	Crew	Duty	Time Up	Time Down	Details of Sortie or Flight	References
1944. 18/19th APRIL.	Lancaster. Mark II. [KO]W.DS.781	P/O. G.H.R.TREASURE (NZ.411609 RNZAF) F/S. GOULD. N. (NZ.41896 - RNZAF) P/O. A. SCOTT. SGT. HOLLINRAKE. SGT. CASSLET,A. SGT. DAWSON.J. SGT HOLLAND.F.	Captain. Navigator. A/B. WOP/AIR. R/G. MU/AG F/ENG	22.44.	03.17.	A/C.J.LL.867 (Captain F/L. C.EDDY)Results of bombing unknown. Shot down by enemy aircraft over base at 03.48 hours. No survivors. / A/C.G.ND.698 (Captain P/O. S.W.HOLDER) Target identified by green target indicators and flares on which bombed from 13,500 feet. Bombs seen bursting. Should be a concentrated attack. Photo attempted.	
	Lancaster Mark II [KO]Y.DS 734	F/S CAGIENARD.R SGT FOSTER. R. SGT McLEOD.J. (R:121066-RCAF) SGT SHORTEN.W. SGT LETCHER.A. SGT KING.F SGT KELLY.C.	Captain Navigator A/B WOP/AIR R/G MU/AG F/ENG	22.49	03.02	A/C. C.ND.809 (Captain P/O. D.CAMERON) Identified target by PFF. Bombed red and green target indicators from 13,000 feet. PFF seemed to be concentrated in two areas. Bombing scattered. Photo taken. / A/C.H.LL.864 (Captain P/O. S. MAUDE,R.) Target identified by River and PFF. Bombed concentration of red and green indicators on instructions from Master of ceremonies. One good fire observed. Photo attempted.	
	Lancaster Mark II. [KO]Z.LL.725	P/O. B.A.ROWE-EVANS F/O. G. STEER. (R:125946 - RCAF) SGT. DIDCOTE,W. SGT. SPRUCE,J. SGT. WYATT,E. SGT. LEVI, R. SGT. LEWIS, A.	Captain. Navigator. A/B. WOP/AIR. R/G. MU/AG. F/ENG.	22.36	03.05.	A/C.Z.ND.755 (Captain P/O. R.CHANTLER) Identified green and red target indicators from 14,500 feet. Several fires burning. / A/C.D.ND.745 (Captain P/O. C. CLAREY) Target identified by PFF. Bombed concentration of red and green target indicators on instructions from Master of ceremonies. Many bursts seen. White flares seen over Channel on homeward run.	
	Lancaster. Mark III. [A4]F.ND.760.	F/S. STEWART, R. F/O. J. LEWIS SGT. WOODEN, K. SGT. GRUND, J. SGT. THOMPSON, SGT. LODGE, V. SGT. PLUMB. I.	Captain. Navigator. A/B. WOP/AIR. R/G. MU/AG. F/ENG.	22.40	03.25.	A/C.A.ND.728 (Captain SGT. QUINTON G.) Bombed on red target indicators from 12,500 feet. Fairly successful attack. Indicators scattered. Photo expected.	
	Lancaster. Mark I. [A4]J.LL.867	F/L. C. EDDY (NZ.59503 - RNZAF) F/O. A. SMITH F/S. PUGH, I. F/S. MADDOX, J. W/O. BENNIS, H. (R:176571 - RCAF) SGT. LANGRIDGE, A. SGT. MURPHY, W.	Captain. Navigator. A/B. WOP/AIR. R/G. MU/AG. F/ENG.	22.43	03.48.	26 aircraft had returned to base by 03.48 hours.	

215

Date	Aircraft Type & Number	Crew	Duty	Time Up	Time Down	Details of Sortie or Flight	References
1944. 18/19th APRIL.	Lancaster Mark III. (A4)A.ND.758.	SGT. QUINTON, C. SGT. RICHARDSON,R. SGT. MILLIGAN, R. SGT. INGRAM, C. SGT. EDWARDS, G. SGT. MILLINGTON,P. SGT. FIELDER, R.	Captain. Navigator. A/B. WOP/AIR. R/G. MU/AG. F/ENG.	22.26.	03.36.		

Date	Aircraft Type & Number	Crew	Duty	Time Up	Time Down	Details of Sortie or Flight	References
1944. 18/19th APRIL.	Lancaster Mark III. (KO)H.ND.790.	F/S. TAYLOR, H. F/S. GARSIDE, S. SGT. CARTER,P. F/S. WHITTON, J. (R.161486 - RCAF) F/S. LAWRENCE, W. (AUS.42-171 - RAAF) F/S1 JOHNSON,G. SGT. ASHLEY, A. SGT. GIBBS, S.	Captain. 2nd Pilot. Navigator. A/B. W/AIR. R/G. MU/AG. F/ENG.	22.35.	02.45.	A/C. A.IM.510 (Captain W/O. HEMMING,L.) Target identified by PFF. Bombed red and green target indicators from 13,500 feet. Indicators concentrated.	
						A/C.C.ND.500 (Captain S/L. J.R.GRANT) Identified target by PFF. Bombed centre of green target indicators from 14,000 feet. Bombing concentrated, aircraft coming in from all directions. Defences negligible. Photo attempted.	
	Lancaster. Mark I. (KO)J.HK.542.	F/L. C.D.RASH F/S. FRANKLIN,D. F/S. ENGLAND, C. SGT. KILMURRAY,W. SGT. RICE, S. SGT. MOORE, K. F/S. McCABE, J.	Captain. Navigator. A/B. W/AIR. R/G. MU/AC. F/ENG.	22.50.	02.00.	A/C.F.ND.754 (Captain P/O.E.MOON) Identified target by PFF and River. Bombed on red target indicators from 13,500 feet. Bombing seemed concentrated. Big explosion seen. Two small fires observed.	
						A/C.C.G.MK.718. (Captain F/S.BURDETT,M.) Target identified by green and red target indicators on which bombed from 14,000 feet. No results observed. Photo taken.	
	Lancaster. Mark I. (KO)X.HK.545.	F/L. W.D.SHADFORTH SGT. PARKYN, R. SGT. WEIR, R. SGT. BRADLEY, W. R.207257 - RCAF. SGT. SHARPE, T. SGT. VEALS, A.	Captain. Navigator. A/B. WOP/AIR. R/G. MU/AG. F/ENG.	22.48.	02.04.	A/C.G.MR.718 (Captain F/S.FRANCES,G.) Target identified by red and green target indicators on which bombed from 14,000 feet. Bomb bursts seen in target area. Marking did not seem too good, bombing scattered.	
						A/C. H.ND.790 (Captain F/S. TAYLOR,H.) Target identified by PFF and bend in river. Bombed on red and green target indicators from 13,000 feet. Raid considered fairly successful although there were two concentrations.	
	Lancaster. Mark I. (KO)B.ND.631.	SGT. LEMOINE,R. SGT. JONES, R. SGT. FALLIS, C. R.132618 - RCAF SGT. GUARD, D. SGT. OLIVER, E. R.198814 - RCAF SGT. BRENNAN, J. SGT. WATSON, H.	Captain. Navigator. A/B. WOP/AIR. R/G. MU/AG. F/ENG.	22.53.	02.09.	A/C. J.HK.542 (Captain F/L.C.D.RASH) Identified target by red and green target indicators on which bombed from 14,000 feet. A few explosions seen. Attack appeared to be going well. Photo attempted.	
						A/C. B.HK.545 (Captain F/L. W.D. SHADFORTH) Target identified by target indicators on which bombed from 13,500 feet. Attack rather wide spread in westerly directions. Indicators definitely scattered. Photo taken.	
	Lancaster. Mark II. (KO)N.LL.718.	S/L. C.H.RAIGENT DFC-Bar.Capt. (NZ.411923 - RNZAF) F/O. I.C.BAYLY, (NZ.42560 - RNZAF) F/O. J.R.CROANKILL (NZ.411977 - RNZAF) F/O. W. THOMSON, F/O. N.G. POWELL (R.200729 - RCAF) F/O. R. PHILLIPS	Capt. Navigator. A/B. WOP/AIR. R/G. MU/AG. F/ENG.	22.49.	02.58.	A/C.B.ND.631 (Captain SGT. LEMOINE,R.) Target identified by river and target indicators. Bombed red target indicators from 13,500 feet - explosion seen in centre. Raid believed to be successful. Photo flash failed to release.	

The images above are a Copy of Operations

216

Pining Pets

There were two other unusual victims of the incident: The dogs that were left with WAAF Daphne (Val) Valentine shortly before take off on the raid to Rouen.

Sadly Sandra and Timmy would not see their masters again. Val took Sandra home to her parents and she lived to be nineteen. Timmy was taken in by another WAAF and given a good home. Photos via Daphne Hogg (née Valentine)

Sergeant Ernest Abbott

Sergeant Ernest Abbott poses with a Blockbuster bomb at
Witchford January 1945

Ernest Abbott, formerly of East Acton W3 now residing in
Canada, completed his training as a Wireless Operator at No. 2
Radio School on 16th June 1944.

Further training continued at No. 8 (O) Air Flying Unit, Mona,
Anglesey, and North Wales moving on to No. 28 Operational
Training Unit at Wymeswold in Leicestershire. It was here that
he became the regular Wireless Operator to Flying Officer
George Stone. On 27th November Stone's crew moved to No.
1656 Heavy Conversion Unit at Lindholme in Yorkshire, before
joining 115 Squadron B Flight as an operational crew on 30th
November 1944. They flew their first operation from Witchford
on 13th January 1945, target Saarbrucken.

Raids to Langdendreer, Duisburg, Cologne, Munchen
Gladback, Wiesbaden, Dortmund (aborted), Hohendbudberg,
Dresden, Chemnitz, Gelsenkirchen, Dessau, Dortmund,
Henrichshutte, Hulse, Hamm, Kiel, Potsdam Berlin, Heligoland,

Bad Oldesloe followed before they took part in their first Manna food drop.

Ernie Abbott (right) with Bill Wheatley

Ernie remembers what he calls the `Somewhat more rewarding operations during the months of April and May 1945.

After a period of low level practice drops with sand bags we were one of the squadrons to take part in the Manna Food Drops to the people of Holland who were desperately in need of food. Our first Manna trip was on 29th April. I remember our bomb bay was packed with emergency food enclosed in what looked like ordinary sand bags. Our orders were to fly in across the coast north of The Hague, and then turn across what had been a German air base. We were in the third wave and were all thrilled to know we were doing something worth while. I was up front with the flight engineer and our orders were to fly as low as safety would allow and drop the stuff inside a circle marked with white paint. The German troops were all around to keep the Dutch people from getting hurt but as we approached many brave souls rushed into the drop zone to gather some food. I often wonder if any got hurt. After four supply dropping operations we were then sent to France to help in the repatriation of British soldiers who had been released from various Prison camps. In my log book for 9th May 1945 I entered it as repatriation of POWs Juvincourt. Juvincourt was a former Luftwaffer Fighter base and I recall seeing smashed up Messerschmitts and Focke-Wulfs just bulldozed to one side to allow us to land. We were then directed around to one side for a check on our undercarriage to ensure that it had not been damaged when we landed as the runway had many bomb holes which had hastily been filled in. On our second trip to Juvincourt the next day we were told that we would have to stay over night, so that they could replace one of the oleo legs on our aircraft. We slept in the Lancaster and later borrowed a jeep from some American soldiers so that we could go and scrounge something to eat and drink. Most of the ex POWs were British soldiers who had not been briefed as to what was happening. When we taxied around to the pick up area I opened the door and let the ladder down, the POWs were ushered up and told to embark. They had no idea what was happening and I recall one saying to me "Where in the hell are we going?" I replied "Where is home?" Canterbury came the reply. "Well," I said, "You will be in England in two hours and back home in a day or two", he was speechless. On 15th May 1945 I flew my last trip with Flying Officer Stone in our regular Lanc KO-Q as we had completed our first tour of ops. After a spot of leave I returned to Witchford with 115 Squadron joining Pilot Officer Godleman as his Wireless Operator. We did several Baedeker trips or Cooks tours as they came to be known taking ground crew personnel over some of the devastated German cities. On 7th September we flew to Bari in Italy on the Adriatic coast to take part in Operation Dodge bringing home POWs as there was a shortage of shipping at the time. We did the trip to Bari twice.

I completed my time at Witchford on 11th December 1945 moving on to No. 1381 Transport Conversion Unit at Desborough, Northamptonshire on 28th March 1946 flying in Dakotas.

Above – Flying Officer George Stone and crew

Left to Right:

Sergeant Bill Wheatly	*Flight Engineer*
Sergeant Ernie Abbott	*Wireless Operator*
Sergeant Rip Herriott RCAF	*Rear Gunner*
Sergeant Tom Knapp RCAF	*Mid Upper Gunner*
Sergeant Maurice Anderson RCAF	*Navigator*
Flying Officer George Stone RCAF	*Pilot*
Pilot Officer James Cox RCAF	*Bomb Aimer*

Flying Officer George Stone RCAF

Flying Officer George Stone RCAF

Operation Dodge 1945

On 2nd May 1945, just before V.E. Day, a proportion of 115 Squadron Ground Crew were flown from Witchford to Bari in Italy. There were twenty ground crew in each Lancaster, all sitting on the cold metal floor for the eight hour journey. Corporal Charles Wyatt was a 115 Squadron Electrician and remembers the journey well:

We were able to move around a little during the flight and could see where we were going through the windows. We had to fly at 1,000 feet all the way. We crossed the Channel, and went on to the West of Paris and South down to the Mediterranean. We flew just off the coast along the French and Italian Riviera to the West coast of Italy, and down to Rome and showed the Vatican City what a Lancaster looked like. (This was a banned flying area so we did not tell anyone about it). Down to Naples we saw Mount Vesuvius (smoking a bit), and on to the East coast of Bari.

When we landed it was very hot and we still wore our UK Blue. We had to service and refuel all the planes before we could change into Tropical kit as they had to fly back to Witchford the next morning. When we had finished our work it was dark. Our camp had been a rest camp for the 8th Army. We had a pier out to sea and a swimming pool. We could get fresh fruit like grapes, which we had not seen for five years and the weather was wonderful, it was just like being on holiday. The purpose of all this activity was to repatriate our troops from Italy back to the UK. A similar operation was also taking place in Naples.

Corporal Wyatt also remembers an incident that took place at Bari, when a 115 Squadron Lancaster was taking off on the return journey to England.

Lancaster KO-G landed at Bari on 15th August 1945. Serviced and re-fuelled, she was ready for the return journey on the 17th to take back more troops to England. At 07.30 hours Pilot Flying Officer Gibbons opened up the throttles and roared down the runway when suddenly a tyre burst causing him to lose control. KO-G slewed off the runway and crashed into a line of Lancasters on dispersal. 115 Squadron's Lancaster HK 798

KO-H and 35 Squadron's Lancaster PB 754 TL-D were both extensively damaged as was ME 834 KO-G. All on board escaped injury, except for a Soldier sitting in the front turret who received slight abrasions.

HK 798 was delivered to 115 Squadron on the 18th February 1945, and was coded IL-L, later IL-B and shortly before the crash KO-H.

ME 834 was a Witchford veteran having arrived on 6th June 1944. The aircraft had several changes of Squadron Codes KO-K, A4-M, KO-M and finally KO-G.

Leading Aircraftswoman Esme Melrose Stott

Leading Aircraftswoman Esme Melrose Stott

Now Mrs. Schuldes, Esme lives in Florida USA with husband Dick. In 1944 Esme was stationed at RAF Witchford in the parachute section.

She recalls some of her memories:

The Parachute section had a shallow well running down the centre of the room, with an eight inch raised edge all around. The parachutes were hung on pulleys in the well to air them out. Sometimes they would be wet, or we would get new ones in and they needed to be hung and inspected before being packed. The packing table ran the length of the room enabling two parachutes to be packed at once, one at each end. New crews would come in and get fitted for a parachute harness, which they would sign for in a book which we kept. Everything was numbered, and we each signed for every chute that we packed. Sometimes we had to go over to the hangars and locker rooms to find parachutes that were overdue for inspection. If a chute came in with the pack shot up or someone had opened it in flight to staunch a wound, then we would pack it up and send it off to M.U. (Maintenance Unit).

One nice thing was that the section was always warm, to dry the chutes so it was often a favourite place for the aircrews to come and warm up and maybe get a cup of cocoa while one of us girls would mend a hole in a jacket or stitch on new tapes. They were always very grateful and we were glad to do it for them. Whenever there were ops, one or two of us would stay behind until take-off, in case there was a need for another chute, it did not happen very often but you never knew. In the early days of the war parachutes were made of a soft beautiful silk and were very nice to pack, then the nylon ones came in and they were very stiff and bulky. You needed all your muscle and strength to get them into the little pack.

Anytime there was a dance on camp, we were there, as most of us loved to dance. There was a lot of activity in our huts after teatime with button polishing, shoe cleaning, putting curlers in our hair, looking for that one iron to press our skirts and putting on our best thin lisle stocking that we had to buy with our precious coupons, rather than wear the heavy ones we were issued with. We were not allowed to wear jewellery of any kind so we had to make ourselves look as attractive as possible in our shirt, tie and lace up shoes. We guarded our makeup like the crown jewels. Once my great-coat was taken at a dance, I was more upset with loosing a new lipstick which was in the pocket than loosing the coat, which I had to pay for.

My friend and I would ride our bikes into Ely for tea in a little café in the High Street, hoping no one would catch us in our battle dress which was only worn on camp, it was worth the risk though to get a nice pot of tea and beans on toast and even some cake if we were lucky. Sometimes when we had an afternoon off we would hitch into Cambridge for curry and rice and if we had enough money we would go to a movie, the flicks as we used to call it. If we could get an overnight pass it gave us time to go to a dance at the Dorothy, there were a lot of little bed and breakfasts in our price range in Cambridge and if we felt daring we took our civvies with us to wear at the dance. We had a lot of fun and our respirator case was used for a lot more than our gas mask.

I remember RAF Witchford for mud, mud and more mud, the cold and wet clothes. We lived in our gumboots, when the weather was bad which most of the time in winter was. The mud got brought into the hut on our boots and whoever was hut orderly that week had to scrape up all the dirt off the concrete floor and wash it which was quite a job. You also had to knock the clinkers off the side of the coke stove which stood in the middle of the room. The beds nearest to the stove were always in great demand because the rest of the hut would be freezing.

I was in the WAAF four years and eight months and even though there were hardships there was a lot of fun and comradeship, which I think we all felt would never be experienced again. There were sadness too when a crew you got to know failed to return from a raid. Some of us lost boyfriends we cared about, but I do not think any of us would have missed the experience of the WAAF. It was the most exciting and memorable time of my life.

Before Witchford I served in the parachute section at Scampton in Lincolnshire. One day I received a card accompanied by a £5 note, (a lot of money in those days); it was a gift from a grateful mother whose son had made a safe descent with a parachute I had apparently packed. Needless to say I am very proud of that card.

The friend I mentioned previously was Cynthia Nunnerley, she was indirectly the reason I now live in Florida. We met on our first Bomber Station when we were barely eighteen years old. Our lives to that point had been very similar so we had much in common; we saw the funny side of things and laughed a lot.

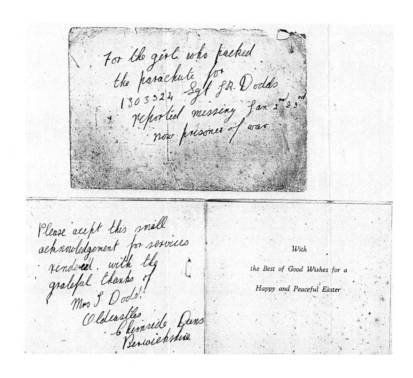

For the girl who packed
the parachute for
1303324 Sgt JR. Dodds
reported missing Jan 2nd 3rd
now prisoner of war

Please accept this small
acknowledgement for services
rendered. with the
grateful thanks of
Mrs J Dodds
Oldcastles
Chirnside Duns
Berwickshire

With

the Best of Good Wishes for a

Happy and Peaceful Easter

The card received by Esme

The parachute section building at RAF Witchford
Photograph taken in 1960s

One instance I recall at Witchford was when we had just been to collect our clean sheets, we carried them on our bikes, balancing them on the handle bars, a precarious business and due to the recent rain the mud road was hard to navigate and my sheets fell off the handle bars, the bike and I followed the sheets into the mud. What a mess I was! Cynthia, who was ahead of me, stopped her bike and when she saw me burst out laughing, tears running down her cheeks, she said, I looked so funny, my cap askew and mud splattered like freckles over my face. I too had to laugh also when we got back to the hut and I saw my face in the mirror. Between us we managed to clean up my battle dress, taking things to the cleaners was not an option for us in those days.

Sometimes, on rare occasions, we got a package from home, Cynthia had received a nice one from her mother and had the contents spread over the packing table. There was some sort of meat paste in a tin, homemade biscuits and several other little items we were anxious to try, so we scrounged some bread slices and some butter from the cookhouse anticipating toast and some of that tinned meat paste. Cynthia was sitting on a bench in front of the coke stove with the bread and butter beside her, busily toasting the bread, when the door opened and in came an officer from Headquarters; I had a parachute on the table so I could not warn her. He marched down the aisle between the table and the hanging parachutes. He was sniffing the air as he went; Cynthia was humming a tune completely unaware of what was about to happen until he was standing behind her. "What do you call this Airwoman?" Cynthia was so startled she almost dropped the toast, however deciding to brave it out, said "Making toast Sir", she set the bread and fork on the bench and stood up. Cynthia had a habit of hooking her thumbs in her trouser pockets, which she did then – unfortunately I had stopped packing my chute and was standing near by, staring at the scene. The officer's face was a picture of icy rage as his eyes swept over the assortment of goodies on the table. "Take your hands out of your pockets and stand at attention" he snapped. Cynthia complied, not as rapidly as he might have liked, which seemed to anger him even more. He caught sight of me "What are you staring at? Get back to work". Now Cynthia, never afraid to speak her mind, drew herself up and glared at him. "There is no need to speak to her like that". Well I am afraid that did it as far as he was concerned, his teeth clenched, he wagged his finger at both of us. I was still standing rooted to the spot, "I will separate you two if it is the last thing I do", and he turned on his heels and headed for the door. Calling over his shoulder with a parting shot, "You will be very sorry for this insolence I assure you". Out he went, the door banging behind him. There was silence after he left. I said, "Think he meant it". "Of course he did, what did he want in here anyway" she said. "Who knows, unless he smelled the first piece of toast you burned, I did open the window". I went over to close it. "If it had been anyone else but him; he had a bee in his bonnet that's for sure", I said. We did not feel much like eating after that.

A month later I was sent on a dinghy course to Credenhill near Hereford. Further down the road was an American army camp and, during the course of my stay there, I met my future husband. After the war we married and eventually moved to Florida. After the dinghy course I was posted to Marham, near King's Lynn. Cynthia went to Credenhill a few weeks later and was posted to Peterborough. We visited each other once and then she was sent down south. It was a long time before we would meet again.

Cynthia went to South Africa after the war but even though there was a lot of water between us, we kept in touch with letters and photos. In later years we were able to meet several times, and it was like we were back in the parachute section again.

Remembering the friends we had made along the way and a lifetime of events crammed into a few short years.

During my time at Witchford I had been dating or "going out with" as we use to say, a Sergeant Air-Crew from Canada. While I was home on leave, I had such a vivid dream, I saw a plane going down in flames, I woke up, my heart hammering, I could not get it out of my mind, I really wanted to get back to camp. I was surprised to find Cynthia waiting for me at the station. On the way back she told me that my friend Pat had gone missing. I asked her when it was and she said a couple of nights ago, which was when I had dreamed about the plane going down in flames. Nothing like that ever happened to me before or since and yet I knew that during wars, strange things like that seem to happen.

I remember a young air gunner who had a strange experience. He shared a room with his chum who was on ops that night.

The air gunner, who was sitting on his bed writing a letter, looked up and saw his chum in the doorway. "Hey I thought you were on ops tonight", he said. The man just stared at him for a moment and then was gone. The air gunner rushed to the door, there was no one in sight. He said he went back and lay on his bed, the letter writing forgotten, half expecting his friend to show up again, but later in the mess he learned that his room mate had indeed "Bought it" the night before. There is no explanation for some things.

The Meteorological Office

L.A.C.W. Carol Holt, now Mrs. Thomas, was a Meteorological Assistant Observer at RAF Witchford from November 1944 to September 1945, when the station closed. Her main memory of Witchford was how cold the hut she shared with several other WAAFs was, infact she described it as one of the most wretched concrete constructions ever invented. Among the other WAAFs sharing her discomfort in the hut were several cooks, one photographer, several mess girls and a bat woman. The Meteorological Office was another important part of the station and was situated on the ground floor of the Control Tower.

Carol Holt and the other five WAAFs that shared Carol's concrete billet

Many of the cold concrete WAAF huts at Witchford would continue to be used for many years after the war, to accommodate families during the acute housing shortage.

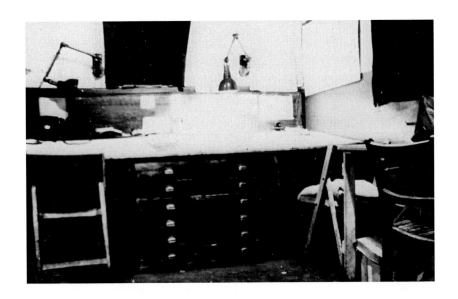

The photograph above shows the Meteorological Office Plotting bench

Blackouts can be seen over the windows. The Meteorological Office was a very important part of the airfield, as often weather predictions would determine whether a bombing operation would take place or not. As we all know, even today our weather is very unpredictable and can change in a very short time. During World War II no satellites were orbiting the earth, sending back pictures of cloud formation and movements.

During wartime the weather forecasters relied heavily upon a piece of equipment called a `Stephenson Screen`, which was situated several metres to one side of the control tower. This unit contained thermometers, water gauge and a wind gauge.

This badly faded photograph shows two forecasters, Flying Officer Starr and Flying Officer Esdaile, inspecting the thermometers in the Stephenson Screen. The balloon filling shed was to the right of the photo, and the fire tender was in the distance

A clearer photo of Flying Officer Esdaile and Flying Officer Starr
leaning on the fire tender

ROUTE FORECAST (for period.............hours to.............hours): Date.............

Time of Origin.............................hours.

Synoptic situation (Fronts, etc.) at ....hours		BASE – TARGET – BASE					
Stage	From	Base – 3 E –	3 E – 6 E	6 E – T – 6 E	6 E – 3 E	3 E – Base	Base – 3 E	3 E – 6 E
	To	3 E –	6 E	T – 6 E	3 E	Base	3 E	6 E
Wind at Surface 2000		270/30	270/30	290/25	270/30	290/25		
" " 5000 feet		270/3	270/35	280/27	270/32	260/37	Zero	Zero
" " 10000 feet		270/0	270/40	270/37	270/40	260/47	-10	-10
" " 15000 feet		280/38	270/50	270/50	280/51	270/60	-19	-19
" " 20000 feet		290/70	280/65	270/65	280/70	270/70	-30	-30
" " 25000 feet		290/75	280/72	270/70	290/71	280/75	-40	-40
Weather		Fair generally but slight rain or drizzle over Base area on Return.						
Visibility		5-10 miles or more generally.						
Cloud (all heights above M.S.L.)		Small amounts of Sc at 2,000 ft or nil at Base for take-off, increasing over Continent to 4-7/10 Sc. 2,500 ft to; a locally to 8-10000 ft. 7-10/10 Sc 1500-2500 ft tops about 6000 ft over Base on Return falling to 1000 ft in main. MEDIUM AND HIGH Broken thin Ac at about 20000 ft with some clearances over Eastern half of Route. High and medium cloud						
Icing Index		Mod. to high in Cu, Mod. in Ns above F/L.						
Freezing Level (above M.S.L.)		4,5000 ft.						
*Pressure at Station Level (Q.F.E.)		Est. pressure at Base on Return 1002 mbs plus or minus 3 mbs.						
*Pressure at M.S.L. (Q.F.F.)		Target 1009 mbs plus or minus 2 mbs.						
Remarks (warnings, contrails, state of sea, etc.)		CLOUD CONTINUED Above 15000 ft over North Sea on Return thickening and lowering to 10/10 Ns. approaching Base area, but some lanes expected.						

*Indicate time, place and tolerance (+.............mb.) and whether expected to be rising or falling.   (P.T.O.)

Issued by............................at..............................Meteorological Office at.............hours.

A weather forecast for period 11.00 hours to 17.00 hours on 4/1/44 issued at 08.00 hours by C. Hinkel at Witchford

Leading Aircraftswoman Jennie King – Now Mrs Sunnock

Meteorological Assistant

LACW Jennie King Meteorological Clerk

My job, while just a very small cog in the wheel that made up a working RAF Bomber Command station, was nevertheless an interesting one. The several assistants who worked in the office in the Control Tower for the Meteorological Officer were engaged on making detailed reports on the current temperature, wind speed and direction, cloud cover and type etc. and sending this information to Group Headquarters.

Another part of the work was converting information relating to weather sent in from other stations onto large charts, and of course, making tea at regular intervals.

We worked in shifts keeping cover for the twenty-four hours as the information came in regularly and the charts needed to be kept up to date. The reports came from all other RAF stations plus Naval and Coastal Command stations. These reports were collated at Headquarters and passed to every Met. Office via the teleprinter, which buzzed and clacked away in the back room. The simple encoding consisted of one line per station sending the information and on this line were details of temperature, wind speed and direction, cloud amount and types, any precipitation and, of course, visibility. The lists would be ripped carefully from the teleprinter and taken through to the office where a fresh chart waited. The assistant would sit on a high stool and work at a tilted, very similar to the ones used today by architects and graphic designers.

With the aid of two pens, one red and one black, neatly tied together at the ends with an elastic band tight enough to hold the unused pen steady but loose enough to enable the switch to be made from the red to black in an instant, the job was done. The method was to draw a circle around the station sending the information, fill the circle with detail relating to the cloud cover and arrange the other figures closely around the circle. This presented the Met. Officer with (we hoped) a picture from which he could proceed to complete the synoptic chart by joining the isobars, plotting the anticyclones and depressions, drawing in the fronts and decide whether each front was occluding and so dispersing, or deepening into a problem area-perhaps making the night's raid into enemy country even more hazardous than it already was.

Records were taken even at night of the weather details. The Stephenson Screen was about fifty yards from the Control Tower where the thermometers were housed and the visibility would be checked with various identifiable buildings or trees. The most contentious visibility aid was a red light fixed on the spire of Ely Cathedral and switching this on was not undertaken unless essential and then only for a second or two, as the Bishop would soon be ringing the station if the light was left on *too long. If you were late in sending the information through to Group there would be a loud tapping and buzzing on the teleprinter to ensure you had not nodded off.*

Being shift workers we were not subjected to parades, kit inspections etc. as there would usually be someone asleep in the hut at any time. We all had bicycles for getting from the WAAF accommodation to the Control Tower and village or Ely, and we were lucky in having a most pleasant and helpful man* in Witchford village who worked very hard for us fixing our broken bike chains, smashed front or back lamps and mud encrusted gears.

Sergeant Pamela Hayden

Watch keeper

Some of Witchford's operation staff – taken in the Control
Tower on 22.12.1944. Photo via Pam Hayden

*Back row- L. to R. Squadron Leader Smith, Navigation Officer
Flight Lieutenant Jack Bawden, Squadron Leader Humphries
Senior Flying Control Officer.*
*Front row- L. to R. Sergeant Pam Hayden Watch keeper, Group
Captain Reynolds Station Commander and Sergeant Val Buck
Watch keeper.*

Pam Hayden was stationed at Witchford from September 1943
until September 1945 as a Watch keeper in the operations room
situated in the Control Tower.

Pam recalls what her job entailed and other memories of her
time in the Royal Air Force.

You had to complete three month training for this job, at the end of which you had to pass an exam. Before the war the duties of Watch keeper were carried out by male Squadron Leaders. Other Watch keepers I remember at Witchford were Jean Buchanan, Val Buck and Flo Wilkinson, although I believe that was her married name after she left the WAAF.

Basically the job consisted of receiving all the information from Group Headquarters (on a secret `scrambler` telephone) about the operations for that night, target, route, type of bombs etc. and passing it on to those on the station who needed to know. The Watch keepers knew everything and were like a nerve centre for the whole squadron, because later we had to pass back to Group Headquarters all the information they needed such as number of planes available, pilots etc. The messes also needed to know the number of men involved on ops and return times so that they could have meals ready.

The Armament Officer needed to know what type of bomb was to be carried and which planes were detailed for the attack. The Station Commander of course had to know everything. We worked shifts over three days, so each day varied. The first shift was from 1.00pm to 5.00pm on the first day, then on the second day we did 8.30am to 1.00pm and back again from 5.00pm until 8.30am on the third day. Then we were off duty for the rest of the day until 1.00pm the next day. Sometimes after night duty we did have to get some sleep in, but not always as, if there were no ops on we were able to sleep for part of the night. Although, fully dressed.

The Watch keepers and other WAAF Sergeants shared a Nissen hut in the Waafery. If we were off duty at any time on a Monday, that was domestic night. We cleaned our bed spaces, polished the floor etc. and cleaned our buttons, buckle and cap badge. We also often pressed hard the seams of our skirts into knife edges to make them look smarter. The hut got very cold in winter and there were often lumps of ice on the blankets we used to cover the table, so we had to get a good roaring coke stove going, which was not easy to light, but very effective when burning well.

During off duty time we often cycled into Ely (we were all issued with bikes as it was about a mile from the Waafery and the Mess to the Control Tower and about 2 ½ miles into Ely), and to the Church Army canteen, which soon became known as

241

the `Charmy`. Here we used to order `One Baked Beans on Toast`, much to the amusement of the Sister, or we could have Toast and Jam or one or two other goodies.

When we had a whole day off we often went into Cambridge on the train from Ely and visited various Service clubs. If we had a S.O.P. (Sleeping out pass), there was a very good W.V.S. (Women's Voluntary Service) hostel where we stayed. I still remember it was run by a lovely lady called Miss. Roseveare. We used to look round the shops and buy Van Heusen collars with our coupons as they were so much smarter than Service issue.

Occasionally we went to London (even if we came off night duty with no sleep), and were sometimes wined and dined by our current boyfriends before catching the last train back to Ely. How we got back to camp I cannot remember unless we walked - by now feeling pretty tired, but able to sleep in the next day by missing breakfast.

We ate in the Sergeants Mess with all the Aircrew and other Sergeants on the camp. When we came off duty at 8.30am, if there had been ops on that night we were sometimes lucky enough to get a huge ops meal, the same as the aircrew who had returned. Bacon, egg, tomato, beans etc. What a treat. Most weekends there was some sort of camp dance - either all ranks or (slightly more posh) in the Sergeant's Mess. I learnt to dance in those days in my clumping airforce shoes.

Another enjoyable jaunt on a free afternoon was to cycle to Littleport about six miles from Witchford where there was a wonderful place where we could have boiled eggs and home-made bread for tea - a real luxury.

In July 1945 all the op and control WAAFs flew in turn to see the bomb damage in the RUHR. This was known as Operation Baedeker.

The heart of Witchford's control room

Photo via Pam Hayden

Centre of photo – Left to Right: Flight Lieutenant Finlayson, Flying Control Officer Lynn ? and Arthur Hayward.

Corporal Daphne Valentine WAAF

Corporal Daphne Valentine

Former Map Clerk Daphne Valentine or Val as she was better known, now lives in Canada with husband Leon whom she married at St. Andrew's Church, Witchford in 1944.

Val recalls her posting to Witchford in 1943:

I was posted to RAF Witchford as Map Clerk in March 1943 from RAF Waterbeach. I arrived with many others who were to form the new stations personnel in various departments before the first squadrons were due to arrive in June. Many of the station's buildings were still under construction at this time. We first set up the Intelligence section in huts which later became crew rooms. Our first store of maps became decimated by dispossessed field mice, and we then moved to the hut at the south end of navigation. During a visit to England and

Witchford in 1990 I was delighted to see the old building was still there and used as a stable for horses.

With other WAAFs I was lodged in the Nissen huts vacated by the Irish workmen who had been building the airfield. We were warned to leave a window open at all times, despite cold weather, as some of the workmen in one of the huts had been asphyxiated by coke fumes from the stove. A new social hall was being built near the NAAFI, with planks laid on cement blocks as temporary seats. Unfortunately during the first concert ironically "Murder in the Red Barn", the form on which my friends and I were sitting collapsed just as the ghost appeared, spoiling the dramatic moment entirely.

I was on duty on the night that the ammunition train blew up at nearby Soham, and also when Pilot Officer Birnie was shot down on his approach to the airfield. I was taking care of two puppies that night; one was Birnie's cross golden labrador/greyhound, the other a golden spaniel whose master also did not return. I also remember a plane that over shot the runway and made a belly landing in a potato field behind the church. They tried to bring the fuselage back along Grunty Fen road into the airfield, but it got stuck turning the corner and gouged the brick work on a house and was there for quite a while.

Gliders practising for the invasion used to glide silently in the night over Witchford – One making a force landing near our WAAF site.

One of my jobs was to receive the "flimsies" that arrived at the last minute with information for the aircrews; often changing instructions after the crews had been briefed and were out at their aircraft. There would be a frantic rush around by jeep, handing them in to the rear gunners` turret, as the planes prepared to taxi out. There would also be last minute changes to the huge packets of leaflets to be loaded on the planes, to the disgust of the bomb aimer who had to pile them through the hatch in his nose compartment. We would then stand on the runway to wave the planes goodbye, often sadly for the last time.

I had the interesting job, just before D-Day, of delivering the secret Invasion maps to the group stations which had been flown into Witchford for 3 Group. Secret waste went to a place near Newmarket, where it was shredded. At Christmas it was tradition for officers to serve the food to other ranks. I still have a menu and although it was customary to complain, we really did not have bad food at all, and the aircrews were especially taken care of. All of us being young had good appetites so meals off camp in Ely at the Church Army hostel or at the Kum-In-Café were always welcome. We would always enjoy a cup of cocoa before cycling home after a visit to the Rex cinema. The laundry in the Market Square at Ely did a wonderful job of washing and starching our shirts. Our days off were spent in Ely or Cambridge. The Dorothy in Cambridge was a popular spot for tea dances, although I went only once myself. To travel further on the train, we would cycle to Ely station and leave our bikes unlocked in an old coal shed behind a pub near the station, and have to search in the dark for it on late night return. Our bikes were invaluable as transport, and were often glued up with mud from short cuts across the sites. A man living in a house at the corner of the main road and the airfield entrance would repair them at very minimal charge. I was told he was still living in the village when we visited in 1990.

Our Intelligence Officers included WAAF Flight Officer Dickinson from the Argentine, and Flight Officer Maria Bluett. There were also Flight Lieutenant Nugent, and Flight Lieutenant John Heffer who now owns book shops in Cambridge.

I was on duty the day of the Royal visit and got called out to the parade ground because my cat had climbed up the flag pole, much to my embarrassment.

My husband was with 115 Squadron at Witchford from mid-August 1944 until January 10th 1945. He did his full tour of operations as navigator with Ted Adam's crew, usually flying Lancaster NG122 KO-W of B-Flight. Statistics from his log book on 115 Squadron shows a total of 78 hours day and 64 hours night operations. He recalls one wild take off when they barely cleared the perimeter fence, taking up some barbed wire on the tail wheel and narrowly missing the roof of a car driving on the road on the other side of the fence. On another occasion he and his crew were sent for a discipline refresher course for re-landing after take off, with full bomb and fuel load aboard after the front hatch had fallen off. There was some official and probably not unfounded opinion that they could have blown up the airfield and Witchford village too if the re-landing had not been successful.

Fonty, Daphne's cat, who caused her embarrassment on the
day of the Royal visit to RAF Witchford

*Leon and I were married on January 7th 1945 at St. Andrews
Church in Witchford, and we believe that we were the only
squadron members to do so. Unfortunately, we have no
photographs of that day.*
*I left Witchford shortly after for RAF Feltwell, and my husband's
crew and several other Witchford crews left for India at the end
of January for a second tour on Liberators. Leon completed
fifteen raids before the S.E. Asia war ended. Flying Officer
Adams, my husband's skipper at Witchford, was killed on take
off to a Red Cross mission to Singapore. None of the others of
the original crew were involved.*

An RAF Wartime Wedding at Witchford

This story is how Daphne (Val) Valentine, map clerk, and Leon (Len) Hogg, navigator met, and married while serving with 115 Squadron at Witchford.

Marrying in wartime posed many problems. The shops were empty, one could not buy clothes without clothing coupons, and members of the forces were not issued with these. Food was all rationed and not many hotels would take on the task of putting on a wedding reception, especially at short notice.

Daphne and Leon first met in October 1944 when Len, who was held off flying through sickness, came to help in the map office where Val worked. They started to go around on days off and when Len was not flying, cycled to Ely in the evenings to sit around the coal fire with other service people at the Salvation Army Café, or at the Kum-In Café where they went for egg, spam and chips. They met at the briefings before a raid, and on return, when the aircrews were served coffee laced with strong rum.

After Len's crew completed their tour over Europe in December they were informed that they were posted to India, to leave in the next few weeks. Val and Len became engaged at the New Year's party in the Sergeant's Mess, and planned to be married before Len went abroad.

The first hurdle came when they found that Len, being under twenty one, would require parental permission, but this was soon resolved. A licence was obtained and the vicar at St. Andrew's Church in Witchford, the Reverend Hadrill, agreed to perform the ceremony.

Val arrived home on the 4th January with barely three days to plan a wedding. Friends rallied around, and one loaned her a white wedding dress and veil, and another some silver shoes.

Flowers were another problem, but the local florist went up to the London flower market early Saturday morning, the day before the wedding, and produced a bouquet of pink carnations.

Fire bombing was heavy at the beginning of 1945 so Val's father decided to stay home and come up to Ely on Sunday, the day of the wedding. He had been up most of the night before with raids, and woke very late for his train. He rushed to the station with his razor in his pocket to shave on the train.

Len's friend was able to get a 48 hour pass from the Navy to appear in time as best man and they were married at St. Andrew's Parish Church on Sunday January 7th 1945. As the vicar was marrying them, he was obliged to stop for some minutes, as twenty six Lancaster Bombers of 115 Squadron took off over the church on their way to bomb Hamburg. They stood silently waiting for the thunderous roar to cease.

Because of wartime restrictions, film was almost unavailable, and the few photos taken with illicit Air Force film did not come out, so there are no pictures of the wedding day. They had booked several rooms for guests at a local hotel, but the hotel was unable to put on any sort of reception for them.

The friends who ran the Kum-In Café volunteered to close for the afternoon and put a meal on for the wedding party. Val's mother still had her Christmas cake uneaten, so she re-iced it over in white icing that she had got from somewhere, and turned it into a wedding cake. Someone else produced some Australian wine from an unidentified source, and the menu for the wedding breakfast was ham and spam.

Len was sent off a few days later, and Val followed with the other wives of the crew to Morecambe, where the honeymoon was interrupted continually with parades, medicals, shots and kitting up for overseas. A few days later the crews left and were sent to South East Asia, where they spent the remainder of the war bombing Japanese positions and the railway in Burma.

Val was not demobilised until late 1945, and it was almost two years before they saw each other again, when Len returned home in November 1946, and they were finally able to begin their life as a married couple.

On 7th January 1999, along with their son and daughter and families, they celebrated their 54th wedding anniversary at their home in Canada, to where they had emigrated in 1952.

The Kum-in-Café

Photo of the Kum-In Café circa 1953. Photo via Ely Museum

The Kum-in-Café was owned by the Powell family who had originally lived in Osbournby in Lincolnshire. Hubert John Powell and his wife Ethel May had seven children, five girls and two boys. The family eventually moved to Ely and rented a place in Market Street, which was being used as a store for building materials. Mr. Powell set to work on turning the builder's store into a home plus getting part of it ready for his new venture, a Tea room called the Stage Coach Tea room. The building had originally been a stopping point for Stage Coaches en-route from London to York. After three or four years Mr. Powell decided he wished to expand his business and moved to new premises in St. Mary's Street. After much hard work on yet another historic building he eventually opened his new venture, a café called the Kum-in-Café and a Bed and Breakfast establishment.

During the war the café became very popular with RAF personnel as it was situated in a position that the airmen and women had to pass on their route back to their airfields at Witchford and Mepal. The café was also very popular with service personnel from the Convalescent Home situated in the

250

old Bishop's Palace, adjacent to Ely Cathedral and was only a short walk away.

The Powell family were very friendly people and made everyone feel at home, especially those who were thousands of miles away from their homes in New Zealand, Australia and Canada. Mr. & Mrs. Powell's daughter, Muriel, became friendly with a Scotsman called Henry McCartney who worked in the Photographic section at RAF Witchford (see Photographic section). Henry was posted abroad to Batavia in the Far East, but before leaving he and Muriel became engaged. While Henry was away they kept in touch with endless letters. Eighteen months later Henry returned to this country calling in at the Café to discuss getting married to Muriel before continuing up to Glasgow to see his family.

On November 2nd, 1946 Henry and Muriel were married at St. Etheldreda's Church in Ely, where Henry placed a wedding ring on Muriel's finger which he had bought from a little jeweller's shop overlooking the Indian Ocean. The reception was held at the Kum-in-Café.

During the war a large wooden teapot, made by Mr. Powell, was situated above the door of the Café to advertise the business. On opening the café one morning, Mr. Powell noticed the teapot had disappeared. Many rumours about what happened to the teapot were put about, including one that it was dropped from a Lancaster over Germany. Mr. Powell made another teapot which stood in front of the building, but he made sure that it was in a place of safety at night. Sometime later, the original teapot turned up in front of the Officer's Mess at Witchford. Although the café was built in the 16th Century it did not prevent it being demolished in 1962 to make way for a development, but that is not the end of the story, for in 1978 the second teapot resurfaced in a Cambridge Scrap Yard.

The replacement teapot which stood outside the café until its closure in the late 1950s, made a reappearance in 1978 as the press cutting below explains.

Teapot teaser

MEMORIES of his lorry-driving days came back to wealthy Cambridge businessman Gordon Cave, when he stumbled across this outsize teapot in his scrapyard the other day.

"If I remember rightly, I got it 16 or 17 years ago — we got the scrap out of the cafe when they pulled the place down . . . Maybe it was 20 years ago."

Anyone remember the teapot. It used to hang outside a cafe on the way into Ely on the A10, and was apparently a well-known landmark.

"I have asked a couple of people. They remember seeing it somewhere, but they don't know where".

The teapot appeared in The Cambridge Evening News on 28 April 1978

Nos. 43, 45 & 47, ST. MARY'S ST., ELY

CAMBS.

ALL WITH VACANT POSSESSION

PARTICULARS OF THE

OLD-ESTABLISHED FREEHOLD

CAFE PREMISES

Well known as

"THE KUM-IN CAFE"

(No. 43) Together with the

EXTENSIVE FURNISHINGS & EQUIPMENT

AS A GOING CONCERN

and the

OUTHOUSES, LARGE YARD, FLAT & COTTAGE

(Nos. 45 and 47), the whole of which occupies an important site at the junction of St. Mary's Street and Cambridge Road (A.10) with a total frontage thereto of 109 Ft. 2 ins. The main building is detached and of brick stud and plaster construction with tiled roof. Internally there is a number of exposed beams and studs which are well preserved and the Cafe Premises (No. 43) are well equipped for extensive daily catering and for sleeping parties of up to 40 persons. The accommodation comprises—

Ground Floor: Entrance Lobby; OFFICE with fireplace and built-in cupboard; TEA ROOM, 14' 8" × 12' 10", with fireplace; PANTRY with fitted shelving; CELLAR; DINING ROOM, 29' 8" × 16' 10" with brick fireplace in ingle nook, 2 windows and a second fireplace (disused); KITCHEN, 30' 9" × 16' 4", with 'Tayco' independent boiler, deep sink and tap; W.C. and BED SITTING ROOM, 16' × 16'.

First Floor: 6 BEDROOMS measuring 18' × 14' 8", 13' 10" × 5' 9", 13' 10" × 9' 10", 17' 4" × 13' 3", 18' 4" × 14', and 18' 6" × 14'. Five open on to Corridor and Landing, and there are some built-in cupboards.

OUTSIDE: Built-in W.C.; Brick-built and iron roofed STOREPLACE with concrete floor; Concrete-built GARAGE with similar floor and LARGE YARD with double entrance gates.

THE FLAT (No. 45) contains Entrance Lobby, LIVING ROOM with cooking range and 2 cupboards, BEDROOM formed by boarded partitions and KITCHEN with tiled fireplace and recess cupboard. All on the Ground Floor and in good decorative state. THE COTTAGE (No. 47) contains Large Lobby, SITTING ROOM with fireplace and 2 built-in cupboards, SCULLERY (off Lobby). *1st Floor:* 2 BEDROOMS opening on to Landing. OUTSIDE: Timber and pantiled Block of 2 Store Places, 2 Brick-built W.C's. and Small Enclosed Yard (serving Flat and Cottage).

ALL MAINS SERVICES ARE LAID ON THROUGHOUT

General and Water Rates £17 17s. 2d. (Total Rateable Value £20). Tithe Redemption Annuity as assessed (if any).

NOTES:

1. The purchaser shall have the option of taking over the Cafe Business at 6 p.m. on the day of sale (subject to accommodation being reserved for Mr. J. L. Powell and his family), otherwise the business will be carried on as at present by Mr. J. L. Powell until completion of the purchase on 1st October, 1954.

2. On taking over the Cafe Business on the 2nd September or 1st October, 1954 the purchaser shall take all the consumable stock by valuation in the usual way.

3. An Inventory of the Furnishings and Equipment in the Cafe Premises (No. 43) which are included in the sale may be inspected at the offices of the Vendor's Solicitors and Auctioneers and in the Sale Room. No Chattels of any description in the Flat and Cottage (Nos. 45 and 47) are included in the sale.

4. The property is listed as of special architectural and historic interest under the Town and Country Planning Act, 1947.

5. Orders to View may be obtained from the Auctioneers.

FOR SALE BY AUCTION IN ONE LOT BY

GEORGE COMINS & SON

AT THE WHITE HART HOTEL, ELY

THURSDAY, 2nd SEPTEMBER, 1954. At 4 p.m.

(Subject to Conditions of Sale to be then produced).

Vendor's Solicitor:

WALTER METSON, ESQ.

LITTLEPORT (Tel. 246). And at Ely and Cambridge.

AUCTIONEERS' HEAD OFFICES: ELY (Tel. 2265/6). Branch Office: 30, Churchgate Street, SOHAM (Tel. 264). And at Ely Cattle Market and Burwell.

W. JEFFERSON & SON, LTD., PRINTERS, ELY.   72381

For Sale notice

RAF Witchford Photographic Section

The Photographic section was another very important part of an RAF Bomber base. One of the duties was the setting up and maintenance of the F/24 aerial cameras and the developing of the film when the aircraft returned. The cameras would be fitted and tested by the section before the aircraft took off. After a predetermined delay, the camera flash would activate. The Photographic block was situated on the airfield complex itself in Hut No. 35. The staff actually lived in the hut due to the need for them to be close to the aircraft at all times.

Some members of the Photographic Section

Left to right: Henry McCartney, Mary Taylor, Mary Price and Corporal Douglas (Dicky) West, who had his own photography business after the war. Another member of the section was Cornel Lucas, who after the war would become a famous photographer of the Stars of the Stage and Screen in America.

Henry McCartney of RAF Witchford's Photography Department remembers an incident he will never forget

It was 1944 and we were preparing the Lancasters for a night raid to Hamburg. As a member of the ground staff my duties included checking the 'Bomb Button' in the Bomb Aimer's compartment. This was a triple action button. When the Bomb Aimer pressed it the following events took place: The high explosive load was released; A special flash bomb was released – it was a sort of glorified flare which illuminated the target area; The planes aerial camera was set in motion to record the scene when the flash bomb exploded in mid air twenty seconds later.

That is what happened when the plane was over a German target, but while it was on the ground I had to push the bomb button to make sure that the photographic equipment was functioning properly. Naturally, I had to check first that there were no high explosives in the bomb bay and no flash bomb in the chute near the tail of the plane. After checking the bomb bay and flash bomb chute, I clambered to the nose of the Lancaster, checked the camera and pushed the bomb button. Sure enough the camera whirred as expected but, something unexpected happened too. There was a muffled thud from somewhere below the plane and a yell of terror from the tail area. I hurried aft to find myself staring at a white faced Armourer. Unbeknown to me, he had climbed aboard and loaded in a flash bomb, before I had pressed the button. Neither of us uttered a word, but we both realised what had happened. I bet my face had turned white too.

On the tarmac underneath the plane lay a 40lb flash bomb, timed to explode twenty seconds after its release. We both knew that, as soon as it exploded, the Lancaster was going to flare up, but there was nothing we could do except make a dash for safety. Instead we just froze there, staring at one another in blank despair. Twenty seconds-Forty seconds-Sixty seconds or was it Sixty years? Another minute passed and we began to breathe again. Gingerly, we crept out of the bomber and found that the flash bomb's delicate timing mechanism had been damaged when it landed on the ground.

There was a humdinger of a row about the damaged mechanism; it cost a fiver to repair.

I often wonder what the Wing Commander would have said, if we had set the Lancaster alight.

Vic White of Witchford's Photography Department recalls an incident which he has never seen recorded or reported anywhere

He is unsure of dates for, he said, "Days were not dates to me, just events 7 days a week – week after week for 5 ½ years".

I was duty dog that night. The squadron had taken off about 8 or 9 pm and I had been to supper and the cinema, to lock up and collect the cans of film to go away on the night transport that called twice a week. Around about midnight, while cycling back up to the village to the drome, I heard aircraft coming nearer and nearer right over the road. I realised that they were going to cross each other. I could not be sure if the heights were the same for it was as dark as pitch, but I knew they were Lancs, and very close. I dived off my bike into a ditch on the left of the road and as a tearing sound of metal came from above, a body landed beside me saying "Keep your head down".

It was a Sergeant from the drome with the same thoughts in mind as me, but to our surprise the two aircraft droned on in different directions, one orbiting the drome and by the time I reached the perimeter, the path was lit up and a Lanc was coming in. It touched down and as it ran along the runway sparks followed. It was Lancaster E-Easy and the rear gunner had to be lifted out. He was not injured but very shocked for the port fin had been nearly severed by the outside prop of the Mepal Lanc that had passed beneath E-Easy. It had also passed through the port wall, cutting through the floor of the aircraft just behind the rear gunner and out through the port wall, cutting the Ammo belt trays in its passage, finishing up by slicing the fin off. Surprisingly, the 75 Squadron Mepal Lanc landed safely, also with a shocked but uninjured crew.

With Mepal and Witchford airfields being so close together, it is amazing that more collisions did not take place.

The Y`s 'Owells

The Y's 'Owells

The above emblem was carried by a 115 Squadron Lancaster MKII piloted by Flight Lieutenant Aubrey Howell DFC. Aubrey and his crew flew their first tour of operations with 115 Squadron, joining them at RAF East Wretham in Norfolk, before moving with the squadron to RAF Little Snoring, also in Norfolk, and finally to RAF Witchford, where they completed their tour.

In the following story Aubrey gives us an insight of what life was like for a Bomber crew and how they became known as The Y's 'Owells.

When I finished my training as an RAF Bomber Pilot in America, I was posted in 1943 to an Operational Training Unit at RAF Wing in Buckinghamshire. After a few days of circuits and bumps in a Wellington Bomber it was time to meet my new crew. We spent an hour or so in the crew room and continued to get to know each other over a few pints of beer in the mess. I found I had a Geordie navigator Ron Stewart, a Leicestershire wireless operator Joe Millett, a Scottish rear gunner Jimmy Masson, a Cockney mid upper gunner Tommy Thomson, a Canadian bomb aimer Mac MacWilliams, and at a later date I would have a Suffolk flight engineer Reg Brown. Training together in the Old Wimpey and in the saloon bar of The Sportsman in the village soon showed that I had a well matched confident crew, all keen to get on with the job we had been training for. Our posting to 115 Squadron in 3 Group at East Wretham in Norfolk was greeted with great excitement when we learned they had recently been equipped with the new Lancaster Mk IIs fitted with the Bristol Hercules engines. The first two weeks at East Wretham was spent in 1678 Conversion Flight, familiarising ourselves with the Lancaster and welding ourselves into an efficient team, or so we thought. Our ego was sadly deflated when we learned quite by accident, that the instructors on the Conversion Flight had made an entry in their secret book that we were not expected to survive more than five operations, but it made us more determined to prove them wrong. We moved over to 115 Squadron B Flight under Squadron Leader Bazelgette (later posthumously awarded the V.C.) and met other pilots Flight Lieutenant Tony Prager, Flying Officer Egglestone, Pilot Officer Sammy Small, Pilot Officer Coles and after one 'second Dickie' trip with Tony Prager to Mulheim, we were ready for our first operation as a crew. This was it.

On 24th June 1943 we were briefed to bomb Elberfeld, flying in Z, Zebra DS 631 carrying one 4,000 lb cookie and twelve cans of incendiaries. Everything was going fine until we were suddenly coned by several searchlights simultaneously. I rammed the control column forward much too hard in my effort to escape the blinding light, because of centrifugal force;

everything not anchored down flew up into the roof, including me. I had forgotten to strap myself into my harness and spent several seconds getting back into my seat, and getting the aircraft back under control. Once under control I found we had lost a lot of height, and incidentally the searchlights as well. We went on to bomb the target successfully and returned to base exactly on track, from which we learned we had a damned good navigator, and a pilot who never again forgot to fasten his harness.

The next night we took off again in Z, Zebra with a similar bomb load bound for Gelsenkirchen. There was a lot of cloud over the target but the Pathfinder Force had done a good job with the target indicator flares and we thought it was quite a good prang. We encountered a bit of flak just after bombing and climbed to about 22,000 ft. to be above it, this seemed to work all right and I stayed at this height. We still had a long way to go over enemy territory and every now and again Tommy would ask me to tip up onto one wing tip so he could have a good view of the sky beneath us. And just as well that we did, for there flying immediately under us about 400 to 500 ft. below was a Junkers 88, just keeping station with us. As we veered off to one side or the other so he did likewise, but just out of effective range. However, Tommy opened fire from his mid upper turret as I banked up again and again, but the Junkers stayed put. Obviously the German aircraft was attracting our attention while he vectored in the night fighters operating with him. Jimmy spotted the first ME 109 just a second before it opened fire, and he screamed out his instructions for me to corkscrew. "Starboard go go" he shouted, but we felt the sickening thud of the cannon shells striking home. Then followed a long series of attacks from both the port and starboard quarters, first from one ME 109 then another, and it was only due to Jimmy and Tommy giving correct warning of each attack that I was able to corkscrew out of their line of fire just at each crucial point of the attack.

We had now crossed the enemy coast and were over the North Sea down to about 12 to 13,000 ft. but they still came at us again and again. By now my arms were just about dropping off with the exertion of the violent evasive action I had been taking for such a long time.

Finally, we were attacked from dead ahead three times in quick succession as the three ME 109s headed for home. The

Junkers 88 was no longer with us either, thank God. Mac in the front turret had a go at them but the closing speed was much too high for accuracy. All the gunners put up a very good show and we were proud of them. We staggered back to base on 2 ½ engines, after landing safely and arriving back at our dispersal point we got out to check the extensive damage to the tail plane, fuselage, port wing and both port engines, and counted ourselves very fortunate indeed to be alive. From this trip we knew we had three top class gunners, a very useful wireless operator and engineer, none of who panicked under fire, but we were badly shaken up, and it made me wonder if the Con. Flight "book" was going to prove correct after all.

Three nights later we flew `Y` Yorker DS 682 to Cologne without any trouble at all, I instinctively liked the handling of this aircraft, and took it again to Cologne on 3rd July, and back to Gelsenkirchen on the 9th. These three trips all went very well mainly because Ron's` first class navigating kept us bang on track in the main stream. Mac did not waste any time on the run up and bombing, straight in and out like a dose of salts, accompanied by Macs` laconic drawl "bombs gone - let's get the hell out of here".

That was the first five ops under our belt, and we had beaten the jinx of the con. Flight `book`, largely because we now had full confidence in each others ability. It also helped to know that `Y` Yorker could now be regarded as our own aircraft, and we had become aware and very appreciative of the efficiency of her ground crew team under Sergeant Dick Ingham, Corporal Jack Furber, Syd Rowe, Ginger and Nobby. They all worked like Trojans in all weathers, and kept her performance right up to specification and spotlessly clean.

The next trip was a short fast one to Aachen, just four hours there and back, it was a very successful operation, and the first time we had carried a `block buster` 8,000 pounder. Then in a course of a seven day period we did three of the four big Hamburg operations which devastated that great city. The first two on the 27th and 29th of July were very accurate concentrated raids which caused enormous fires gutting the whole area of the city. The German radar warning system was made useless by the brilliantly simple idea of using `Window`, bundles of metallic strips of paper which the engineers had to throw out, hundreds of bundles from each aircraft whilst in radar range. Reg spent hours back in the extreme cold of the main *fuselage chucking the loose bundles down the flare chute, and it always amazed me that even at those very cold temperatures he always preferred to sit on his fur lined Irving jacket rather than wear it. He must have been frozen to the marrow.*

Our third trip to Hamburg on August 2nd proved to be a complete wash-out due to a very extensive electrical storm which barred our way to the target. The majority of the squadron jettisoned their bombs at or near the enemy coast and returned to base, sensible fellows. Warrant Officer Noxon flew his Lancaster at a much lower level through the storm along with some of the No. 3 Group Stirlings. I tried to fly through it at around 20,000 ft. but found extreme difficulty due to heavy icing conditions, violent lightning flashes and solid cumulus nimbus clouds which caused by far the worst turbulence we had ever experienced. My efforts to keep out of serious trouble involved constant changes of course with the result that when we emerged to clearer skies our `most probable position` was a circle radius 50 miles. After flying past our E.T.A. (Estimated time of arrival) on target we had to jettison the load and turn round and fly right back through the same storm. To complicate matters the port inner engine began to run very rough and then, due to serious over heating, I had to feather it and run on three, gradually losing height to maintain a reasonable air speed. It was a long slow journey back to base during which Joe's Q. D. M.s`were invaluable and we eventually landed 1 hour 20 minutes late. Wing Commander `Turkey` Rainsford thought we had `bought it`, and at de-briefing we were reminded of the squadron motto `Despite the Elements`.

The squadron moved to the new airfield at Little Snoring on the 6th August and it was a pleasant change to land on a concrete runway again after the completely grass covered field at East Wretham, which was also ringed with damned great trees. How I missed those trees some nights I do not know.

The next three operations to Nuremburg, Milan and Turin were comparatively easy, although they were all long and tiring trips lasting 7 hours, 9 hours 5 minutes and 8 hours 10 minutes, respectively, but flying over the Alps to Italy in bright moonlight was quite a sight.

The next op was a different proposition altogether. One glance at the route marked up on the big wall map at briefing told us it was Berlin, the `Big City`. I think this one meant a bit extra to Tommy and myself both being Londoners, our families had had *to put up with month after month of sleeping in air raid shelters, windows and doors being blown in, and neighbours and friends killed by our German counter-parts in the Luftwaffe. Our route took us straight through the middle of Germany, we were in the first wave of the attack meeting very heavy defences of searchlights and flak, but fortunately we got in and out again before the night fighters got up in force. It was the later waves of bombers that were intercepted and caught it very badly as they were silhouetted against the glare of the fires in the city and the P.F.F. (Path Finder Force) marker flares still falling. I believe Bomber Command lost 58 aircraft that night.*

August 30th was a nice quick op, 3 hours 30 minutes to Munchen Gladbach on which we took Flying Officer Newcombe as second `Dickie`, he was to be posted missing from a subsequent trip. By this time Squadron Leader Jim Starkie had taken over as our `B` Flight Commander, he was well liked by all. We had been trying to think of a suitable crew emblem to decorate our `Y` Yorker and to give us some identification as a crew. The basic idea of using my surname, `Howell` along with the aircraft letter `Y` eventually led us to `The Y's `Owells` the original sketch being done by my father. Then an artist friend was pressed into service and he eventually came up with a magnificent canvas 3 ft. x 3 ft. depicting baby owls as the crew members `operating` from the back of the mother owl flying across a huge yellow moon. I collected it during my leave early in September but on return to the squadron I was shattered to hear from Squadron Leader Starkie that my `Y` Yorker had pranged and was a right off. He had taken it on a trip while we were on leave and was badly shot up by fighters. The aircraft was diving out of control when he gave the order to bale out, and only after some of his crew had actually jumped did he managed to regain control at a very low level and fly the badly damaged aircraft back to crash land it at Ford in Sussex. He managed to salvage Joes` St. Christopher medallion which we had pinned above the doorway, and as he handed it back to me with a rather guilty look on his face, he said, " Sorry that`s all that is left of your aircraft". Fortunately, a brand new Lancaster DS 734 had just been delivered, so we christened another `Y` Yorker, the ground crew doped the new emblem onto the fuselage just below my window on the port side, and we were back in business again.

For the remainder of September and the first week in October the squadron was stood down from ops in order to test out some new navigational radar equipment, and although we flew every day for about three weeks it was all daylight flying and a welcome change from operations all at night. Then it was back on ops again on the 7th of October to Stuttgart, followed on the 8th when we took Squadron Leader Roberts as second `Dickie` to Hanover, and back again to Hanover on October 18th, all three trips being reasonably quiet and successfully completed. Next it was Düsseldorf, with Sergeant Trevor coming along for the trip, which was a quick one in and out and home again in 3 hours 20 minutes. After another spell of leave came the toughest part of our tour of ops.

November 18th was the start of the Battle of Berlin and during the next six weeks, we completed eight successful operations to the `Big City`, and one to Leipzig and Frankfurt. They were all long, cold; tough, tiring trips during which we could not relax for a moment because of the increased use of enemy fighters, and of course Berlin was one of the most heavily defended targets in Germany. Bomber Command losses became very heavy indeed and many of our good friends and comrades failed to return. It was generally considered at this phase of the Bomber offensive that only approximately one third of Bomber Command crews finished a tour of 30 ops, two thirds `got the chop`.

It took us between 6 and 7 hours to complete each of these trips, and most of that time we were vulnerable over enemy territory with the odds stacked against us, as there was no easy route to the `Big City`. On all of them we carried one 4,000 pounder and either 8-10 or 12 cans of incendiaries.

On one of these operations in November, we had an indicated air temperature of -58 F, Jimmy suffered frost bite on his face and the microphone in his oxygen mask froze so he neither could nor answer our repeated attempts to contact him. I sent Joe back to check what had gone wrong, but unaware that his portable oxygen bottle had not been refilled he was very soon semi-conscious and unable to report back to me. In desperation I sent Reg back to find out what the trouble was, with strict instructions to get on to main oxygen and the intercom immediately he got to them. With Tommy's` help Reg restored the oxygen supply back onto main oxygen and with Joe having recovered Jimmy's` microphone they all returned to their respective positions. While all this had been going on only

Mac, Ron and I were minding the shop and not in a position to see any enemy fighters. Had they attacked we would have been a sitting duck.

On another occasion we took Squadron Leader Baigent as second `Dickie` just prior to his taking over as our `B` Flight Commander. He paid us the compliment of falling asleep during the return journey but was rudely awakened when the starboard engines cut out. Before dozing off Baigent had omitted to change the petrol cocks over to the other tanks. I gave him a few choice phrases at the time, but we remained good friends and I was later very sorry to learn of his illness and early death back home in New Zealand after the war.

Early in December we moved to another airfield at Witchford near Ely, and continued our nerve sapping trips to Berlin culminating in consecutive flights on 1st and 2nd of January 1944 at the end of which we were very tired indeed. On the first one of these we were nearly chopped out of the sky by a Halifax diving down out of nowhere, we just did not see each other and he missed us by only a few yards. After bombing I opened up the throttles and came back at a high rate of knots, and very high petrol consumption, we did not have a lot left in the tanks when we got back to dispersal. On the next we had to climb through a lot of cloud with icing conditions, and we did not see much of the target, we just bombed on the P.F.F. markers, and got the hell out of there as fast as we could. We saw a lot of fighters but they were busy with other Lancs. not as fortunate as us, and we belted for home. That made 29 operations altogether and we anxiously awaited the last one to finish our tour. Several trips were laid on and then cancelled due to bad weather and we were all on edge at this time. Then we were briefed again for a trip to Berlin, but before we went out to the aircraft I was sent for by Wing Commander Bobby Annan to be told that a signal from Bomber Command had temporarily reduced the number of operations for a heavy bomber crew from 30 to 25 ops due to the very heavy losses in recent months. We were immediately stood down from duty, but could not leave the base for security reasons as we knew the target, so we relaxed with a few beers while the rest of the squadron took off, but I think each of us wished we had been able to do the last one to finish off our tour of ops. Perhaps it would have been one too many. Flight Lieutenant Barnes and his crew had also completed 29 ops at the same time, but opted to go straight on to No. 7 Squadron P.F.F. at Oakington for another tour. They failed to return from their first trip.

Reg, Mac and I went to No. 3 Lancaster finishing school at RAF Feltwell to train new Lancaster crews. Ron and Joe went to RAF Finningley to train navigators and wireless operators and Jim and Tom went to RAF Brize Norton to train new gunners.

On July 5th 1944 Ron and I were recalled to Witchford for an investiture and were both very pleased to receive the DFC from H.M. King George VI in the presence of Queen Elizabeth and the Princess Elizabeth. The investiture concerned only 115 Squadron whose crew members had been awarded decorations during the last few months of hectic operations. Men like Ray Milgate, Geoff Hammond, Len Halley, Bert Boutillier, George Mackie, Bobby Annan, Cyril Baigent and many others we were proud to have known and flown with. Later that same month I received another surprise in the shape of a presentation wrist watch together with a letter from Air Vice Marshall R. Harrison C. in C. No. 3 Group, explaining that Senor Adalbert Fastlich from Panama had given a number of watches to the Air Ministry for the recent bombing of Berlin. Apparently, his brother had been killed during a German air raid on London in 1940.

During our twenty nine operations we carried 86.7 tons of high explosives. Flew with six second pilots and carried three passengers.

Flight Lieutenant A.H. Howell DFC	Pilot
Pilot Officer R.S. Stewart DFC	Navigator
Pilot Officer H.T. MacWilliam	Bomb Aimer
Pilot Officer R.F. Millett	Wireless Operator
Warrant Officer E.J. Thomson DFC (on 2nd tour)	Mid Upper Gunner
Pilot Officer J. Masson	Rear Gunner
Pilot Officer R.S. Brown	Flight Engineer

The Y's 'Owells, 1943

Left to Right: Sergeant R.S. Brown, Sergeant R.F. Millett, Pilot Officer H.T. McWilliam, Sergeant E.J. Thompson, Sergeant J. Masson, Flight Sergeant A.H. Howell, Sergeant R. Stewart.

Headquarters No.3. Group,
Royal Air Force,
Exning,
Suffolk.

3G/S.8738/RH/DO.   21st April, 1944.

Dear Howell,

         Sr. Adalbert Fastlich, a Panamanian subject
of Austrian origin has given a number of watches to
the Air Ministry for presentation to Captains of
aircraft who have been instrumental in the recent
heavy bombing on Berlin.

         Sr. Fastlich gave as a special reason for
the gift, the fact that his brother was killed during
a German raid on London in 1940.

         You have been chosen as a representative
of this Group to receive one of these watches.

         Sr. Fastlich would appreciate a letter of
thanks, his address is:-

                  c/o His Britannic Majesty's Legation,
                  Panama.

                  Yours sincerely,

                  R. Harrison

Flight Lieutenant A.H. Howell,
No. 3. Lancaster Finishing School,
R.A.F. FELTWELL.

Above, the letter received by Flight Lieutenant Howell in 1944
from Air Vice-Marshal Richard Harrison CB, DFC, AFC, AOC of
3 Group informing him that he had been chosen to receive a
special presentation wrist watch

Flight Lieutenant Aubrey Howell DFC

The Y`s `Owells meet up at a reunion at RAF Watton in 1968

Left to Right:

Joe Millett, Reg Brown MBE, Tommy Thomson DFC, Aubrey Howell DFC, Mac MacWilliam, Ron Stewart DFC, Jim Masson.

Remembrance Sunday November 1999

The four surviving members of the Y's 'Owells and their wives
at the 115 memorial in 1999

Left to Right:

Ron Stewart DFC, Aubrey Howell DFC, Joe Millett and Reg Brown.

The 115 Squadron memorial is situated at a point where two of the three runways converged. This fine memorial was erected by squadron veterans in 1989, to honour their comrades who paid the ultimate sacrifice for victory and the freedom we enjoy today.

Wreath laid in memory of the fourteen members of 115 Squadron killed in the Witchford intruder incident on 19th April, 1944

War and the Law at Witchford

With the extra duties that would fall on the Police at the outbreak of war in 1939, Special Constables were recruited to help with the extra work load.

Witchford was no exception and six Special Constables and one Sergeant assisted the Witchford Village Bobby, PC44 Cecil David Sutton, with upholding the law in and around the villages of Witchford, Wentworth, Coveney and Wardy Hill. The Specials were recruited from Witchford residents either too old for call up for the services, or in reserved occupations.

A photograph taken in the vicarage garden at Witchford of PC Sutton and the Specials

Back Row Left to Right: George Dunham, Bill Nicholas, Bert Mitcham and Harry Spencer.

Seated Left to Right: Alfred Pearson, Sgt. Brand Richardson, PC Sutton and Richard Emments Wallis.

Brand Richardson was a Blacksmith and local Builder whose house and yard was situated opposite to Marroway Lane, a turning off the Main Street. On the left hand corner of the turning of Marroway Lane was the Police house.

Richard Emments Wallis was a farmer who lived in Common Road, an area that would see the construction of many of the domestic buildings for the new airfield.

With the thousands of construction workers and later RAF personnel that would come into the area to build and run Witchford and nearby Mepal airfields, it would be inevitable that petty crime and the occasional more serious incident would take place. In the following pages and throughout this book you will find reports made by PC Sutton to Superintendent F.G. Wells at Ely Police Office on some of the incidents that took place throughout the war years. In these reports you can see how differently petty crime and minor incidents were viewed in those days, compared with today. Some are now quite amusing, while others are as tragic as the day they happened. I have, through further research, been able to expand on some of the incidents which took place.

Superintendent F.G. Wells to whom PC Sutton's reports were sent at Ely Police Office. Superintendent Wells would later become Deputy Chief Constable for the Isle of Ely Constabulary

I am indebted to Roy Sutton, son of the late PC Sutton, for allowing me to use the following copies of the reports his father kept.

Police House,
Witchford,
Ely, Cambs.
28th July 1943.

Wing Commander. N. Alexander.
R.A.F. Station,
Witchford,
Ely, Cambs.

Sir.

With reference to the fact that it might be necessary for Police Officer's stationed locally, in the course of their official duties to visit the R.A.F. Station, Witchford. I hereby make an application for a pass for each of the following six Police Officer's.

Superintendent. F. G. Wells, Police Office, Ely.

Sergeant. J. R. Bent. Police Office, Sutton.

P.c. J. O. Seymour, Police House, Mepal.

P.c. C.D. Sutton, Police House, Witchford.

P.c. W. H. Green, Police Office, Ely.

P.c. C. W. Taylor, Police Office, Sutton.

If this request is granted it is understood that on a visit they would report to the Guard Room.

Thanking you in anticipation,

Your faithfully,

P.c. 44.

To. Supt.F.G.Wells.
    Police Office,
    Ely, Cambs.

Ely

8th September   43

Report from D.A.P.M. Office, Cambridge, re petrol from
R.A.F. Station, Witchford, being supplied for use in civilian
cars.

Sir.

I beg to report that as a result of a telephone message
from Sergeant Bell, at 3-30°P.M. on Wednesday 8th September
1943, I met Ft Lt Stevens, Pilot Officer Tickner and two
sergeants from the D.A.P.M. Office, Cambridge, I was informed
that they were making enquiries about petrol which was being
obtained from the M.T. Section, R.A.F. Station, Witchford, for
use it was alleged in two civilian cars E.L.Y.893 and C.K.H.
601, in company with them we visited the R.A.F. Station, and
interviewed several members of the R.A.F. M.T. Section, but
we were unable to find any person who had actually witnessed
any petrol being supplied for use in any private car, one man
L.A.C. James Arthur Burnley. NO.614787 stated that it was
common knowledge in the M.T. section that these two cars were
having petrol which was coming from the M.T. pump, it appeared
this has been talked about in the huts but so far their is no
direct evidence that this is so.

At about 5-20.P.M. in company with Ft.Lt. Stevens and Sergeant
Milne, I saw Frank Stanley Cleminson, Foreman for South London
Decoraters, on the R.A.F. Station, this man uses car E.L.Y.893
which is the property of his firm, he was in charge of this
car at the time. I told him that we were making enquiries about
petrol the property of the R.A.F. which it was alleged was
being supplied to civilains for use in their cars. He replied.
I know nothing about any R.A.F. petrol, I have my own petrol
coupons sulipied to me from London". When asked if he had any
objection to a sample of petrol being taken from his car. He
replied. "No, you can take a sample if you like".

Petrol coupons in his possession. No.E/2.K.45730, stamped on
front South London Decoraters, issued at London.

I am, Sir.
Your Obedient Servant,

P.c.44.

To. Supt. F.G. Wells.
   Police Office,
   Ely, Cambs.

       Witchford

         Ely

     24th February 46

Archie James Rogers, age 37, Licensed Victualler, of
the 'Cross Keys' Public House, Main Street, Coveney,
Ely, Cambs.
Did permit 506347.'Spada' Luca, Rank Sold.
        23236. ' Cinelli' Ginnato, Rank Sold.
       193599.'Rotonno' Liborio, Rank Cap.
      506339.'Saroli' Antonio, Rank Sold.
      216225.'Frontini' Amileare,Rank Sold.
      505200.'Bonanomi' Angelo, Rank C.M.
      283034.'Cibelli' Loreto, Rank Sold.
       25275. 'Imperetore,Aesquete, Rank Sold.
       73041. 'Frinzi' Giovanni,Rank Sold.
     F.3106.'Lojecono' Domenico,Rank Sold.
     F.3113.'Mireroh' Giovanni,Rank Sold.
in certain Licensed Premises called 'Cross Keys'
certain intoxicating to be consumed on the premises
otherwise than during the hours permitted by the
Licensing Act 1921, at the'Cross Keys' Public House,
Coveney, Ely at 3.25.P.M. 24th February 1946.

Sir.
    I beg to report that at about 3.25.P.M. on Sunday 24th
February 1946, in company with Sergeant Goodwin, I visited
the 'Cross Keys' Public House, Coveney, we entered by the back
door, which was unlocked.
    I want into the taproom and saw the 11 Italians(named
above) they were sitting at the tables and each one had a pint
glass which contained beer.
    Whilst I was taking particulars all the men drank up
their beer in my presence.
    There were also 4 other Italians in another room.
    See attached report of Sergeant Goodwin.
    The Landlord 'Rogers' was in his living room. I asked
him if he cared to give any explanation as to why he
had permitted intoxicating liquor to be consumed during
non-permitted hours.
    He said. " I know I am wrong in letting them consume it
during prohibited hours, but they had only been here about
five minutes and they had one drink each"
    One of the Italians seen by Sergeant Goodwin. No. 41579,
'Suffer' Lodino, had some money in his hand and 'Rogers' was
present when this man wanted to pay for his beer and 'Rogers'
said to him. "It is alright, I will give it to you".
    I told 'Rogers' that he would be reported.
    Both the statements made by 'Rogers' were made in the
presence of Sergeant Goodwin.

                I am, Sir,
            Your obedient servant,

                P.c.44.

Flight Sergeant Tom Noel Fogaty DFM

On the night of the14th January 1944 Flight Sergeant Tom Fogaty and crew took off on an operation with 115 Squadron at RAF Witchford. Twenty three of 115`s aircraft were detailed for the attack – eight from A-Flight, seven from B-Flight and eight from C-Flight. The target that night was Brunswick and Fogaty was pilot of one of A-Flights MKII Lancasters, DS629 KO-H. The target was identified by means of red and green markers and Fogaty dropped his bombs from 22,000 feet. After leaving, the plane was attacked from below by a JU88. The enemy aircraft not being seen until it broke away. The starboard inner was hit by cannon shells and caused violent shuddering of the aircraft. The engineer, Sergeant Life, was wounded in the leg and hand and the mid upper and front turrets were put out of action. Hydraulic oil and smoke filled the aircraft. In a second attack the starboard wing was hit again. A third attack was made by the JU88 but was unsuccessful. The Lancaster by this time was down to 12,000 feet and it was observed that the starboard inner engine had been shot away. Fogaty remained calm throughout the attacks and encouraged his crew. A course was set for home, with the aircraft now down to 5,000 feet. Nevertheless, Flight Sergeant Fogaty was determined to bring his aircraft and crew home or ditch rather than fall into enemy hands. Skillfully, he flew his damaged aircraft back to the emergency landing airfield at Woodbridge, executing a successful landing with a burst tyre, without further damage to aircraft or crew. This was Fogaty's fourth operation as Captain and only his first on Lancasters. He was recommended for an immediate award of the DFM. Flight Sergeant Pugh, who flew as a spare bomb aimer on this trip with Fogaty, would lose his life on the night of the 18th/19th April when his aircraft was shot down over Witchford during the Intruder Incident.

Sergeant Life, Fogaty's flight engineer, recovered from his wounds but sadly died later in 1944 when he drowned at Denver Sluice during a Dinghy drill. After several successful operations Tom Fogaty took off from Witchford in LL704 KO-H – one of ten 115 aircraft to take part in a raid to Nuremburg. Hit by flak over the target they were attacked by a Night Fighter. The crew now on their fourteenth operation were ordered to bale out while Fogaty held the aircraft steady. Considering that he was now too low to bale out himself, Fogaty decided to make an emergency landing in the dark. When asked how he managed to escape from a crash like this, Tom said, "I have no idea, I came to, several yards from the aircraft and have no recollection of even hitting the ground."

Image of crashed Lancaster

CONFIDENTIAL.   IMMEDIATE.

RECOMMENDATION FOR HONOURS AND AWARDS.

Christian Names...TOM NOEL HEYWOOD..........Surname....FOGATY.

Rank....FLIGHT SERGEANT....................Official Number....1315284.

Group....NO.3 GROUP.....Unit....NO.115 SQUADRON.

Total hours flown on operations...........31.43.

Number of sorties.....SIX.

Total hours flown on operations
since receipt of previous award...N/A.

Number of sorties since
receipt of previous award.........N/A.

Recognition for which recommended..DISTINGUISHED FLYING MEDAL.

Appointment held.....PILOT - CAPTAIN OF AIRCRAFT.

On the night of 14th January, 1944, Flight Sergeant Fogaty was Captain of a Lancaster which attacked Brunswick.

After leaving the target at a height of 22,000 feet, the aircraft was attacked from below by a JU.88, the enemy aircraft not being seen until it broke away. The starboard inner engine was hit by cannon shell and caused a violent shuddering of the aircraft; the Engineer was wounded in the hand and leg, the mid-upper and front turrets put out of action. Hydraulic oil and smoke filled the interior of the aircraft.

In a second attack, the starboard wing was hit again. XXXXXX XXXXXXXXXXXXXXXXXXXXXXXXXXXXXXXXXXXXXXXXXXXXXXXXXXXXXXXXXXXXXXXXX XXXXXXXXXXXXX A third attack was made by the enemy aircraft but was unsuccessful. The aircraft was by this time down to 12,000 feet and it was observed that the starboard inner engine had been shot away.

Throughout the attacks, Flight Sergeant Fogaty remained calm and encouraged his crew. A course was set for base, the aircraft losing height to 5,000 feet. Nevertheless, Flight Sergeant Fogaty was determined to reach this Country or ditch, rather than fall into enemy hands.

By skilful airmanship he flew his damaged aircraft and executed a successful landing with a burst tyre at Woodbridge without further damage to aircraft or crew.

This N.C.O. was on his fourth operation as a captain - his first on Lancaster aircraft. His masterly handling of a difficult situation and fine crew co-operation saved both his crew and aircraft.

Date.18th January.1944.   Wing Commander Commanding,
                                           No.115 Squadron,   R.A.F.

COVERING REMARKS OF STATION COMMANDER.

This N.C.O. displayed great skill in handling his aircraft under very trying conditions setting a fine example to his crew.
Date....................   Group Captain Commanding,
20.1.44.   R.A.F. Station, Witchford.

COVERING REMARKS OF BASE COMMANDER.

            Strongly recommended.

Date...21st January. 1944.   Air Commodore Commanding,
                                            No.33 Base, R.A.F. Waterbeach.

COVERING REMARKS OF AIR OFFICER COMMANDING.

I recommend the immediate award of the Distinguished Flying Medal.

Date..24 Jan 1944.   R. Harrison
                                            Air Vice Marshal,
                                            Commanding No. 3 Group, R.A.F.

Recommendation for Distinguished Flying Medal

A Special Target

On the 30th June 1944, 115 Squadron took off from Witchford to take part in an attack on a special target; a road junction in France through which tanks of the 2nd and 9th Panzer divisions would have to pass in order to carry out a planned attack on the British and American armies. The attack on the road junction near Villers Bocage by 151 Lancasters, 105 Halifaxes and 10 Mosquitoes of 3, 4 and 8 Groups was so successful that the planned German attack did not take place. The following day, on Saturday 1st July, Wing Commander W.G. Devas Commanding Officer of 115 Squadron based at RAF Witchford gave the following report on the attack in a B.B.C. Home Service programme called `War Reports` which followed the 21.00 hours news. The talk was broadcast to the Empire and was included in special overseas programmes and war recording units.

It was in the afternoon, and we were standing by for a normal night attack. Some of our aircraft were either preparing for their night's work or were sleeping. Suddenly, the message came through that we were to bomb a special tactical target at short notice. Aircraft had to be recalled, crews summoned from all parts of the dispersed camp. Bomb and petrol loads had to be changed and cameras and ammunition altered for daylight work. Every man of the squadron was working at full pressure. Minutes sped by. Crews assembled for their briefing without even time to eat their meals. The target, so we were told, was a concentration of German tanks, troops and guns which were trying to hide in the area near Villers Bocage. They were preparing a counter attack against the second army, and they were not going to be allowed to get away with that. After the briefing the last hurried preparations were completed, and it was a great relief to see the whole squadron in the air on time. En route, other squadrons joined the stream and it was a most impressive sight to see hundreds of heavy bombers flying steadily towards the target in daylight. There above, we saw a vast demonstration of air power, below we saw an armada of countless ships, and so to France, with hundreds of our own fighters on guard above us. The actual target was small as it was vital. When we got there we saw bombs streaming down *ahead and on either side and all landing smack in the right places. It was 12 minutes of precision bombing, done exactly as it should be done, and what flak there was, made not the slightest difference to its accuracy. The weather was good and we were able to make clear bombing runs. Underneath, the dust and smoke and flying debris which had been raised by the first bombers to go in, surged up into the air in constantly thickening clouds blotting out the target indicators. We turned for home and then I saw something below me which I shall not easily forget. It was in a way like some unexpected reward. British tanks were again on the move, nosing forward towards the enemy. Before the last bomber in my squadron had got back to the airfield, the first photographs had been developed, all showing remarkably accurate bombing. One of the Lancasters in another squadron based near us did not get back. It had been damaged by flak and we were afraid it might have been lost. Then the news came through that for the first time, one of our heavy bombers had touched down on a landing strip in France.* It was a memorable raid with many outstanding features, and there is no doubt that we gave the enemy a nasty knock and helped our own armies at just the right moment.*

* The Lancaster that was reported to be missing and was then reported to have touched down on a landing strip in France was from 75 Squadron based at Witchford's near neighbour RAF Mepal. Squadron Leader Williamson`s aircraft had been damaged by flak and his engineer Sergeant McDevitt wounded. In order to get Sergeant McDevitt urgent medical aid, Williamson landed on one of the landing strips being prepared hastily in France.

Flight Engineer Sergeant Frank Rutter

Frank now lives in Australia where he emigrated in 1949. He wrote to me in 1998 in answer to my request for information about his time in the RAF and the period he was stationed at Witchford. Never a great fan of authority, Frank explains below what his war was like.

Frankland's crew taken on completion of a tour with their Lancaster HK598 KO-J (HK598 was lost on the 20th April 1945 while serving with 1660 Conversion Unit, when it crashed while flying on two engines at Claypole, Nottinghamshire)

Back row left to right:
Sergeant Frank Rutter   *Flight Engineer*
Flight Sergeant D. Stewart-Smith   *Bomb Aimer*
Flying Officer P. Frankland   *Pilot*
Flight Sergeant H.H. Skinner   *Navigator*
Front row left to right:
Sergeant E. Martin   *Wireless Operator*
Flight Sergeant J. Dorling   *Mid Upper Gunner*
Sergeant Bayly   *Gunner*

I left school and started as an apprentice plumber at 14 years of age. I did not want to be a plumber, I wanted to be a chemist because I used to get 98% for chemistry and was fairly good on science, but I was told I was going to be a plumber so a plumber I became. My pay as an apprentice plumber started at 7s 6d (37 ½ p) for a forty four hour week, that was from the age of 14 to 15, from 16 to 17 it was 10s (50p), from 18 it was 12s 6d (62 ½ p) and the most you could make I think when you finished your apprenticeship was 28s (£1.40). I also had to attend night school at Technical College, three nights a week. I had to pay for my own books and do it in my own time at night, so I used to finish work at 5 o`clock, have tea and I would be in the technical college at 6.30pm and I think we used to knock off at 9.30pm. I was a keen dancer and I then used to pop straight into the dance halls and possibly meet up with a girlfriend, and walk her a couple of miles home. I used to walk home myself about four miles, get home just after midnight and I had to be on the bus or on my bike at 7 o'clock in the morning to start work again. We were fit in those days. I volunteered for the Air Force but did not tell anyone as I was in my last year of my City & Guilds. Six months before I was due to sit for the examination my calling up papers came up for the Air Force and I went in to train as Flight Engineer, but first of all I was sent to London for basic training. The first thing they did was march us across the Lords Cricket ground, it was pouring with rain and I was still in civvies. They shoved an RAF great coat over me, took an identity photo and served us some green stuff they called soup. It was more like gruel than soup, I do not know what it was, shocking stuff and could have been chopped grass for all I knew; it was the colour of grass. They then marched us back to where we were staying. We were staying at some flats near London Zoo, in a place called St. James Close. We were then taken to the swimming baths after which we marched back to the flats and I thought if this is the Air Force this is not for me so I went back to Kings Cross Station and I said to a guy on the platform, " When is the next train back to Newcastle", he said "You have just missed one, the next one is 10 o'clock tomorrow morning". So I went back to the billets and woke the next morning and then just continued on doing my initial training in London, that is where they cut your hair, did all your injections, you did your square bashing, and they issued you with your uniform and things like that. Unfortunately there had been a murder by one of our RAF blokes in London and in their wisdom the RAF decided to put a time clock in our flats. They were actually flats overlooking St. James Close in St. Johns Wood, quite near to London Zoo as our Mess Hall. The RAF decided to put a clock in, so that people had to clock in and out and so that if anyone was in after 11.59pm which is nearest to midnight, they would then be on charge. Because I always liked dancing I went to the Hammersmith Palais and duly came in at 1 o'clock in the morning. Before I went out I thought, well if I do not clock out, I will not have to clock in and of course, when I came back I got caught, so I was in the RAF fifteen days and I was on Jankers for three days, which meant that I then had to do kitchen duties in our Mess Hall (which was London Zoo restaurant), peeling potatoes. After square bashing we then had to report at 6 o'clock where we were given a boiler suit and taken across to London Zoo, to bash spuds. After my kitchen duties were completed I put my boiler suit in my gas mask bag and then hopped off to the dances again, so I was dancing instead of being confined to barracks for three days. I used to go out, bash potatoes, hop off to the dance halls and then come back again, which did not please a lot of the chappies there because they had all their injections and they were confined to Barracks for three days and could not get out, but I was out dancing. So right from the start I was a rebel. I always wanted to be in the Air Force and to be flying, but when I saw the mindless way in which they marched you round, I thought these guys have got peas for brains and so the Air Force was a challenge for me, so as a rebel I was not only fighting the Germans, I was also fighting the RAF most of the time. So you are really asking the wrong bloke when you ask me for my experiences of the RAF and Witchford.

I continued my training in Wales at St. Athans and passed out as a Flight Engineer. They then sent me to a Heavy Conversion Unit and that is where I met up with my crew. Well actually the first crew they gave me were a New Zealand crew and we were doing heavy conversion training on Stirlings. I did not get on very well with this crew, as they played their cards close to their chest, and also wanted to stay on flying Stirlings. I said to the flight engineer leader, "I am not flying with that crew", and of course the flight engineer leader said, "You cannot please yourself who you are flying with". I said, "Well, I am not flying with them". So he said, "I will put you with another crew". He gave me another crew whose pilot was a flying officer and another New Zealander. He had been flying with Air New Zealand, a civvy airline, but I could not get on very well with them either. So I said to the flight engineer leader, " I am not flying with that crew either". Of course all hell broke loose, and he said, "You just cannot please yourself". I said, "Well look, I am just not flying so please yourself, I want another crew or else". He said," What the hell do you want?" I said, "I want an English sergeant as a pilot", so I got my crew and that was Frankland. We then did our heavy conversion on Stirlings and that was the first time I had ever flown in an aircraft, which was surprising because I only had to watch a swing to make me sick, let alone ride on an aircraft. I thought well this is where they are going to find me out and of course when I got flying I was not sick and so I was able to perform and I got on well with my pilot and we were great mates. We arrived at Witchford after we had passed our heavy conversion course and our first night flying at Witchford was on May 27th 1944 which was my 21st birthday, so I always remember that. Later on I went on leave and I realised I needed some transport so I started looking around. I was going to buy a SS Jaguar, it was a nice black Jaguar with red leather upholstery and I could have bought one for £60, then when I had a look at the thing, I thought well if I get posted I have got to transport that thing around so I decided to buy a motorcycle which was a BSA 500 Blue Star for which I paid £15. I had never driven a car or motorbike in my life so when I got the motorbike I said to the bloke, "Which handles and knobs do you turn, how do you kick it on and which gear?" So he showed me and I picked this motorbike up, drove it through my town which is North Shields, took it home and then drove the thing down to Cambridge and on to Witchford. I had never had a licence and did not have the time to get one. The pilot also had a motorcycle and we used to go around to the local dances and we would travel all over the place to the local hops. Unfortunately, one day I was going through Witchford village to go to Cambridge and an RAF truck in front of me with a learner driver, stuck his hand out of the window and gave a little wavy sign, I do not know what it is like now, but a little wavy sign and a flick of the fingers used to mean overtake, so I duly put my foot down and tried to overtake this truck just when he decided to turn right into Bedwell Hey Lane which was the entrance to

288

the airfield, so I pranged the motorbike straight into his petrol tank, he stopped and I could not stop my motorbike. Eventually I got the damn engine stopped and got myself pulled out of it. I was in hospital for a month. All I had was a burn on the foot where the friction burnt a hole in my shoe where it had more or less tilted over, scraping it along the road. The police came along and wanted to see my driver's licence and of course I did not have one and they wanted me to make a statement. About a month later he came to see me and said, "Why have you not got a driver's licence?" I replied, "How can I get a driver's licence? I am flying all night and sleeping all day", so I got fined a shilling (5p). I duly got my driver's licence. So that is the only injury I ever got in the RAF and that was on my motorbike in Witchford. The RAF tried to make me pay for the petrol tank on the lorry. I refused to pay and they are still waiting to this day. Unfortunately, the burn on my foot would not heal up, so I was accompanied by a WAAF nurse to the RAF Hospital at Ely. When the ambulance arrived I was put on a trolley and the WAAF nurse pushed me along to the lift, as the specialist I had to see was on the first floor. When we got to the lift the nurse could not operate the lift so I got off the trolley, got the door open, pushed the trolley in and got back on it and we went up to the first floor where the doors were a problem again, so I had to open the doors again, then got back on the trolley so the nurse could push me in to see the doctor. The specialist decided the foot injury would need a skin graft and he would take the new skin from my bottom. I told him I already had one sore spot and did not need another. So I was taken back to Witchford sick bay where they continued to bathe my foot in salt water and it eventually healed. I cannot tell you a lot about Witchford because I used to go to the operations room and say, "Any operations on?", and if they said no, I would jump on my motorbike and say right I am off to Cambridge. I became friendly with a girl who I later became engaged to. She was a farmer's daughter and lived in Cambridge. I used to meet her from work and we would go to the farm in Madingly Road and have tea. She would then get changed and off we would go dancing at the Dorothy Cafe and then I would take her home on the motorbike and leave at about 1 o'clock in the morning to get back to the squadron, have a couple of hours sleep, get up for breakfast and then have a look to see if there was any operations on. If there were any I would just go out and check the aircraft, make sure that everything was right, check the form 700 and then do the op, come back, have bacon and eggs, have a bit of sleep and if there was not any ops on the next day, I would then be on my motorbike and down to Cambridge. So basically that was the story of my life in the RAF. We lived in a Nissen hut with another crew. The officers were in the Officers Mess, (my pilot eventually became an officer). On two occasions the other crew who shared our hut failed to return and I never got to know their names, for they lasted only a few weeks. I was recommended for a commision but I did not take it up because I wanted more freedom which I had with my motorbike, and as I said I never had a lot to do with the squadron, mainly because, I do not know if you are aware of it, but the RAF 's airfields were split up, the air crew were totally seperated from the ground crew, this was done deliberately because they did not want to see the WAAFs mixing with the air crew. In fact, if you were an officer you were not allowed to have a WAAF girlfriend and they more or less discouraged the WAAFs from mixing with the aircrew because they did not want it to be known just how many men were lost on operations. One day I went into our hut to pick some stuff out of my kit bag which was alongside my bed, and this chappie came up to me who was in another crew who I did not know anything about, because he must have been just new in. He said he had been there six weeks, he said, "What are you doing?", I said, "I am getting stuff out of my kit bag", he said," I have been here six weeks and I have not seen the bloke who sleeps in that bed, so I said "You are looking at him now, it is me". So he had not seen me for six weeks and we lived in the same Nissen hut, so that is how little I had to do with the squadron itself. A lot of the aircrew when off duty used to go out to the local pubs. I did not believe in drinking, I used to drink a little bit, but not very much because you had to have your wits about you. I did not believe in drinking and flying. Just like they say now, do not drink and drive, if you do you are a bloody idiot! Do not drink and fly otherwise you are a bloody dead idiot! I was unlucky one day, in the morning it was very foggy, it was too thick for flying so I went to Cambridge. It was 6 o'clock when I left Witchford and the fog was one of those typical fen fogs, but I managed to get to Cambridge ok. When I got back to the squadron the boys said, "Boy, you are in strife, they have been calling you on the tannoy all night because there is an op on". Well I knew something must have been on because just when I got to the squadron I could hear the Lancs revving up and saw the last one take off in thick fog, so I thought to hell with it and went back and had a bit of sleep. I got up later, went back down to the mess for tea and here was trouble. The flight engineer leader was walking towards the mess and said, "Rutter you bugger, where have you been?" I said,"I have been to Cambridge". "Did you know there was any ops on?" "No, I did not", I replied. So he said, "If you have not got a good excuse you are on a court martial. Do you know I had to do your op?". I said,"It must have been an easy one, you got back didn't you". The flight engineer was a flight lieutenant, Onslow was his name. We used to nickname him Junior, Junior Onslow. "Well I could not have flown", I said. "Why not?", he said. "Because I saw white spots in front of my eyes and then I blacked out so I could not have flown". "Have you been to the medical officer?" "No I haven't". So he said, "Well you should have". I said, " Look I am going to finish my tour of operations, I am disappointed I missed the op and I would have been there if I had been able, I do not know what the complaint is". "I do, it is kidney trouble", said the flight lieutenant, I have got it and I sometimes see white spots and blackout". "Oh", I said, "Isn't it bloody awful, I have never experienced anything like it before". Of course I never had anything wrong at all and just said the first thing that entered my head. He said, "Good job you have got a good excuse otherwise you would have been on court martial". So I was one of the few blokes that missed an operation and got off scot-free. We did have a couple of scary ops. One night over Stuttgart we got mixed up with the night fighters which shot a Lancaster down in front of us, shot another one behind, missed us and hit the bloke behind us. So there is four of us and we were the only ones that they did not hit, so we corkscrewed for about half an hour and got back home OK. The next night we went to Stuttgart again and I said to the skipper, we are not going to take those nightfighters on, we are going to fly through flak, so this is what we did, and lo and behold up came a shell on the port wing and exploded about twenty holes in us. No-one was injured and no real damage was done to any of the vital equipment. We did our operation and came back again so I was leading a charmed life up to then. That first crew of New Zealanders I refused to fly with because they wanted to fly Stirlings, went on to fly six operations. One night they were carrying mines and the mines exploded and that was the end of them. The other crew with the New Zealand pilot went to Mepal and he did twenty six and then was shot down, so I think someone was looking after me. On another occasion we came back one morning and I saw this Messerschmitt 110 on the starboard wing. I said to the crew, "A Messerschmitt is on the starboard wing and if you move your guns I will come down and thump the lot of you. Just sit and do nothing", which we did and this Messerschmitt came alongside of us, flew parallel with us from about sixty yards away. This was over the English Channel and when we got to the English Coast he just accelerated and sped off and left us. I do not know why he did not come back and just shoot us down, because we only had 303 Brownings and he had point 5 cannons so we were useless to offer any resistence, so we were better to just stay dumb and it worked. So, I got through thirty ops, at the time as aircrew my life expectancy was thirty days. Maybe I am shooting the line but as I say, it was just a matter of getting up, doing your ops, checking the aircraft and either you got back or you didn`t. I believe the figures are six out of ten people got shot down and killed or were taken Prisoners of War or injured. Only about four ever got out without a scratch on them and I was one of them. Because of my motorbike accident I was in RAF Witchford sick quarters for a month, so I did not do all my operations with my crew so I was flying spare. I flew with the wing commander one day, I had a blue with him and swore at him, he was doing something which I should have been doing and he had me in, and finished up apologising to me because I had it all down on my log sheet, so that was another run in with authorities. My pilot Percy Frankland went on to train other pilots. Unfortunately one day he took up an Airspeed Oxford, the weather clamped in, and he was on his own, ran out of fuel and pranged into the side of a hill and was killed. I did not know that until few years later when I got in touch with my navigator Skinner, and he told me the story.

I consider myself a lucky man to have survived a tour of operations. In the period I was stationed at Witchford, the squadron lost 29 Lancasters and I was not on any of them. I consider every day of my life a bonus.

At home in Australia Frank's hobby is wood turning, and over the last few years since I first made contact with him he has become a good friend and has produced many wood turned pens which he has sent over to England to raise funds for the RAF Witchford Display of Memorabilia. Another item he made is a squadron clock, dedicated to his crew, which now has a prominent position in the display.

In 1999 when Roy Sutton presented me with copies of his late Father's (PC 44 Cecil David Sutton) Police reports while he was Witchford's village policeman, I was amazed to find amongst the reports the motor cycle accident described by Frank Rutter. I sent a copy of the report to Frank, who is now delighted to show his friends in Australia his criminal past.

To. Supt. F. G. Wells.   Witchford
    Police Office,
    Ely, Cambs.   Ely

                              8th September   44

      No.1892875. Sergeant Francis Wallace Matthew Rutter
age about 24, R.A.F. Station, Witchford, Ely. Being the person
who was not the holder of a licence did drive a motor vehicle
(Motor Cycle B.R.9213) on a road, on the Witchford Road, Ely,
at 16.40hrs 28th August 1944.
Sir.

    I beg to report that an accident occurred on the Witchford
Road, Ely, at about 16.40hrs on Monday 28th August 1944, in
which a B.S.A. motor cycle. No.B.R.9213 was involved. The
particulars of this accident were reported to me by the R.A.F
Police and I was informed that the above-named was the owner
and rider of the motor cycle when the accident occurred and
that he received injuries in this accident.
At about 11.30hrs on Wednesday 30th August 1944, I interviewed Sergeant Rutter, in the presence of Ft/Lt Brawn, at the
Sick Quarters, R.A.F. Station, Witchford. I told him that I
was making enquiries about an accident which occurred on the
Witchford Road, Ely, at about 16.40hrs on Monday 28th August
1944, in which I understood he was involved whilst riding a
motor cycle B.R. 9213. He said, "Yes, but that as nothing to
do with the Police, the accident was on the R.A.F. road".
I told him that the accident occurred on the highway and
asked him if I could see his driving licence and cautioned
him. He said, " I cannot show it to you now".
I pointed out to him that he must produce it within 5 days
and issued to him an HO/RT/1 to produce it at Witchford.
As a result of being informed that 'Rutter' wished to make
a statement, at about 14.30hrs on Friday 8th
September 1944, I again interviewed him, in the presence of
Flying Officer Frankland, I cautioned him and he made the
following statement:-
               I very much regret to say that at the
time of the accident I was not in possession of a Driving
Licence, Road Fund Licence or Insurance. I have tried to
obtain these locally, but was unable to do so, when the
accident occurred I was taking advantage of a brief spell
from my operational duties in order to go and obtain them at
Ely. My only object in taking my cycle was to take it to a
local garage to obtain a certificate of serviceability
necessary to take out an insurance. As I had only obtained
the bike a few days previous I was eager to have these
matters cleared up and I did not realise the seriousness of
my action until it was pointed out to me.

                      (Signed) F. Rutter. Sgt.
I told him that he would be reported.

He is now in possession of a Driving Licence No. E.2767.
Provisional. issued by Tynemouth C.B.C. 2nd September 1944,
giving his address as:- 8. Rake Lane, New York, Shiremoor.

                     I am, Sir,
                 Your Obedient Servant,

                         P.C.44.

Police report

The History behind a Photograph

In 1944 I was given two photographs of RAF Witchford by Madge Baxter (née Leonard) whose parents had kept a shop in the village during World War II. Both photographs had been taken by Corporal West of Witchford's Photographic section and these two copies had been given to Madge by him, as he had been friends with Madge's family both during and after the war. One photograph was of a Lancaster landing at Witchford with the Cathedral in the background and has been used on the front cover of this book and the other was of a crew. On the back of the crew photograph was written 115/195 Squadron. Witchford Airfield October 1944. Shot down over Homberg 2nd October 1944.

Photograph of Peter Funk's crew

Left to right:

G. Flower	Dublin, Ireland
H. Major	Canada
B. Lumsden	Australia
P. Funk	Canada (Pilot)

N. Price	Leicester
S. Didley	Yorkshire
G. Kenny	Trinidad

My interest in this photograph prompted me to pay a visit to the Public Records Office at Cambridge, where I was able to obtain the following information:

RAF Witchford 2nd November 1944 Target Homberg

19 Aircraft left Witchford to bomb target. 2 Aircraft missing

Lancaster MK I HK663 Pilot Flying Officer P. Funk RCAF and Lancaster MK III LM743 Pilot Flying Officer R. Palmer RNZAF did not return.

An added note to the report stated it was later learned that Flying Officer P. Funk had been admitted to No. 52 Medical Field Hospital British Liberation Army. Nothing has been learned of his crew.

The Official Raid Report:

Clear patch over target. Target bombed at 14.10 hours at 20,000 feet visually and by P.F.F. (Pathfinder Force. Bombing appeared scattered. Plenty of black smoke. Medium to intense. Heavy flak up to 21,000 feet.

The next step was to check the Roll of Honour for 3 Group of which Witchford was part. It revealed that Rear Gunner Sergeant Kenny had been killed on the night of the raid. No mention was made of the other crew members, which meant they had survived and were possibly taken as prisoners of war.

A Stroke of Luck

I received a telephone call from Madge Baxter to say that she had remembered meeting a Gerry Flower in the village about two years ago and that he had said that he was revisiting his old airfield. Madge had taken him into her back garden where you could still see some of the old wartime huts. Madge said that they exchanged addresses and that she received a Christmas card from him that year. When Madge gave me the address I was disappointed as it was in Canada and not in Ireland as was written on the back of the old photograph. I decided it was worth writing a letter to Canada for after all there could not be so many Gerry Flowers that served at Witchford.

A few weeks passed and the reply to my letter arrived.

Dear Mr. Aldridge
How interesting that history should catch up with me after more than 50 years. It gives me great pleasure to answer your questions and remember a time when we were all so young and indestructible, or so we thought. The oldest member of the crew was Peter Funk at 30 years, I was the baby at 20 years The rest of the crew's ages fitted in between. You ask about what happened to us and I will try to answer to the best of what I remember and what I was able to pick up from Peter Funk when I came to Canada in 1956. We used the old Lancaster for about ten operations, mostly night and all big ones such as Bremen, Stetten, Dusseldorf etc. Then they gave us a new aircraft when 195 squadron was formed from C Flight of 115. I believe that at the time 115 was considered a chop squadron which was not too good for moral. However, we took off on November 2nd 1944 to destroy the oil plant at Homberg. This was our 21st mission and we were all confident that it was going to be a piece of cake, but right from the beginning something went wrong. We were the lead aircraft and suddenly we began to lose power from one engine. A short discussion took place between the crew and we decided to carry on, by relinquishing the lead and slowly moving back into the formation which was behind us. However, this did not happen and we arrived over the target on our own. Just as we were about to drop our bombs we were hit by flak which knocked our aim off. So we went round again, lined up and let our bombs go. Then the

German's guns really let us have it. I think they were radar controlled because no matter what evasive action we took they kept hammering us. First we lost the starboard outer engine, then the starboard inner. We were in a dive at the time, then they got our port outer and the captain gave the order to bail out. Finally the port inner went haywire, but the captain held on to the aircraft until each and everyone of the crew got out. He managed to get out through the top hatch and just about saved his life because of being so low. However, he was badly injured and was later picked up in a ditch by a Canadian tank crew. He never knew much about it except waking up in hospital before being sent back to Canada, where he spent several years recovering from various injuries. He passed away about twenty years ago. Gerry Kenny, the rear gunner was killed while parachuting to the ground. In regards to the rest of us, well we nearly made it to our lines but we were captured and got a taste of what it's like to be in the middle of a battle field. The Sergeants were gathered up and put in a local gaol where we were interviewed, but it was by regular officers of the German army so there was no problem. After that we were taken to some interrogation place, the name of which I forget. We were kept there for about two weeks which was an unpleasant experience. We were then sent to Dusseldorf and marched through the streets, guarded by German guards and the people called us terror flyers. From here we were sent in crammed box cars to Stalag Luft 3A Breaslav – somewhere on the Polish border. Sometime in January 1945 the Russians were advancing towards the camp and the Germans decided to move us on the march in the middle of winter to Berlin. The Russians finally caught up with us on May 10th 1945. The Russians were not keen to let us go, so we escaped and jumped on an American truck which took us to Hanover, where we saw white sheets and good food for the first time in many months. My weight at that time had gone down by 85 lbs, but on reflection I feel fortunate I was young and healthy and managed to survive where others like myself survived one accident only to lose their lives in the misery of that terrible march. Peter Funk never did get recognition for saving our lives. As far as I know I am the only surviving crew member left, the rest having passed on. I suppose that's what happens to baby crew members. I am enclosing some documents which may be of use to you.
Regards

Gerry Flower.
P.S. The bomb aimer later said that it was the best hit on a target he ever made.

Flying Officer Funk and Flying Officer Palmer's aircraft were the first losses of the reformed 195 squadron. Flying Officer Palmer's crew were also taken as POWs with the exception of Sergeant E.G. Paradise who was killed. The photograph that started this story was taken of Peter Funk's crew, during the time when 115 squadron's C Flight was being used to form the basis for the reforming of 195 squadron. The aircraft in the picture is Lancaster ME 803 A4 D-Dog of 115 squadron's C Flight. This aircraft stayed at Witchford, changed flights and was relettered several times. It eventually completed 105 operations before being struck off charge on November 27th 1946.

Royal Air Force Station,
WITCHFORD,
Nr. Ely,
Cambridgeshire.

6th. November, 1944.

Dear Mr. Flower,

It is with deep regret that I have to confirm the news that your son,
1798759. Sergeant Gerald Walter Flower, has been reported missing.

There is unfortunately very little definite information that I can
give you at the moment. He went out on an operational flight on the day,
2nd. November, 1944, to attack an important target in enemy territory
and up to the time of writing nothing further has been heard of his aircraft.

Your son had proved himself a very capable Air Gunner and had become
a popular member of the Squadron. His loss will be keenly felt by all
his comrades.

It is desired to explain that the request in the telegram notifying
you of the casualty to your son was included with the object of avoiding
his chance of escape being prejudiced by undue publicity in case he was
still at large. This is not to say that any information about him is available, but it is a precaution adopted in the case of all personnel reported
missing.

Air Ministry instructions preclude my enclosing the addresses of the
Next of Kin of the other members of the crew, but in the event of any
news coming to hand regarding your son, rest assured it will be communicated
to you immediately.

In the interim, please accept the most sincere sympathy of myself
and all the personnel of the Squadron in your period of anxiety.

Your son's personal effects have been carefully collected and
forwarded to the R.A.F. Central Depository, Colnbrook and in due course
you will a communication from them.

Yours faithfully,

Mr. A. Flower,
100 Elford Terrace,
Donore Avenue,
S.C. Road,
Dublin,
Eire.

300

Royal Air Force Station.

Witchford.

Ely. Cambs.

Ref: WFD/C.2603/597/P.1.   15th November.1944.

Dear Mr. Flower.

As the Officer supervising the safe keeping of your
son's personal effects on this Unit, please accept my
sincerest sympathy in your present anxiety.

In accordance with Air Ministry instructions, his
personal effects have been forwarded to the Officer Commanding
The Standing Committee of Adjustment. R.A.F. Central Depositor
Colnbrook. Slough. Bucks, in order that certain formalities ma
be complied with. All enquiries regarding these effects shoul
be made to that address.

Your son's bicycle is being held in safe custody on
this Unit, pending Air Ministry authority for its release. I
should be glad however, if you would be good enough to let me
know your wishes with regard to its disposal so that there may
be the minimum of delay when the release authority is granted.

Yours sincerely.

Group Captain. Commanding.
R.A.F. Station. Witchford.

A. Flower.-Esq.,
100. Elford Terrace.
Donore Avenue.
S.C.Road.
Dublin.
Eire.

301

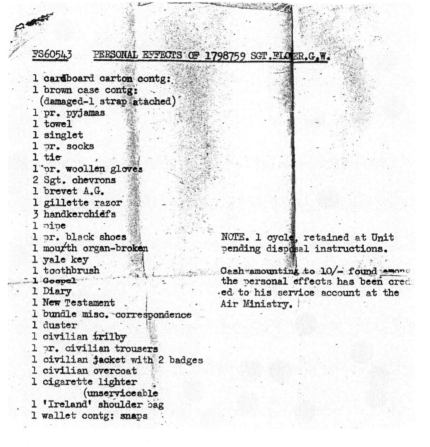

FS60543   PERSONAL EFFECTS OF 1798759 SGT. FLOWER. G. W.

1 cardboard carton contg:
1 brown case contg:
  (damaged-1 strap atached)
1 pr. pyjamas
1 towel
1 singlet
1 pr. socks
1 tie
1 pr. woollen gloves
2 Sgt. chevrons
1 brevet A.G.
1 gillette razor
3 handkerchiefs
1 pipe
1 pr. black shoes
1 mouth organ-broken
1 yale key
1 toothbrush
1 Gospel
1 Diary
1 New Testament
1 bundle misc. correspondence
1 duster
1 civilian trilby
1 pr. civilian trousers
1 civilian jacket with 2 badges
1 civilian overcoat
1 cigarette lighter
          (unserviceable
1 'Ireland' shoulder bag
1 wallet contg: snaps

NOTE. 1 cycle, retained at Unit
pending disposal instructions.

Cash amounting to 10/- found among
the personal effects has been cred-
ed to his service account at the
Air Ministry.

The above images detail letters sent to Mr. Flower concerning his son

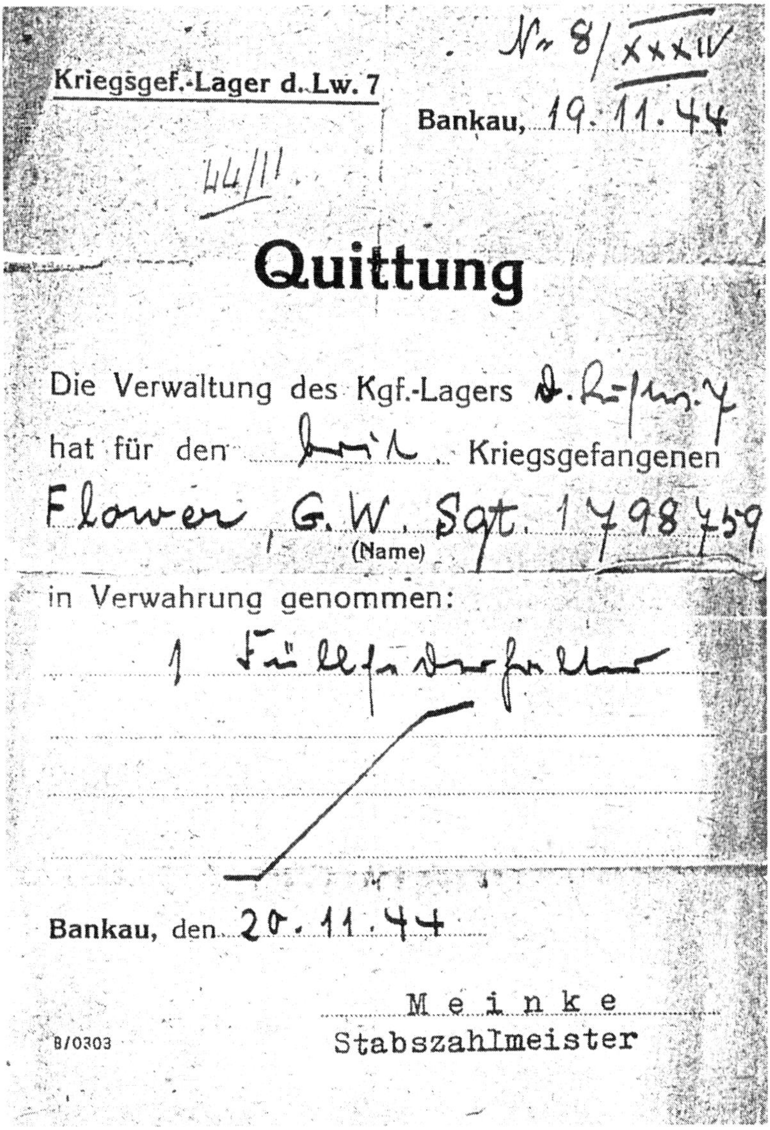

Kriegsgef.-Lager d. Lw. 7

No 8/XXXIV

Bankau, *19. 11. 44*

44/11

Quittung

Die Verwaltung des Kgf.-Lagers *d. R-/m. 7*

hat für den *____* Kriegsgefangenen

Flower, G. W. Sgt. 1798759

(Name)

in Verwahrung genommen:

1 Füllfederhalter

Bankau, den *20. 11. 44*

M e i n k e

Stabszahlmeister

B/0303

German receipt for Sergeant Flower's fountain pen

303

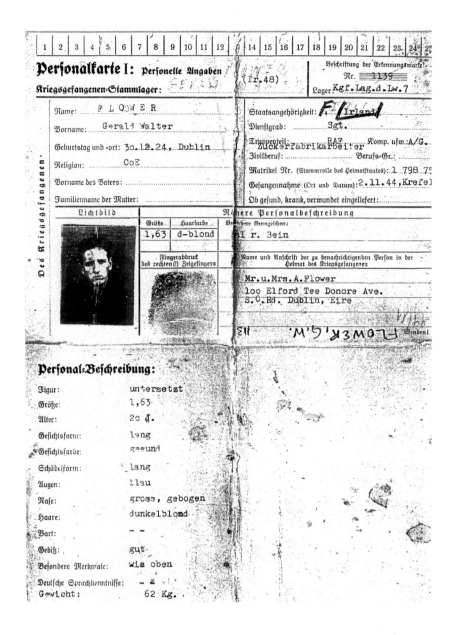

German Prisoner of War record for Sergeant Gerald Flower

German Prisoner of War ID card

The Night We Bombed Little Downham

Former 115 Squadron Flight Sergeant Rear Gunner John Carter recalls how his aircraft accidently dropped an 8,000lb cookie on the outskirts of the village of Little Downham.

It was the night of the 18th/19th March 1944, my birthday as I was born just after midnight on 19th. We took off from Witchford at 19.55 to bomb Frankfurt in our Lancaster MKII KO-A DS682. This was our fifth operation. We were carrying an 8,000lb cookie, (the only time we did). After take off we circled the base to gain height before setting course. At 6,000 feet our Bomb Aimer Arthur Stoneman said," I will put the heater on for the cookie skip". Our Pilot, Warrant Officer Howard Hemming said," OK". The aircraft rolled and lifted and Arthur said," I think the bomb's gone – it is not fused, so it will not go off". Looking down from my turret I saw a flash and I said,"It has you know". As we were under radio silence our pilot decided that we should fly with the bomber stream as far as the enemy coast and then return as we had 6,000lb of incendiaries left, so it was not worth going to target.

We landed back at Witchford and taxied to our dispersal, followed by the Wing Commander in his car. The wing commander said," What is the matter Hemming?" Howard told what had happened. The wing commander said," Oh! We saw a flash but thought a kite had gone in". Our navigator had taken an accurate gee fix, so our pilot, navigator and the wing commander went away to look for the damage. Luckily, it had dropped on the edge of Little Downham making a large hole, which I am told is still there. Only half of the bomb had gone off (an 8,000lb bomb was made in two sections), or the effect would have been much more severe. There were no human casualties, although we were told that a horse and a number of chickens had been killed and several windows in the village were blown out.

At the enquiry next day, it was found that during our aircraft's 50 hour service inspection the day before, two similar plugs, one yellow (for heating) and one red (for release circuit) had been put in the wrong sockets. Our aircraft went into dock to have the damaged bomb doors replaced. Our aircraft had been fitted with the only special 12,000lb bomb doors on the squadron. We got DS682 back on the 22nd and this time got to Frankfurt without incident.

Flight Lieutenant Hemming and crew

This photograph is believed to have been taken on 22/6/44, the day after the crew completed their first tour of operations with an attack on Domleger. The crew are seen here with Lancaster KO-A PB130 with which they had flown their last four operations. At the time of the accidental dropping of the bomb on 18/3/44 Howard Hemming was a Flight Sergeant and between then and the above photograph being taken some crew changes had taken place. Sergeant Ernie Buckley had taken over the mid upper gunner position some time after the incident, and completed his tour on 12/6/44 and is not in the photograph. Sergeant John Carter is third from the left and Flight Lieutenant Hemming fifth. Other crew members in unknown order are: Navigater Flight Sergeant Groom; Flight Engineer Sergeant E. Haddow; Bomb Aimer Sergeant A.Stoneman; Wireless Operator Sergeant H. Howie; Unknown Mid Upper Gunner and Mid Under Gunner Flight Sergeant J.

McCue. A few of Witchford's Lancasters had been adapted to accommodate a mid under gun to cover a blind spot under the Lancaster. The original crew members had begun their tour on 18/2/44 in Lancaster MKII DS699 with an operation to Leipzig, six hours fifty five minutes.

Little Downham resident, John Glover remembers the explosion well and how it got him out of a spot of bother with his mother. John was 11 years at the time and his mother reared chickens. She had just bought a new thermometer for checking incubation temperatures. John decided to heat up the new thermometer over a candle to see how far he could make the mercury climb. Unfortunately he over did the heating up and the thermometer burst. Just as John's mother began remonstrating with him, the bomb exploded, shaking the ground and breaking windows. John's mother quickly extinguished the lights, the thermometer incident forgotten. John remembers that the bomb made a large crater on land owned by Farmer Johnny Brooks at Hirst Lane. The next day he and his friends went to investigate the crater only to be told off by the village Bobby PC Dewsbury.

Another Little Downham resident, Ken Jefferson also remembers the explosion. He had travelled the three miles into Ely to see a film at the Rex Cinema, where he was seated when the bomb went off. So violent was the explosion that several people ran outside believing Market Street, in which the cinema was situated, had been bombed. He remembers that the crater was left for some considerable time until Johnny Brooks complained to his local M.P. and the hole was then quickly filled in.

George Larham was a Foreman Ganger on the railway at Black Bank Station near Little Downham. He was biking towards Ely about 300 yards from Foxes Lane when the bomb exploded and was blown into the dyke by the blast. The man who would many years later become George's son-in-law, 13 year old John Casbon, was standing near an archway in Little Downham's Main Street, close to Proctor's shop. The blast from the bomb created such a wind through the archway that it nearly blew John off his feet. Moss was blown off the roofs of the houses into the road.

Former Electrical Officer at Witchford, Flight Lieutenant Douglas Humphery explains what went wrong and his involvement in the incident.

I was concerned in the incident right up to the hilt. I should explain that at the time when we were at Witchford they were increasing bomb loads and the Lancaster was adapted and modified many times. It was adapted to take a 4,000lb bomb and then later an 8,000lb bomb. The 8,000lb bomb was two 4,000lb bombs bolted togeter with appropriate modifications to the fusing arrangement. The fusing arrangement of a bomb worked as follows, a little windmill on the front was driven round by the air pressure of the falling bomb, which wound through some gearing. It wound a disk with a hole in it, round until the hole was opposite the firing pin so that when the bomb hit the ground the firing pin, which was spring-loaded, would shoot forward, hit the detonator and up would go the bomb. Well, that was how it worked if it was fused, but in order to do that it had to turn this little windmill that was on the front of the bomb so many revs. Now if you did not want it to go, you put in a little clip which held the windmill from turning. It was a little circlip which you could pull off and that went to a piece of straining wire which hooked up into what we called a fuse unit which was in effect an electromagnetic hook. When the electricmagnetic hook was energised, the bomb fell away and the hook hooked on the bit of trailing straining wire, released the circlip which was holding the little windmill and the bomb fell free and the windmill started to whirl until it fused. It used to take probably a 1,000 feet of dropping before it got to the point where it was fused. If you did not want it to be fused and you wanted safety around the aircraft, of course you did not energise the little electromagnetic hook and if the bomb did fall away, it came complete with its wire and the circlip which held it from being fused. That was the arrangement with the 8,000lb bomb and all the bombs come to that, except the incendiaries, so you could not drop it live unless you wanted to. The bomb racks which were detachable from the aircraft had a 5 core cable and this cable was divided into a sort negative return. Wire number 2 shall we call it, was the fusing unit which energised the little hook which made the thing fused or unfused according to whether you energised it or not and a release unit which we will call cable number 3, which was again an electromagnetic thing which fits by a mechanical advantage, this threw the hook backwards and let the bomb go free from its moorings, now that was the release gear. I forget what the other wired from a terminal box with a 5 pin plug that plugged into the aircraft. The units were wired in coloured wiring; the red went to the release unit and that was just a single pair of wires, one for the negative and one for the firing circuit and a yellow circuit went to the fuse unit, they were coloured obviously to distinguish them. Well these units got an awful lot of damage and general hard wear, so we had an electrician in the bomb dump whose job it was to repair the release units and carrier complete with its wiring. On this particular occasion the electrician was given the job of repairing one of these bomb release units and he had damage to the two lots of wiring. Well in theory he should have got a red lot of wiring for the release unit and a yellow lot of wiring for the fuse unit. He found he had not got any twin wiring of those colours so he had to use black which was common general purpose cable and, in the process of putting the black wires into place of the yellow and red wires, he got them crossed. Now that meant that the release unit would not fire when they fired the bomb and the release fuse circuit was energised when the fuse unit was energised. It was common practice for crews going off on operations when they got about 5,000 feet up to open the bomb door and out the fuse units on and test the release unit by the indicator lamps, (a system to indicate that the release units were there and were 'live'). Of course they were circling for height on this particular aircraft and they opened the bomb doors and put the fuse unit on. They use to leave them on because the fuse units were then ready and could not be forgotten and they were shut off when they shut the bomb doors by the limit switches anyway. But, what happened in this instance was once they opened the bomb doors and put the fuse unit on, away went the 8,000lb cookie. Well that meant the release unit went but the fuse unit did not, so the fuse was still clamped and this little windmill was clamped as the bomb was falling. Well we know it fell at Little Downham but we did not know then of course and it fell about 6,000 feet and exploded on impact because it was a thin cased bomb. The Armaments Officer said later that it was the first half of the bomb that had gone off but not the second, so in fact the second half of the bomb was blown to bits by the first half but did not explode otherwise the explosion would have been even worse. At the *time of the explosion I was driving up to flying control, just after the Lancaster had taken off. I used to buzz around the aircraft, just before take off and see if there was anything unserviceable that I could deal with at the last minute. Anyway, I was coming up to flying control and there was a terrific flash in the sky and I thought Christ what is that and then there was a rumble. I did not think the explosion was all that loud at the time but when I got up to control they said it had rocked the building, but did not know where exactly it was. We used to have a system of telephones in the airforce that by co-operation with the Post Office telephone people, gave us an emergency call which meant that you could ask for the next line in to wherever it was you were phoning or you could have a crash call which meant that anyone who was on the phone at the time you wanted a number had his plug pulled out and yours plugged in immediately and that was called priority one. Well the flying control officer was up in control and we thought the explosion was somewhere north of the drome, so he rang round all the police stations and on the fourth call which was Little Downham the policeman's wife said," Yes". Her husband had just gone out as they had just had an explosion somewhere nearby and it had blown their windows out. Well that was the incident and of course the follow up from it was that the C.O. Insisted that we investigate. I was given the job of what they call `Investigating Officer`. I had to make a report out, a summary investigation it was called. I did protest to the C.O. that if you investigate technical staff who were under me theoretically I might be responsible, but he said, "No, that does not matter, you do the investigation". So, I did the investigation and I duly found out what had caused it. I felt sorry for the airman who was responsible because there he was faced with doing repairs, he had not got any yellow wire and he had not got any red wire so he used black wire and he had got them crossed, and of course there was a technical failure, but the C.O. Insisted that he was charged. He was charged and I had to come and give evidence about it and I do not think he got anything more than about seven days or something, but it was considered very serious as a technical matter in the airforce.*

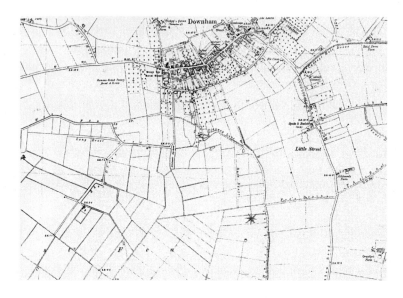

✴ marks the spot

Place	Date	Time	Summary of Events	SECRET.
WITCHFORD	18.3.44		aircraft completed operations successfully. One mid-upper gunner baled out over enemy territory.	
			ADMIN. - The aircraft which returned early on account of the accidental release of one 8,000 lb bomb was found to have badly damaged bomb doors.	
	19.3.44		OPERATIONS - One aircraft was detailed for Air Sea Rescue duty. 17 aircraft detailed to attack Brunswick. Operation cancelled at 16.55 hours.	
	20.3.44		OPERATIONS - 20 aircraft were detailed to attack Munich. Operation cancelled 16.55 hours.	
			ADMIN. - Court of Inquiry opened by Squadron Leader P.H.G. Rice, No. 33 Base, Waterbeach President, and Squadron Leader H.W. Cambell, No. 32 Base Mildenhall - Member, into accidental release of one 8,000 lb bomb on 18th March 1944.	
	21.3.44		OPERATIONS. - 20 aircraft were detailed to attack Berlin. Operations cancelled at 18.17 hours.	
	22.3.44		OPERATIONS. - 21 aircraft were detailed to attack Frankfurt. One aircraft failed to take off (bogged), 1 aircraft returned early. 19 aircraft completed operation. 1 aircraft overshot on landing at Base. 1 aircraft crashed 4 miles from R.A.F Woodbridge.	
	23.3.44		OPERATIONS. - 2 aircraft were detailed to carry out Windowlite Exercise. Exercise complete successfully.	
	24.3.44		OPERATIONS. - 18 aircraft were detailed to attack Berlin. 4 aircraft were reported missing. 1 aircraft landed at Tangmere, 1 aircraft landed at Ludford Magna. 12 aircraft completed operation.	

Log entry

Summary of Events

Only two nights after the accidental dropping of the 8,000lb bomb close to Little Downham, it appears that another similar accident took place on the 23rd March 1944, when 75 New Zealand Squadron based at nearby RAF Mepal dropped a mine on the outskirts of Witchford, causing damage to properties in the villages of Coveney and Wardy Hill.

Author's note:

Several Witchford residents have informed me that two parachute mines were dropped by the Germans on Witchford one evening. (Date uncertain). One exploded on the outskirts of the village, the other failed to explode, having landed at nearby village of Wentworth.

Was the incident confused with the Mepal accidental dropping of a bomb as mentioned in the Police Report as it seems most unlikely that two bombs should be accidently dropped within a few days of each other?

To. Supt. F.G. Wells.   Witchford
     Police Office,
     Ely, Cambs.   Ely

                       24th March   44.

Explosion of Mine, at Witcham 23rd March 1944.

Sir.
     I beg to report that with reference to the exploding of
a mine at Witchford, which was dropped from an Aircraft from
R.A.F. Station, Mepal on the 21st March 1944, I have received
reports of damage to house property in the occupation of the
following persons which it is alleged was caused by this
explosion.
Cecil Walter Bye, 6. Council Houses Coveney, approx 1 square
yard of plaster of bedroom ceiling fallen down.
Samuel George Dewsbery, Wardy Hill, Coveney, approx 1 square
yard of plaster of Kitchen ceiling fallen down, plaster of
Bedroom ceiling loosened, 1 pane of glass 2 feet by 1 foot in
Kitchen window broken.
Albert Henry Maltby, Queens Head Public House, Wardy Hill,
Coveney, 1 pane of glass 1 foot by 9 inches in Bedroom window
broken.
On Friday 24th March 1944, I telephoned to the Station Adjutant
R.A.F. Station, Witchford, regarding who was responsible for
the damage caused, he stated that if he could have a report of
the damage caused he would then decide who was responsible.
In view of this I respectfully suggest that a copy of this
report be forwarded to the Commanding Officer R.A.F. Station,
Mepal.

                          I am, Sir.
                  Your Obedient Servant,

                          P.c.44.

Police report

314

Pilot Officer David Leslie Pirie

Pilot Officer David Leslie Pirie

Pilot Officer David Leslie Pirie, seen here in Flight Sergeant uniform, joined 115 Squadron at RAF Little Snoring on 23rd August 1943. His training started in 1940 at RAF Leuchars with 224 Squadron as a fitter/rigger but previously he had been an apprentice at RAF Harlton from the age of 15 ½ years. Further training took him to Aldergrove and Limavady in Northern Ireland before being posted to RAF Clare College, Cambridge on 26th February. This posting was his remustering to air crew where his pilot training would begin with No. 22 E.F.T.S. (Elementary Flying Training School). No. 22 E.F.T.S. flew from

Newmarket Road Cambridge, now Marshall's airport and also used a small airfield at Caxton Gibbet. In March 1942, Pirie was posted to Canada and then the USA. He returned on 30th March 1943 and was posted to RAF Lulsgate Bottom near Bristol. Further postings to South Cerney, Bibury and Finningley took place before his posting to 115 Squadron at Little Snoring as an operational pilot. Pirie and his crew flew several operations from Little Snoring before the squadron moved to Witchford in November 1943. The early months of 115 squadron's stay at RAF Witchford in 1944 were to see the squadron lose many aircraft and men, as this was the period of heavy raids on the larger German cities – especially Berlin. On 24th December 1943, Pilot Officer Pirie and his crew took off from Witchford at 00.55 hours in Lancaster MKII DS773 KO-T. The target that night would yet again be Berlin. This was the first operation that the squadron had flown since Wing Commander Annan had taken up his post as the new Commanding Officer on the 21st. Complete cloud cover over Berlin did not make this a successful raid, although it did help keep the losses of aircraft down to sixteen. Sadly Pilot Officer Pirie's aircraft was one of those that would not return. There were no survivors.

Crew of Lancaster MKII DS773 KO-T

Pilot Officer David Leslie Pirie	Pilot
Sergeant Jack Heal	Flight Engineer
Pilot Officer Kenneth David Pearce	Navigator
Flight Sergeant William Hardaker	Wireless Operator
Sergeant John Ronald Davidson	Bomb Aimer
Sergeant John Southwell	Mid Upper Gunner
Sergeant Joseph Calvert	Rear Gunner

Pilot Officer William Donald Crebbin 188647

Pilot Officer Crebbin taken during his training in Canada

21 year old Pilot Officer Wiliam Donad Crebbin arrived at RAF Witchford to join 115 Squadron on 31st October 1944. His pilot's training had taken him via Canada, 84 O.T.U. No. 3 Lancaster Finishing School and No. 31 Base. Pilot Officer Crebbin and crew took off in Lancaster PD293 KO-O from

Witchford on 26th November 1944 at 12.10 on an H2S training exercise and disappeared without trace. It is believed they may have got into difficulties over the North Sea.

Pilot Officer Crebbin's crew were:

Sergeant John Edmund Parkin
              Flight Engineer   *Age 22 years.*
Flight Sergeant Harry Donald Hooper RCAF
              Navigator
Flying Officer Edward Alfred Tragheim
              Wireless Operator/AG Age 30 years.
Flight Sergeant Thompson
              Bomb Aimer
Flight Sergeant Ian McKinnon RCAF
              Mid Upper Gunner   *Age 27 years.*
Sergeant Mathew Blenkinsop
              Rear Gunner   *Age 22 years.*

They are all commemorated on the Runnymede memorial.

Two Australian Gunners

The two Australian Gunners in the photograph also became regular members of Flying Officer Martin's crew.   Peter Champion (left) eventually replaced mid upper gunner Sergeant Hollis, who baled out during a raid to Frankfurt on the night of the18th/19th March.   The aircraft LL646 was damaged under the fuselage through to the top which caused damage to inter-communication.

Leigh Johns (right) replaced Sergeant Jeff Payne who had flown four trips with Martin.   On the fourth trip Payne suffered frostbite during a raid to Frankfurt on the 22nd/23rd March 1944, when the connection of his electric gloves became detached.   He had blistering of two fingers and was transferred to the RAF Hospital Ely.

`Tim` the Lancaster Chaser

This photograph of Tim the dog, a cross breed with no tail was given to me by Mr. Barry Rutman who now lives in London. Barry was an evacuee during World War II and lived with Mr & Mrs. H. Gillett at Redhill Farm Stretham. Mr & Mrs. Gillett managed the farm for Mr. Robert Driver who also owned Ely Fields Farms, most of which was taken over to build Witchford Airfield. Barry recalls that Tim spent most of his early years on the airfield, where he developed the habit of chasing incoming and taxi-ing aircraft. Eventually it was decided that his practice was potentially dangerous for both him and RAF personnel, so he was given into care of Mr. & Mrs. Gillett at Redhill Farm, where he became the house/farm dog and where he lived for many years until his death. Tim was an extremely fast runner, despite having no tail. Although this hampered his manoeuvrability, he could still run like a hare. Tim never got out of the habit of chasing planes when they flew over the farm. Barry also remembers the sails and cap of Stretham Windmill being removed so that it could be used as an Observer Post.

Another Dog in Trouble

The case of the chicken snatcher

PC Cecil Sutton received a complaint at 10am on Sunday 9th May 1943 from Mr. John Fairchild, The Homestead, Main Street, Witchford, to the effect that sometime since 8pm the previous night he had lost seventeen young chicks from his farmyard at the rear of his house. PC Sutton visited Mr. Fairchild's yard and made search and enquiries. He found the chickens were missing from three different broods in seperate coops and were aged between 1 and 2 months old. Apparently, they had been taken by a dog or rats. At 1 pm PC Sutton received more information from Mr. Fairchild to the effect that he had seen a Brindle coloured dog in his yard. The dog then ran away through the hedge in the direction of the camp, and that it had something in its mouth. In company with Mr. Fairchild, PC Sutton visited the camp and, in a kennel by the side of No. 51 hut, saw a Brindle bitch with three puppies. The Constable examined the kennel and found a white chicken which was quite warm. The chicken had been badly bitten and had only been dead a very short time. The owner of the dog was not present at the time and on further investigation PC Sutton and Mr. Fairchild found another five chickens dead in the yard. All of the chickens were found to be torn as if killed by a dog. At 2.40pm on the same day, PC Sutton returned to Hut 51 to interview Mr. Frederick William Flooks aged 32 years, a labourer involved in the building of RAF Witchford. Flooks was informed of the nature of PC Sutton's enquiries and shown the carcas of the chickens. PC Sutton also informed Flooks that he was responsible for the dog, and that he would give Mr. Fairchild his name and address so that he could take action to recover compensation. Advised by the constable to contact Mr.Fairchild, first an agreement was settled by the two men and Flooks agreed to pay Mr. Fairchild 5/- shillings (25p) each for seven chickens at 2 months old and 3/- shillings (15p) each for sixteen chickens at 1 month old. However, Mr. Flooks was not out of trouble yet, for having been asked by PC Sutton to produce his dog's licence, he had to admit that he did not have one as he said that he had only recently bought the dog from a man for 5/- shillings (25p). Flooks had nothing to say when PC Sutton said that he had knowledge that the dog had been at the hut since 17th February 1943.

To. Supt. F. G. Wells.   Witchford
    Police Office,   Police Office
    Ely, Cambs.   Ely

                                    9th   May   43

Chickens killed by dog at Witchford .

Sir,
        I beg to report that at about 10.A.M Sunday 9th May 1943, I
received a complaint from John Fairchild, The Homestead, Main
Street, Witchford, to the effect that sometime since 8.P.M. the
previous night he had lost 17 young chickens from his farmyard
at the rear of his house, I visited the yard and made search and
enquiries, the chickens were missing from 3 differents broods in
seperate coops and between 1 month and 2 months old, apparantly
they had been taken either by a dog or rats.
        At about 1.P.M. I received information from Mr. Fairchild that he
had seen a brindle coloured dog in his yard, the dog ran away
through the hedge in the direction of the camp, and that it had
something in its mouth. In company with Mr Fairchild, I visited
the camp and in a kennel by the side of No.51. Hut, I saw a
brindle bitch with 3 puppies, I examined the kennel and found
therein a white chicken, this was quite warm, it had been badly
bitten and had only been dead a short time, the owner of the dog
was not present at this time. 5 other chickens were found dead
in the yard all of them being torn as if killed by a dog,
        At about 2-40.P.M. same date I saw Frederick William Flooks, age
32, Labourer, No.51.Hut, Camp Site, Witchford, I told him the
nature of my enquiries and showed him the chicken which I had
found in his dog kennel and also the other fine which had been
found in the yard and told him that he was responsible for the
chickens killed by his dog and I should give Mr. Fairchild his
name and address for him to take action to recover compensation
for the damage and advised him to see Mr. Fairchild.
        I understand that he has seen Mr Fairchild and they have made an
agreement to settle this matter.
        I understand that 'Flooks' is having the dog destroyed.
        7 chickens 2 months old, value 5/- each, 16 chickens 1 month old
        value 3/- each.

                                    I am, Sir,
                            Your Obedient Servant.

Police report concerning the chickens

322

To. Supt. F. G. Wells.   Witchford
    Police Office,
    Ely, Cambs.   Ely

                              9th   May   43

          Frederick William Flooks, N.R.I.No. W.O.V/1017983, age 32
Labourer, No.51. Hut, Camp Site, Witchford. Keeping a dog over
the months old without having halfoenees licence authorising him
so to do, at Witchford 9th May 1943.
Sir,
       I beg to report that at about 1.P.M. on Sunday 9th May 1943

whilst making enquiries with reference to some chickens which

had been killed by a dog I visited the Camp Site, Witchford, inta

immediby the side of No.51. Hut, I saw a brindle bitch with 3

small puppies, this dog is the property of 'Flooks'.

At about 2-40.P.M. same date I saw 'Flooks' I asked him if he

was the owner of the dog. He replied "Yes". I asked him if I

could see the licence for it and he said. " I havn't got one".

I asked him why he was keeping a dog over six months old without

a licence. He replied. " I havn't had it long".

'Flooks' to my knowledge had this dog in the hut on the 17th

February 1943, and I understand he gave a man 5/- for it.

                                I am, Sir,
                         Your Obedient Servant,

                                P.c.44.

Police report concerning the licence

More Police Reports

Police House,
Witchford,
Ely, Cambs.
28th July 1943.

Wing Commander. N. Alexander.
R.A.F. Station,
Witchford,
Ely, Cambs.

Sir.
    With reference to the fact that it might be necessary for Police Officer's stationed locally, in the course of their official duties to visit the R.A.F. Station, Witchford. I hereby make an application for a pass for each of the following six Police Officer's.

Superintendent. F. C. Wells, Police Office, Ely.

Sergeant.   J. R. Bent. Police Office, Sutton.

P.c.   J. O. Seymour, Police House, Mepal.

P.c.   C.D. Sutton, Police House, Witchford.

P.c.   W. H. Green,   Police Office, Ely.

P.c.   C. W. Taylor, Police Office, Sutton.

If this request is granted it is understood that on a visit they would report to the Guard Room.

                    Thanking you in anticipation,

                        Your faithfully,

                            P.c.44.

Police letter applying for passes

324

To. Supt. F. G. Wells.
Police Office,
Ely, Cambs.

Ely

8th September   43

Report from D.A.P.M. Office, Cambridge, re petrol from
R.A.F. Station, Witchford, being supplied for use in civilian
cars.

Sir.

I beg to report that as a result of a telephone message
from Sergeant Bell, at 3-30 P.M. on Wednesday 8th September
1943, I met Ft Lt Stevens, Pilot Officer Tickner and two
sergeants from the D.A.P.M. Office, Cambridge, I was informed
that they were making enquiries about petrol which was being
obtained from the M.T. Section, R.A.F. Station, Witchford, for
use it was alleged in two civilian cars E.L.Y.893 and C.K.H.
601, in company with them we visited the R.A.F. Station, and
interviewed several members of the R.A.F. M.T. Section, but
we were unable to find any person who had actually witnessed
any petrol being supplied for use in any private car, one man
L.A.C. James Arthur Burnley. NO.614787 stated that it was
common knowledge in the M.T. section that these two cars were
having petrol which was coming from the M.T. pump, it appeared
this has been talked about in the huts but so far their is no
direct evidence that this is so.

At about 5-20. P.M. in company with Ft. Lt. Stevens and Sergeant
Milne, I saw Frank Stanley Cleminson, Foreman for South London
Decoraters, on the R.A.F. Station, this man uses car E.L.Y.893
which is the property of his firm, he was in charge of this
car at the time. I told him that we were making enquiries about
petrol the property of the R.A.F. which it was alleged was
being supplied to civilains for use in their cars. He replied.
I know nothing about any R.A.F. petrol, I have my own petrol
coupons sullpied to me from London". When asked if he had any
objection to a sample of petrol being taken from his car. He
replied. "No, you can take a sample if you like".
Petrol coupons in his possession. No. E/2.K.45730, stamped on
front South London Decoraters, issued at London.

I am, Sir.
Your Obedient Servant,

P.c.44.

Police report concerning petrol

Witchford A Most Primitive Village

RAF Witchford's Medical Officer Flight Lieutenant Brown wrote the following report on the 12th September 1944, after an outbreak of Sonne Dysentry broke out on the camp:

The outbreak appears to have spread from the neighbouring village of Witchford. The sanitation of this village is very primitive with few facilities for bathing and plug toilets being almost unheard of. The infection started among the civilian community some six weeks before a spread to the camp was noticed. The disease in the camp was a mild type, starting with a headache and in one or two cases with conjunctivitis rather like predominal measles. Temperature 102 – 103 lasting 3 days. Sulphaguanading did not appear to be very effective. Controls stools were negative in some, in about the same as where the drug was not used, also systems subsided and stools became formed in about the time routine. Sulphaguanading dosage – 3 hourly for 24 hours then 3, 8 hourly until stools formed.

Jack Tarran's Memories of Witchford and Mepal from Down Under

In response to a letter I wrote to him in early 1998.

It was with surprise and pleasure that I received your letter carrying the Ely address. My time in that area is tucked away in the back of the mind and not known to most current friends, hence seeing it on the envelope proviked thoughts of ` hey what's this?`.

I read of your display of memorabilia with much interest. Those of us who served on RAF Squadrons as `Odd Bods` have an association called the `Odd Bods UK Association (RAAF) 1939-1945`. At a luncheon on 10th February 1998, I mentioned your letter to another 115 Squadron `bod`, Frank Rutter. That name will be familiar to you and he was able to fill me in further on *your activities and the display at Witchford. At the same function, I mentioned your letter to the Hon. Secretary of the Odd Bods Association and he asked for an extract of it to be published in the next newsletter. I have now sent that information to him. There are approximately ten 115 Squadron members listed as members of the Odd Bods Association in Victoria, so hopefully you may hear from some of them.*

Incidently the print of the 19-4-44 disaster has arrived in good order and condition for which I thank you very much. I was not on the squadron at that time and in fact did not recollect having heard about it. So much was happening from day to day that such events most unfortunately soon slipped into the background. It is my intention to have the print framed and it will hang on the wall of my study.

I was in the UK in 1981 and again last year in September/October 1997. However it was not possible to make a return visit on either time to Witchford and Mepal. (More about that follows).

The following is a summary of my service in the RAAF and in particular 115 Squadron and then 75 (New Zealand) Squadron.

After a year as a member of the Air Training Corps (A.T.C.) 1941/1942 I entered the RAAF in July 1942. After training in Australia as an Air Observer (later known as Nav. B) I went to Canada and did a General Reconnaissance course at Prince Edward Island. This completed I arrived in UK in November 1943 with a group of approximately 100 people similarly trained with a view to service in Coastal Command. As Bomber Command suffered heavy losses in late 1943 and early 1944 we waited patiently and smugly for our expected comparatively `safe` postings to Coastal Command. However our smugness was shattered early in 1944 when an officer from RAAF H.Q. in London arrived to tell us that we were to be switched to Bomber Command, half as Navigators and half as Bomb Aimers in both of which skills we had been trained. Then it was to A.F.U. in Wales (Ansons) for familiarisation to UK flying conditions, followed by O.T.U. at Chipping Warden (Wellingtons). Then heavy Conversion Unit at Stradishall (Stirlings) for advanced training. The Stirling, by then phased

out of Bomber Command operations, was followed by
`Lancaster Finishing School` at Feltwell.

We eventually arrived at 115 Squadron, Witchford about mid-
Setember 1944, hopefully fit and ready for `Ops`. Apart from a
hiccup of being allocated as a crew to a hut which still
contained the belongings of a crew shot down the previous
night, we soon settled in and were fortunate to be to take the
traditional six days pre-ops leave. Flight Sergeant Woodward, a
Londoner, was our skipper with a crew consisting of two other
Londoners, a Yorkshire man and three Australians. In those
days that did not seem in the least unusual as we were all
`British`. Naturally there was a certain amount of banter with
regard to test cricket prowess, climates, etc., but no way did
any of us regard others as foreigners. Petty nationalism has
now supplanted that highly satisfactory attitude amongst
younger generations, to the disadvantage of all of us. When I
think of the experiences we went through in the suceeding
months, I wonder how we survived without the current fashion
of `counselling`. Quite frankly, we did not need it! However –
back to Witchford and 115 Squadron.

On 20-9-44 we did our first op. to Calais where German forces
were surrounded but preventing the use of the Port. That was
followed by a further trip to Calais 25-9-44, Cap Gris Nez on 26-
9-44 and Walcheren Island on 30-10-44. By this time our
confidence had grown, probably misguidely, as those four trips
were easy daylight ops. On 5-10-44 we were on a battle order
for our first night op. On entering the briefing room the word
SAAARBRUCKEN hit my mind andhas been firmly implanted
there ever since. (Maybe `counselling` would have got rid of it).
That was our real introduction to ops, with fighter flares floating
down around us, indicating the night fighters were there ready
to pounce. Pounce they did with a Path Finder Lancaster
blowing up in front of us and creating the most vivid spectacle
imaginable as all his marker flares went off at once. There we
were; an inexperienced crew, with no attacks on us and yet a
highly experienced P.F.F. crew gone literally in a flash. The next
night, 6-10-44, Dortmund, again everything went well for us but
unfortunately, as always, not for everyone.

Sunday afternoon 7-10-44, a daylight to Emmerich where there
was a build up of German forces to counter the Arnhem
campaign by the British Army. It was a glorious sunny day but a
very dirty target with extremely heavy flak. Again an aircraft

328

blew up just in front of us. It was strange how our personal reactions developed. You felt sorry for the downed crew but had that feeling 'it won't happen to me'.

On 14-10-44 we were on target at Duisberg in the early morning and again that same night. By this time Jack Woodward, being of small stature, was having severe back trouble resulting from manhandling the heavy Lancaster, such that he was taken off ops. Our last news of him was that he was put on Hurricane fighters used for 'fighter affiliation' exercises with the heavy bombers. Whether in fact he was so employed I do not know. To us he was a very competent pilot able to recognise situation in the air with great rapidity. We remained at Witchford for thr rest of October and most of November as a 'headless' crew. Some further leave was enjoyed in that period, then back to Stradishall to crew with our new pilot Flight Lieutenant Ian (Jock) Taylor, from Glasgow. He was very popular with crew despite our feeling that at age 27 years he was rather old for the job!.(Our previous pilot was 22 years at the time).

Memories of Witchford include the 'electric' atmosphere each day as we checked our aircraft and waited for a battle order. If none, or if we were not on it, if there was one, there would be a feeling of relief and feeling of a whole lefetime ahead- even if expectation was only 24 hours. Much of the detail has faded from memory but is revived to some degree by conversation with others and reading of the events at the time. I remember an occasion at Witchford which boosted our confidence in our flying and operational standards. It was a weather unserviceable morning with fog and/ or low cloud closing the airfield. However a lone lost damaged American B17 spotted it and made repeated attempts to land. Realising he was not going to make it, one of our Lancasters took off, got in front of him and led him in. Maybe there is a record of that somewhere!*

After completing training with 'Jock' Taylor, our expected return to Witchford did not take place. Instead we were posted to 75 New Zealand Squadron at Mepal which of course was next door to Witchford. By this time we were trained on the Gee. H, blind bombing system and carried out mainly daylight ops, without the assistance of the Pathfinder Force. A most vivid memory of Mepal is of an event which occured during the Gee. H.training. It was a beautiful sunny afternoon, a Sunday I think, and not being an operational flight i.e. no bomb load and minimum of *fuel, we took a relaxed and 'this is just too easy' approach to the task in hand. On commencing the take off run a swing developed, was over corrected and we were then off the runway on the grass and heading for the bomb dump (a sand bagged enclosure where many people were employed). By this time Jock had it under control and decided to continue the take off in that direction. However, the bomb dump personnel decided to get out quick and as we went over the top, there were people departing in all directions. I still have this mental picture of arms and legs fully extended and radiating out from the sand-bagged area!*

19-2-45 saw us at Wesel, followed through the remaining months of the war by targets at Kamen, Cologne, Wanne-Eickel, Dortmund, Hattingen, Hamm (twice), Hallendorf, Merseberg, Kiel, Regensburg and Bod Oldesloe. Then on 29-4-45, Operation Manna (food supplies) to The Hague. This was repeated on 1-5-45 and 3-5-45. What an experience that was – the Dutch people out waving, (we were as low as 300 feet and could see it all); German guns standing idle and their crews watching us flying overhead. That experience was equalled on the 9th, 11th and 14th May by visits to Rheims to pick up returning Prisoners of War, Operation Exodus. They were often a pitable sight but were in high spirits at returning home. We took little boxes of barley sugar for them to suck if the confines and smells of the inside of the Lancaster caused air sickness. Not having had such for years, the whole box was gone before they even entered the aircraft! Very soon after that we Australians were taken off the squadron and posted to holding units pending repatriation to Australia. After that our experiences were not talked about very much, as so many people had similar stories to tell and re-establishment was the priority.

Now that we are mostly retired it is talked about more. It is gratifying that younger generations are taking an interest in it at this stage and hopefully projects such as yours and Paul Crucq's on Walcheren Island will help succeeding generations to have a knowledge of those disastrous yet rewarding times.

*   Although I could not find any record of the damaged Flying Fortress being guided in by one of 115 Squadron's Lancasters, I was amazed when, 6 months later in conversation with Henry McCartney, one of RAF Witchford's Photography Department staff that he had two photographs of the damaged Flying Fortress. Henry sent the photos to me and there was no doubt that this must be the Fortress that Jack Tarran mentioned in his letter. In the background under the port wing can be seen Hole Farm Farmhouse which is still there today and gets its name from being built in a hole. The Fortress had damage to its Starboard inner engine and a bullet hole in the nose. The aircraft is in Silver finish which indicates the incident happened later in the war. Henry also recalled that a maintenance crew came out from Bassingbourne to replace the engine before it could be flown back to its base.

The photograph shows the damage to the aircraft's starboard
inner engine and the hole in the nose

Photograph of Flying Fortress

A Fateful Day for a Witchford Crew and the Village of Great Offley

Tuesday 18th July 1944

At 04.20 hours, Pilot Officer Albert Letts took off from the runway at RAF Witchford. This was the seventh time Letts and his crew had taken off from Witchford on an operation since arriving at the fenland airfield in June 1944. Pilot Officer Letts' aircraft was KO-J LM616, which had also arrived new at Witchford in June and was now on its tenth operation, an operation that neither aircraft nor crew would return from. Pilot Officer Letts' aircraft was one of twenty five Lancasters that 115 Squadron were contributing to an operation to bomb enemy positions, concealed in woods at Emieville. The last of the Witchford Lancasters left the runway at 04.40 hours. The total bomb load of the twenty five Lancasters was 275 x 1,000lb and 1x 500lb. On arrival over the target the crews dropped the bombs from heights ranging from 8,000 to 10,000 feet onto the wooded area. Many fires were seen until smoke and dust obscured further visual observation. With all bombs dropped, the Lancasters turned for home and the safety of their respective airfields. It is not known if Pilot Officer Letts' aircraft suffered any damage or mechanical failure over the target or on the return journey, but the next time the aircraft was seen, it was circling over the village of Great Offley, Hertfordshire, on what was a very misty morning. Eye witnesses at the time thought that one engine was on fire, and the pilot was looking for somewhere to put the Lancaster down. The Lancaster had arrived from the direction of Hitchin just after 7.0am going west towards Great Offley, a village that stood on much higher ground. At West End Farm, Great Offley, George Handley and his two sons were in the cow shed carrying out the early morning milking. George's wife Alice and their two daughters, Mary and Elsie, were in the house when a terrible chain of events started to unfold. At 07.10 hours it is probable that Pilot Officer Letts decided to try and crash land the aircraft, unsure of what the terrain was like below the mist. At a spot called Eagles Nest, the aircraft clipped some trees taking several branches with it. Continuing on, the Lancaster cut two furrows across a field and swept up two large water tanks before careering into the farmhouse at West End Farm. The house, although extremely well built, was totally destroyed and the fuel tanks of the Lancaster ruptured and exploded, creating a terrible inferno from which no-one could escape. Villagers and the National Fire Service came to help, but could not do no more than prevent the fire spreading to other farm buildings. More help arrived with fire appliances from Luton and Letchworth to help bring the fire under control. George Handley and his two sons had escaped the disaster, as the cow shed was not damaged in the crash. George, unable to cope with the loss of his wife and daughters, took his own life in 1949. George's youngest daughter Elsie, who was a Private in the A.T.S. had only arrived home the previous evening for a few hours leave from a gun site where she was stationed. Pilot Officer Letts and crew all perished in the crash and ensuing fireball.

The Crew of Lancaster KO-J LM616

Pilot Officer Sydney Albert Letts   Pilot
                    Age 31
Sergeant Keith John Smith
                    Navigator   *Age 20*
Warrant Officer William John Kennedy RCAF
                    Bomb Aimer   *Age 20*
Flying Officer Thomas Richardson
                    Wireless Operator   *Age 23*
Sergeant Isaac Morris RCAF
                    Mid Upper Gunner   *Age 21*
Sergeant Earl Douglas White
                    Rear Gunner   *Age 21*
Sergeant Donald Carpenter Clark
                    Flight Engineer   *Age 20*

Sergeant Morris is buried at New Ground 554 Staveley (St. James) Churchyard, Over Staveley, Westmorland.

Flying Officer Richardson – grave G.3 New Seaham (Christ Church) Churchyard, Seaham, County Durham.

Pilot Officer Letts' grave 13769 and Sergeant Smith's grave 13969 are in Cambridge City Cemetery.

Sergeant Clark's grave is in the south section, 16a Hitchin Cemetery, Herts.

Pilot Officer Kennedy's grave 52.F7 and Sergeant White's grave 52.F8 are in Brookwood Military Cemetery, Woking, Surrey.

. `Mother and two Daughters killed as Plane crashes` were the headlines that accompanied the Press photo of the crash site. The whole village had been woken by the terrific explosion which took place around 7am as aircraft fuel poured into the house causing the explosion and blazing inferno that devoured both aircraft and house.

Wireless Operator Flying Officer Thomas Richardson; one of the
seven crew who died in the terrible crash

Photo of crash site

Charlie's First Op.

Ex 115 Squadron rear gunner, Flight Sergeant Charles (Charlie) Wernham, flew with Pilot Officer Hallam's crew from RAF Witchford and completed thirty operations. Here he recalls the very first operation that they took part in on the 11th December 1944 as an inexperienced crew.

We had listened to the call, had seen the placards 'See Life from a new angle, Join the Royal Air Force and Fly'. We had obliged like the Good Britains of the History Books, and now was the night to fulfil the dream. How did seven men from vastly different corners of Britain and one from Canada come together to be about to face death and mete out death and destruction to an enemy we hated and yet had never met? Would we have the guts to cope with it and look after one another? Ted Hallam our pilot was Welsh and came from a religious background. Greeney (Flying Officer Green) from Canada was our navigator, Flying Officer Eddie Carswell bomb aimer was from Manchester, as was our wireless operator Flight Sergeant Mallen. (Clip) Flight Sergeant Dick Clipsham was our mid upper from Coventry and I was tail end Charlie in the rear gunner's position and came from a tiny hamlet in rural England, in the vale of the White Horse and King Arthur country. (Tommy) Tucker was our flight engineer from Cornwall. Our ages were 22, 21, 21, 22, 22, 18 and 20. Clip and myself – part of the Air Guners Association – had been together since I joined up at Lord's Cricket ground. Clip had re-mustered from ground crew and was like a big brother to me; all our training had been together so we had faith in each other's ability. We had crewed up with Ted and the others at an Operational Training Unit, quite a mixed bag, but it had worked. Ted worked us hard and we felt we were a good crew. He trained us to be able to do a little of each other's job, enough if we were in trouble to get home. We were training on Wellingtons.

When we moved on to a Heavy Conversion Unit (Stirlings) we were joined by Flight Engineer Sergeant Tucker as the four engined aircraft needed a flight engineer. After much training we moved on to a Lancaster Finishing School before joining 115 Squadron at RAF Witchford, situated in the fens not far from Ely and its Cathedral.

Before we became operational as a crew, Ted our pilot went on his second `Dicky` trip (second pilot) to gain operational experience and nearly got the chop. Ted flew with Flying Officer Gibbon's crew on an operation to Duisberg. They reached the target and bombed from 20,000 feet but the ground was not visible. The outer Ruhr defences were heavy and Gibbon's aircraft received flak damage to the port side of the aircraft from mid upper turret to port wing; compass and H2s were unserviceable through damage. The mid upper gunner was wounded in face and hands. They made it back to Witchford at 12.43 hours. Ted had received his baptism of fire.

We, the rest of the crew, were on a seven day leave, to be back at Witchford by 08.00 hours. I decided to have an extra night with the 'girl friend' and arrived back at 13.00 hours, five hours late and was immediately put on charge. In the Sergeants Mess I was asked to phone the Officers Mess and speak to Ted, who was not a happy man, and wanted to know if I was fit for our first trip and to make sure I was at briefing at 14.00 hours. Individual sections briefing was at 14.00 hours while main briefing was at 15.00 hours by invitation only, with an Armed Guard on the door. In the briefing room, the Wing Commander chastised me for my late return and told me to report to see him in A-Flight's office at 09.00 hours tomorrow morning. Taken back by this I retorted that I was entitled to ten hours stand down after an operation. His reply was that I was yet another Barrack Room Lawyer, so I had better report to him at 14.00 hours for a rollicking.

Briefing

Maps were uncovered showing trips to Osterfield via France, missing hot spots if navigators were good enough. (A huge cheer went up). 150 Lancasters of 3-Group were to attack the Railway Yards; 18 of 115 Squadron's Lancasters to take part. The squadron's commanding officer tells us to stray off track or it's death, expect plenty of night fighters and Ack-Ack guns by the hundreds and search lights. The Intelligence Officer takes centre stage, next with all the latest reports on targets and if shot down make for probable help areas. Also to make sure parachute and clothing buried and escape kit and compass ok. The Metrological man is up next telling us probable 10/10ths cloud and temperatures below zero at 20,000 feet – also to expect snow and ice on return. Navigator Leader with bombing, Wireless and Gunnery Leaders all had a little more to add. The Group Captain had his penny worth. All eyes were on us, the new sprog crew, by the old stagers to see if we showed any degree of fear and would we make it, as sprog crews always suffered the most casualties. 115 Squadron's aircraft are detailed to take off from 18.45 hours onwards. We have been allocated Lancaster IL-K. Our bomb loads are 1 x 1000lb, 1 x 500lb and 1,500 incendiaries. Briefing over, there must be no more talking about the target.

We now board the transport to take us to the mess for flying meal – A hearty meal for the condemned; always an egg but a good meal from the cooks. Transport returns to take us to the crew rooms and our lockers, where we don three pairs of long johns, vests and our J L Sullivan heated flying suit, boots, Mae West, chute harness and outer suit. By now we look like Michelin Men, as we waddle, not walk. All personal letters, photos, cash etc. is placed in bags and locked away until we hopefully return. If we don't, everything is collected by Committee of Adjustment Officers. There it will be sorted and returned to next of kin. Flying rations issued of chocolates, gum, barley sugar and fruit. (My ration I placed in my locker). Front of aircraft crew, would take flasks and sandwiches. No point us gunners taking this, as once ensconced in turret, there was no where to store it. Plus no way to have a pee and we always said, if we got scared and shit ourselves at that height, it always froze. The M.O. (Medical Officer) and Padre would be in attendance in case someone was sick or had a cold, or needed 'Wakey Wakey' tablets (But not for me). The Padre asked if we wished to pray, but I saw no point asking God to protect me, as the men on the other side were praying for God to do the same for them. I could not expect him to choose between us or them when we were both on a killing mission, but I had no doubt I would survive.

I sent no last letters from me to my parents and family, friends and girl friend, as they all knew how I felt, but should it happen, help one another and get on with the living. My mother, a devout Catholic, would pray for my soul as she prayed for my brother in Burma and myself to return safely.

17.30 hours the transport takes us out to the flights singing Jerusalem. Our kite was outside the control tower, a spot always reserved for the novices, as new crews all keyed up would usually be the ones to have problems. The good old ground crews were always at hand as they had seen it all before. We all had our customary pee on the tail wheel, a final christening of England for luck.

On board, I slid into my turret, checked sights, guns, intercom, oxygen and bulkhead doors were closed. The rear turret always seemed so remote from the rest of the crew and was always the first target for an enemy aircraft, who knew if they put the rear gunner out of action, the rest were at its mercy. Sitting in space in a graveyard turret, being frozen to the marrow and had a chance of being fried alive in a flying death trap in seconds. The seating was a 15" x 9" pad. Control column between your legs, topped by hand grips to control the turret and triggers – Gun-sight above a red circle and dot superimposed in the sky. I plug in so called heated suit, pull turret doors shut which, when locked, act as a backrest. No oxygen for me or Clip, so the ground crews come in and found nothing wrong, it's called finger trouble associated to new crews. Ted calls the fitters in, claiming a magneto drop. Fitters run up the engines and found no problems (must be no more finger problems) and we are ok to fly. I always carry a tin helmet to cover 'private parts', very essential as I have not used it to its full potential yet.

The engines were now warmed up and checked out for full power. Call from Ted, everyone ok and we taxi out to the runway. We get the green light from the caravan and we are off down the runway with turret turned to port in case of emergency. We stagger off, wheels up, flaps on and climbing. Turret now turning and guns set to fire. The turret in the darkness gives one a false sense of security, enclosed like a bird in a cage and almost robotic feel. We turn over airfield and Greeney gives course for coast and we start to climb. No one talks, it's like a morgue, other than the throb of Merlin. Call from Greeney, change course in one minute over coast. Over sea now, call and test guns, all ok. Climbing to height, Greeney says, "Enemy coast coming up". Bomb Aimer now dropping window to bamboozle German radar. Wireless Operator gives reports from group and bomber command. Bomb Aimer now fuses the bombs. The night is as dark as pitch; wind whistles through turret. (Clear vision panels, no perspex). We are now nearing target, so expect fighter attacks. Ack Ack guns are opening up and search lights weaving, looking for contacts. My intercom obscure, frozen in oxygen mask, I call up the skipper to tell him I am changing helmet. (Not easy, off oxygen for as little time as possible but manage ok). Periodically we hit slip stream from other aircraft. We are in the mainstream and the target is sighted by fires from the first attack.

The searchlights on cloud base are making it like daylight. Ted calls, "a DO 217" is coming on the port side. I turn turret and follow it around to find a JU 88 is close enough to see the radial engines, call out "Corkscrew" to port and fire, see hits on enemy which bucks and dives. I start to float in turret. Ted pulls out, and we go to level flight again. Panic over for the moment. Here and there an aircraft explodes after being hit by fighters, not much hope for crews and no point in dwelling over others misfortunes, everyone for himself. Shells flying around bucking our Lancaster. It did not seem possible to get through the flak. They were hitting us like peas in a can. The worst part was to come, with the run up to the target and to bomb while flying straight and level, plus one extra minute to take a photo. No one is talking now, but getting on with what we had been sent for, but it was the roughest part. Just stiff with fear now and thinking what idiots we were and this was only the first of a tour of thirty.

Plenty of Ack Ack fire coming up and now sweating in fear, a dry mouth and clammy hands. As we run into the target Eddie calls, "Bomb doors open, markers ahead, left, left steady, right a bit". (I was almost expecting Eddie to say, "Back a bit" how much longer. Bomb's gone and one minute, so we can get the hell out of here. It seems a life time. Greenie calls to wireless operator to say, "Gyro's toppled, due to our evasive action". Wireless operator calls Ted, to say, "He will be off". OK from Skipper. Wireless Operator puts on emergency oxygen bottle and climbs over main spar down to gyro, job done, he returns and has slight argument and punch up with navigator who realises the wireless operator is out of oxygen. Sits him down and puts him on to main oxygen. Soon he is ok – oblivious to anything that happened on this trip.

We are heading home but no time to relax. Greenie changes course again and we climb to 20,000 feet. The coast is now coming up. Over coast we start to lose height again. Coffee and sandwiches come out for front crew as oxygen masks come off. Us gunners, still on oxygen, masks still have icicles hanging on them. Back over England at Southwold Gap. Stray outside and our own Ack Ack will shoot us down. Ted calls up 'The

Tower`, with Witchford's call sign `Blackmass`, and is given landing instructions, but warned to watch out for German intruders, so keep alert. We landed safely at 02.46 hours. Seven hours forty five minutes round trip. Ground crew waiting to marshall us in and administer fags to those who smoke to steady nerves, in most cases it worked. (Only Ted and myself were non smokers). One trip completed; twenty nine to go. The ground crew were happy and helpful. Their work would just be starting again in the cold open fenlands. Transport and interrogation. Clothes off and stowed away. Parachutes returned to heated parachute section. We were given a mug of steaming hot tea laced with Naval Black Gold rum which was very sweet and I am now beginning to thaw out. The young WAAF tea ladies were a sight for sore eyes. The interrogation by intelligence officers combats reported all bombs gone and photos taken. Fires visible for up to fifty miles on homeward trip. One Witchford aircraft returned early due to a fault, but seventeen of us from Witchford attacked the target and returned safely.

We walked two miles back to the mess, cold and very tired eyes, red and sore, glad to be back and alive. Cooked meal at 05.00 hours. Then back to our Ritz billet nissan hut, which is freezing cold. No rocking to sleep tonight. 07.00 hours sleep. Wakened at 13.00 hours, washed, shaved and dressed, ready for 14.00 hours to see Wing Commander. I was marched in like a common criminal under escort, hat off. What was my excuse for arriving late asked the Wing Commander. I said that I wanted one extra night with my girlfriend, so left at 05.00 hours in morning, arriving at 13.00 hours. What train, said the Wing Commander, removing his Bradshaw book from his drawer to check times to check my story. He told me to behave more like an NCO. He told me he was admonishing me and did I know what it meant. I replied that I understood he was giving me a warning. I was then marched out and left annoyed, after doing my duty the night before. I hope we will survive the next twenty nine operations.

Photograph of Flying Officer Hallam and crew 1945

Left to right:

Sergeant Clipsham	Mid Upper Gunner
Flight Sergeant Mallen	Wireless Operator
Flying Officer Green	Navigator
Flying Officer Hallam	Pilot
Sergeant Tucker	Flight Engineer
Flying Officer Carswell	Bomb Aimer
Sergeant Wernham	Rear Gunner

A Long Day's Night by Sam Wood

Witchford via Mersberg 4th April 1945

It was great to get back to the old billet after being away for a couple of weeks on Radar course H2S, G.H. and Fishpond at Feltwell, but woke up with a cracking hangover after the binge last night. Peering at my watch, I can see I am late for grub at the mess, so on with a pair of denims and nip under the wire at the back of the billet and obtain a couple of fresh eggs from the farm for a couple of pence. Got the stove going and had eggs on toast with tinned best butter, (courtesy of my Canadian crew) one of the perks of being in a Canadian crew.

Made myself respectable and walked to the mess for mail, read papers and check if I had any daily inspection to do on any aircraft. Found I had KOU-LM 696, my mate Gordon, Australian wireless operator for Flight Lieutenant O'Halloran's crew, also had a D/i so we cadged a lift to the drome, collected helmets from the lockers and out to the dispersal. Plenty of activity going on – looks like there could be ops on tonight. Lucky for me a trolley accumalator is near the kite so plug and start to switch on. While things are warming up I get one of the portable oxygen bottles and start deep breathing (good for hangovers) then put out bottle for refill. Switch on intercom; check all positions, tunes in transmitter to Waterbeach to check signal strength, ok, but my receiver could be better. Finished D/i, so back to mess for lunch.

Conversations and arrangements are interrupted with the arrival of the `Battle Order` being put up on the notice board. Pushing through the crowd, I can see we are on ops tonight, so is my mate Gordon; that settles where we are going tonight for entertainment. We decide to go back to the billets and get a couple of hours' shut eyes. Woken up by the noise of the boys getting ready to go to the mess; 16.00 hours. Quick wash and shave; make up bunk for later and join queue for egg, sausage and spuds (that's if you are on battle order). Shout goes up, transport arrived for briefing. A few cheerios and quips to the WAAFs on duty in the mess and we pile into the trucks.

Wireless Operators briefing room is nearest to drome entrance, so we are dropped off whilst the other members are taken to their briefings. On entering, the first thing is to make a bet, for two shillings (10p) you guess the target write it down, winner takes all, usually about two quid (£2), we have to wait till main briefing to find out the target. We settle down, collect our colours of the day (vary cartridges) depends on the length of flight, how many changes there can be. We are given what frequencies to use, time of broadcast to us (any news etc), collect our codes of the day, disperse and walk over to the main briefing room where all the rest of the guys will be. After being checked in by a couple of M.P.s we enter the smoke logged briefing room. Looking round I find my crew table and join them. Enter flight commanders; we all stand up, at ease, and the board map is uncovered to a buzz of talk as we see the red tape route stretches to the far end of Germany, Mersburg, our longest trip yet, the exact target is given. A petro-chemical plant, details of plant and aiming points are given, our bombing height is given as 19,500 with the master bomber stooging around at 5,000. Intelligence give their briefing; which route, sites of high flak and searchlights concentrations on our track, no problems with the Met. Little bit of cloud knocking about. We finish briefing with take off times, rendezvous times and heights, the usual pep talk from the C.O. and good luck. I happen to say to the skipper it would be our longest trip being the thirteenth one, he replied, it's my fourteenth with having my second dickey trip (first trip being with another crew as second pilot). Orville mid upper gunner said, "I've done twelve, missed one with toothache, so we should be ok, it's not the full crews thirteenth."

We make our way to the locker room, put our flying boots, chute harness and mae west on and go to the hatch to collect our flying rations, flask of tea and our parachute, checking anti tamper thread under clip that it's not broken. Our usual quip to the WAAF Packers, 'Can we bring it back if it doesn't work?' I wonder how many times that's said, to relieve the tension. Outside in the fresh air, the trucks are waiting to take us to our aircraft, race to get in front seat if it is a WAAF driver. Arrive at the dispersal, chat with the ground crew who thank us for the fags. Bomb doors are so 'Red' Harry our bomb aimer checks the load, one 12,000 pounder and four 250s. All clamber in after wetting tail wheel with last pee for luck. I pull ladder in, close door and make my way to wireless operator position. I wait till I hear skipper say, 'start' one, S/inner which has generator for all electrics in, switch the intercom on and call up all positions, all working clearly. Radio is now warming up, all lights showing. Suddenly, there is a smell of burning rubber, lights start to blink and the set gives dying moan then silence. I check main fuses, they are ok, taking the set innards out of its case, I check for damage and can see it's a case of fresh set, beyond me to fix it, calls up skipper on intercom, lets him know I will have to arrange new set. I take the set out and get out of the aircraft to the ground crew, so they can phone up to the radio shack for a replacement and a mechanic. I tell the skipper the mechanics are on their way, the retort being 'They had better pull their fingers out or these engines will blow their tops with over heating`. The mechanics arrive, I take the set off them and go back to position, puts everything back, switches on to sound of morse, in touch with the outer world at last. Informs skipper carry on, we are twenty minutes late, we waddle our way round the perimeter to our take off runway, next to the main road to Ely, looking through the Astra Dome there is quite a crowd of people waving to us over the fence, plenty young ones wondering if their date will show up tonight or if they are 'on'. We get the green light from the trailer and skipper starts to wind up power, a hiss of air compression and we start to move slowly down runway, the tail picks up, and the Merlins start to singin' their own personal Merlin song. Full power, throttles locked, three parts down the runway I can look across at the wing tips as the familiar bow comes into them taking the strain of 67,700lbs take off weight. It seems as though the fuselage wants to stay on the deck and wings and engines take off on their own, I can hear the skipper breathing heavy with the strain and saying, "Come up baby", the boundary hedge is getting closer when the horizon starts to fall away and our long haul starts as we head for the cloud base. If you happen to suffer from `ring twitter` (nerves & s...s), this is where it starts; full load and climbing, knowing there are two or three squadrons taking off at the same time from around Ely.

Still standing in Astra Dome I see the light getting stronger. Suddenly we burst out of cloud into brilliant sunshine and I can see a long line of scattered Lancasters in front of us as they head out towards the Wash. Dropping down in the wireless operator's seat, I tune into base waiting for our first message which is only a time check so signs on in log and settles down on listening watch. After a while Gordon our navigator leans across to tell me to switch my intercom on (when on set wireless operator keeps off intercom, so crew will not be bothered with static and morse), skipper wants to know what a Lanc about half a mile away is flashing on it's Aldis lamp. Getting into dome with my Aldis, I flash across code for 'Who is that?' Reply was, "Gordie KO-E is that timber?" I replied "Yes KO-U". I let the skipper know there is no panic, it's only O'Halloran's wireless operator wanting a chat. Finishing a chat, I settle down at the set again and tune into a bit of dance music. Feeling the aircraft weaving about a bit I switch off and go on intercom. I get in the dome as Harry the bomb aimer is talking to the skipper and giving guiding instructions through a belt of searchlights, quite a bit of flak being thrown up two or three miles away, could be someone off course or there is another party going on to keep the fighters from the main stream. Looking over Gordon's shoulder at the map I can see it could be around 'Happy Valley' the Rhur Valley, around an hour to go yet, so stops in dome, extra pair of eyes for fighters. Hearing Gordon giving skipper new course I can see it's the final leg to the target. In the distance there is a big bank of searchlights, the sky is full of twinkling stars which are really flak bursts. Harry starts to give the skipper his run up to the target, the master bomber relaying what is happening, we are on our final run in, Harry saying, "Bombs doors open, left, left, steady", on reds when a shower of green target indicators go down from master bomber, Harry comes out with the Canadian language expression (s...) as the master bomber says," Bomb on greens, you're starting to undershoot", we will have to go round again so a dicey circle to get in the stream again, the flak seems to be heavier – right height too, shrapnel rattling off the dome, making me keep ducking (for what use it is if a piece hits that isn't spent). Approaching target again and bombs away, stay level for photo flash as master bomber says, "That's better; give the bastards hell". Photo taken, nose down get the hell out here, the old girl leaps away like a greyhound out the trap. Breaking away from the flak belt we are suddenly caught in the new Radar controlled blue searchlights; we knew that we would be in for a few minutes of special attention. Other searchlights started to cone us as Harry shouted, "Starboard go", the skipper went into the best corkscrew we have been in as everything except the kitchen sink came up at us. We burst out of the cone into darkness, Harry guides the skipper through *what could be the Leipzig defences where our corkscrew had taken us. I inform skipper we are getting sparks from starboard engine. Eddie the engineer says, "Temperature and pressure ok, keep an eye on it". Harry said, "We may have a hang-up as there is still a light on my panel". Skipper says, "Go down and check Sammy". Putting on chute and portable oxygen bottle I go down the fuselage with a dim torch to check bomb bay, while I am plugging in my intercom I hear mid upper saying, " Stick that torch somewhere else," I forget where. "It's ruining my night vision". In the dome again I let the skipper know there is heavier spark from the engine, suddenly a flash of flame. Skipper shuts off engine, side slips to port as he tells Eddie to feather the engine, bit of luck the flames die out.*

Time for group broadcast, tunes in and coded message comes to us. I decode, let the skipper know we have enemy fighters up at the front of the stream and I have to start jamming their signals and instructions from their controllers. Al, the rear gunner calls up skipper that his turret is U/s through generator for its power is in starboard engine. I switch on 'fish pond' radar screen to detect enemy aircraft. I can see we are being left behind with only three engines, no fighters, I inform skipper, also tells him I will send a message to base, we will be late back, message sent with E.T.A. Everything quiet, we are below 10,000 feet, so off and into hot drink from flask. Looking through dome I see we are skirting Happy Valley. Harry gives Gordon spot check on Rhine, bang on track, and making for Belgium coast. Sends message crossed coast, last leg, I switch on I.F.F. to identify us (with being late, in the distance a lone searchlight comes on, pointing straight up and then dipping towards nearest airfield in case we have to land).

Skipper calls up base for permission to land. From the dome I spot the red light on top of Ely Cathedral as the seductive voice of the W.A.A.F operator says, "Come right in Burny", to wolf whistles from us all. Flaps down 2750 revs and we drop towards the deck, tyres touch and squeal as we touch down, 8 hours 20 minutes after take off. I switch off all equipment, jump out of the kite to see the ground staff already putting the tower round the engine to repair or replace it.

Transport waiting, across to briefing and hot cup of tea laced with rum. One of the other lads comes across and says Gordon, my mate in O'Halloran's crew, is overdue and never been in touch. Back in the mess for grub and back into the 'pit' straight away and drops off, shattered with the noise of the Merlins still throbbing and Morse and static rattling in my ears and head. Woke up for dinner, to be told a piece of flak the size of sixpence had pierced the Glycol tank and only the quick action of the crew had saved the engine exploding.

Little did Sam Wood know at the time, that his Aldis lamp contact with O'Halloran's wireless operator would be the last contact ever made with Gordie or any of O'Halloran's crew. For the aircraft was in collision with another Lancaster of 186 Squadron. Only one airman, Pilot Officer A.E. Bartlett from the Stradishall based Lancaster, survived. O'Halloran's eight man crew, as he had a second pilot on board, would be the last operational casualty of 115 Squadron.

4th April 1945 Lancaster MK 1 HK555 KO-E

Flight Lieutenant Thomas Anthony O'Halloran   Pilot,
*   183181 RAFVR*
Pilot Officer Laurence Luxton   2nd   Pilot,   33,
*   J94582 RCAF*
Flight Sergeant Charles Edward Marchant   Flight
*   Engineer, 22, 1604373 RAFVR*
Flight Lieutenant Wilfred Gordon Carr   Nav   22,
*   1683518 RAFVR*
Warrant Officer Gordon Reginald Saville   Wireless
*   Operator, 24, 428798 RAAF*
Flying Officer Albert Edward Adams   Bomb   Aimer,
*   149989 RAFVR*
Sergeant Earnest Sheavills   Mid   Upper
*   Gunner, 24, 651465 RAF*
Sergeant John Thomas Buckley   Rear
*   Gunner, 1690398 RAFVR*

Due to being superstitious, the crew having just returned from an airtest of Lancaster KO-J LM696 prior to an operation to bomb the Leuna oil refinery at Meuseberg on 4-4-45, pilot Flight Lieutenant Burnett's photo was cut out from another photo and stuck on after their operations were over.

Operations completed by the crew:

Lancaster	Target
KO-W	Krefeld
KO-M	Munchen – Gladbeck
KO-T	Dortmund
KO-X	Hohen – Budberg
I L-T	Osterfeld
KO-Q	Dortmund
KO-A	Gelsenkirchen
KO-R	Datteln
KO-J	Henrichshutte
KO-Y	Bruchstrasse
KO-Y	Munster
KO-U	Mersberg
KO-J	Dortmund
KO-Y	Kiel (operation that sunk the Pocket Battleship)
KO-Y	Badoldesloe (Admiral Scheer 9/10/45)
KO-Y	Rotterdam (for food drops)

After the war Sam Wood had his own Painting and Decorating business in Pemberton, Wigan. Sam and his wife always attended the 115 Squadron Association reunions held each year. As a young man he served his country well, so it was a great shock to hear in September 2008 that Sam and his wife had both been killed in a road accident.

Crew left to right:

Flight Sergeant A.L. Findley	Rear Gunner RCAF
Flight Sergeant Sam Wood	Wireless Operator
Sergeant Eddie Boyle	Navigator
Flight Officer Gordon Bradley	Flight Engineer RCAF
Warrant Officer Harry Lindhurst	Bomb Aimer
Sergeant Orville Blouin	Mid Upper Gunner
Flight Lieutenant Burnett	Pilot RCAF

Nicholas Alkemade

Nicholas Alkemade was born in North Walsham in Norfolk to a Dutch Father and English Mother. His parents would have no idea then, that their young infant would many years later become famous for an unbelievable escape from certain death. It was 1940 when 21 year old Nicholas joined the RAF and served on Air-Sea rescue launches. Feeling that he needed more excitement, he transferred to Bomber Command and trained as an Air Gunner, which eventually brought him here to RAF Witchford as a 115 Squadron Gunner with Flight Sergeant Newman's crew. Flight Sergeant Newman flew with Flight Lieutenant Seddon's crew on the night of 20th/21st of February 1944, target Stuttgart. This was common practice for a newly trained pilot to gain operational experience, before taking his own crew on a bombing mission.

It was the night of 1st/2nd of March 1944 when Newman and his own crew were to fly together on their first operation. The target was Stuttgart and eighteen 115 Squadron Lancasters took off from Witchford between 23.26 hours and 23.52 hours.

Newman's crew were as follows:

Sergeant J. Cleary	*Navigator*
Sergeant G. Berwell	*Wireless Operator*
Sergeant C. Hilder	*Bomb Aimer*
Sergeant N. Alkemade	*Mid Upper Gunner*
Sergeant G. McDonough	*Rear Gunner RCAF*
Sergeant E. Warren	*Flight Engineer*

Newman's C-Flight Lancaster A4-A DS 795 bombed the target along with the rest of the squadron from 20,000 feet. Their next operation to Le-Mans on the night of 7th/8th of March 1944 was flown in Lancaster KO-C LL 640 of A-Flight. Fourteen 115 Squadron aircraft took part in this operation and had all returned safely by 00.09 hours.

The squadron's next operation was to Stuttgart, on the night of the 15th/16th of March. Newman's crew were not on this operation, from which Pilot Officer Rodger and crew failed to return. It was the night of the 18th/19th when Newman's crew took part in their next operation, when 115 Squadron provided twenty two Lancasters for an attack on Frankfurt. Pilot Officer Frampton and crew failed to return to Witchford from this operation, and another aircraft, piloted by Flight Sergeant Williams, was forced to land at Coltishall having been shot up and the rear gunner wounded. All the remaining aircraft returned safely. Newman's Lancaster A4-GLL 646 received slight flak damage to the starboard fin. The next operation for the crew was a return journey to Frankfurt, in Lancaster A4-K DS 664, when the squadron provided twenty Lancasters for the attack. Flight Sergeant Pope's badly damaged aircraft crashed at Bredfield, while trying to land at the emergency landing airfield at Woodbridge. Only the flight engineer and wireless operator survived.

Target Berlin

The next operation on the night of the 24th/25th of March 1944 would bring more tragedy to the squadron, when they were detailed to provide eighteen Lancasters for an attack on Berlin, in accordance with Form B378 received from H.Q. No. 3-Group. The first aircraft to take off for the big city was Pilot Officer Moon at 18.35 hours, followed at one or two minute intervals by the rest of the squadron. Flight Sergeant James Arthur Newman opened the throttles of his Bristol Hercules powered Lancaster DS 664, nicknamed `Werewolf`, and roared down the runway lifting off into the night sky. Newman's two gunners had taken it in turn on their previous ops as to who took what gunners position. Tonight Nicholas Alkemade was in the rear turret and John Joseph McDonough was in mid upper position. The target tonight was the one most feared by aircrew, and this operation would do nothing to change their opinion. For those making their maiden trip to Berlin like Newman and his crew, they would have no idea of the terrible night this would turn out to be. 577 Lancasters, 216 Halifaxes and 18 Mosquitoes were heading for the target, but exceptionally high winds caused the bomber stream to become scattered. The winds, which had not been forecast accurately, were to cause even more trouble on the return journey, when the bomber force strayed over the Ruhr defences. 44 Lancasters and 28 Halifaxes would be lost on this raid. 14 bombers were shot down by night fighters over the target alone; the rest were destroyed by flak. The

Lancasters bombed the target between 20,000 and 21,000 feet, and turned for home. 4 of Witchford's aircraft would sadly not make the return journey. 23 year old Pilot Officer Thomas Elliott Vipond and crew were shot down by Hptm Martin Drews of 111/NJG1 at 00.20 hours and crashed at Epse, 4km SE of Deventer in the vicinity of Gorssel. There were no survivors. Flight Sergeant Ieuan Glyndwyr Williams and crew were also shot down by a night fighter and crashed at Kropelin. The only survivor was Bomb Aimer Sergeant Meikle, and he was taken as a POW. Pilot Officer Leonard Myles McCann RCAF and crew suffered the same fate as the others. Two of the crew survived and were taken as POWs.

Nicholas Alkemade and his Amazing Escape

As Flight Sergeant Newman approached Berlin they could see the searchlights probing the sky. Soon they saw the red and green markers dropped by the Pathfinders and made their run-in to drop their 4,000lb 'cookie' and incendiaries. Turning for home through the searchlights, the crew kept a sharp look out for night fighters. The crew could see other Lancasters under attack and some going down in a great ball of fire. They were somewhere over the Ruhr when a series of shuddering crashes hit the Lancaster from nose to tail. Two cannon shells exploded on the ring mounting of the rear turret, shattering the plexiglass and sending a large piece slicing into Sergeant Alkemade's right leg. Quickly he depresses his guns and saw not fifty yards astern, a JU 88 blazing away at the Lancaster. Sergeant Alkemade fired at the enemy aircraft and it peeled away trailing flame. It was now that he realised that flaming fuel was running past him, and he started to report to his skipper that the tail was on fire, but he was cut short when Flight Sergeant Newman said, "I can't hold her lads, bale out! Bale out!" Alkemade flicked the turret doors behind him open with his elbows and turned to open the fuselage door beyond. There before him was a giant ball of fire. Flame and smoke came towards him and he pulled back into his turret coughing and blinded by smoke. Nicholas desperately needed to get to his parachute, which was always stowed in the fuselage, a few feet inside the second door. He opened the door again, but it was too late as the case had been burnt off and the silk was coming out in folds and disappearing in puffs of flame. It was decision time, the oil from the rear turret's hydraulic system was now on fire and flames were now burning his hands and face, and it was only time before the plane would explode. He decided it would be better to die a quick death by jumping out, than die being roasted alive. Quickly he rotated the turret, flipped open the doors and in pain and desperation fell backwards into the night. His last recollection was the relief of being away from the searing heat, and the cold air on his face. Nicholas had no feeling of falling but could see the stars below his feet, so he knew he was falling head first. If this was dying, he thought to himself, it was nothing to be afraid of. His only regret was not being able to say goodbye to his friends and girlfriend Pearl, then he blacked out.

Slowly, Sergeant Nicholas Alkemade regained his senses. Above him he could see a patch of starlit sky. Slowly, the dark patch framing the area of sky turned into a hole in a thick group of fir trees. As he gained more of his senses, he realised he was laying on a deep mound of under bush covered in snow. He was very cold and his head and back throbbed with terrible pain, but he was all in one piece, and a feeling of total wonderment fell upon him when he began to realise that he had fallen over three miles, had his fall broken by fir trees and a snow drift and survived. He tried to sit up, but the pain was too much. Looking around, he found that his flying boots were gone and his uniform was scorched and torn. In his pocket he found a badly burnt tin in which he kept his cigarettes and lighter. He lit up a cigarette and looked at his watch; it was still going and the luminous hands showed 3.20am. It had been near midnight when the aircraft was hit.

Nicholas removed the whistle from his collar and from time to time gave it a blow. After what seemed hours, he heard a far off "Hulloo". He kept blowing the whistle and then saw flashlights approaching. Soon some men and boys appeared and ordered him to get up. When they saw he could not, they put him on a tarpaulin and dragged him across the frozen ground to a cottage where an old lady gave him a warm drink. Soon a car arrived and two men came in, dressed in plain clothes. Totally oblivious to his pain, they pulled him up and took him to their car and on to hospital. After coming out of the operating theatre, he learned that he had burnt legs, twisted right knee, a deep splinter wound in the thigh, strained back, slight concussion and a deep scalp wound, first-second and third degree burns on his face and hands, most of which had been received before he jumped from the aircraft. Cleaned up and installed in a clean bed, he was visited by a member of the Wehrmacht. Through an interpreter, Nicholas was asked the usual questions. "What was your target?" "Where is your base?" "How many aircraft are there?" Answering name, rank and number he said that he was not allowed to answer the other questions. The questioning then turned to his parachute. "Where is your parachute?" "Where did you bury it?" When Sergeant Alkemade replied, "I did not use one", the German officer nearly burst with rage, turned on his heels and stormed out. After three weeks, Sergeant Alkemade's wounds were almost healed and he was taken to Dulag Luft near Frankfurt, and put into solitary confinement. A week later a young Luftwaffe Lieutenant led him into Kommandant's Office. "We have to congratulate you, I believe, Sergeant", said the Kommandant in English, and asked Sergeant Alkemade to tell his story once again. After listening to the explanation, he said, "A very tall story I think Sergeant". Sergeant Alkemade said that the story could be proved if the wreckage of the aircraft was found, for the remnants of the parachute pack would still be there, just forward of the rear fuselage door, and also the parachute harness could be examined to prove that it had never been used. The Kommandant, who had listened to the story in silence said, "A really remarkable story, and I have heard many". He then gave the Lieutenant some orders, who then saluted and left. Fifteen minutes later the Lieutenant returned waving Sergeant Alkemade`s parachute harness, accompanied by three other officers, all shouting excitedly in German. The Lieutenant put the harness on the desk and pointed to the snap hooks that were still in their clips, and the lift web still fastened down on the chest straps. The Kommandant leaned back in his chair, studied each of them in turn and said, "Gentlemen, a miracle – no less". He then rose and offered his hand to Sergeant Alkemade and said, " Congratulations my boy, on being alive. Tomorrow I promise your Comrades will be told how you became POW. Next morning back in the Kommandant's office, Nicholas saw that the Luftwaffe had been busy, for there on the desk lay some pieces of scorched metal, including the D-handle of a parachute ripcord and a piece of wire that would be the ripcord itself. "The remains of your parachute pack", said the Kommandant. "We found it where you said it would be; to us this is the final proof". The crash site of the Lancaster lay twenty kilometres from where Nicholas had landed. The bodies of Pilot Flight Sergeant Newman, Flight Engineer Sergeant Warren, Bomb Aimer Sergeant Hilder and Mid Upper Gunner Sergeant McDonough had been found in the wreckage. They had been buried with full military honours in a cemetery near Meschede. Later Nicholas was to learn that Wireless Operator Sergeant Berwell and Navigator Sergeant Cleary had been blown clear and had also survived. Sergeant Nicholas Alkemade was marched into the compound by a German Officer and two N.C.O`s, where two hundred captured alied flyers were assembled and was directed to stand on a bench. The Officer then recounted the story to the assembled men. Sergeant Alkemade was then surrounded by Airmen of all nationalities, all wishing to shake his hand, and offering cigarettes or chocolates. Sergeant Alkemade was then presented with a paper, signed by the Senior British Officer, who had taken down the German authentication in writing and had it witnessed by two Senior British NCOs. It reads as follows:

It has been investigated and corroborated by the German authorities that the claim made by Sergeant Alkemade, 1431537 RAF is true in all respects, namely, that he made a descent from 18,000 feet without a parachute, having been on fire in the aircraft. He landed in deep snow among fir trees. Corroboration witnessed by:

Flight Lieutenant H.J. Moore, SeniorBritish Officer.

Flight Sergeant R.R. Lamb, 1339582.

Flight Sergeant T.A. Jones, 411 Senior British NCOs.

Date: 25/4/44

After the war Nicholas returned to England and married his girlfriend Pearl. Geoffrey Berwell was their Best Man. Nicholas died in 1987.

Cartoon - Echoes of Bygone Skies, unknown origin

Nicholas Alkemade's Whistle

The whistle, seen in the photograph below, is the one that Nicholas Alkemade used to summon help after his remarkable survival of falling 18,000 feet without a parachute.

The whistle was taken from Nicholas as a souvenir by one of the German searchers who with others found Nicholas by following the sound of his whistle. The man who claimed the whistle, was a local named Gottfried Voss. He took the whistle from Nicholas just before they moved him to a nearby house. Nicholas could not walk due to his injuries, so the Germans dragged him there by placing him on an old tarpaulin they had found. The occupier of the house was an old lady with a kind face who gave him the finest Egg Nog he had ever tasted. After Nicholas had been taken away for medical treatment and interrogation, Gottfried Voss returned home and placed the whistle in a drawer where it lay for many years, until ex RAF Police Sergeant Sidney Thatcher and his German, locally-born wife Margot, became interested in the remarkable survival story of Nicholas Alkemade and were shown the whistle, still in the drawer where it was placed in 1944 by Gerhard's father Gottfried.

Mr. & Mrs. Thatcher persuaded Gerhard to let them return the whistle to Witchford and place it in the Display of Memorabilia situated on the Lancaster Way Business Park, formerly RAF Witchford.

On 25th June 2009, Mr. & Mrs. Thatcher returned the whistle to Witchford, 65 years after it left on its fateful journey, attached to Nicholas Alkemade's lapel.

Nicholas Alkemade's whistle in the Witchford Display of
Memorabilia 2013

The photo shows Mr. Thatcher handing over the whistle to
Barry Aldridge, the Curator of RAF Witchford Display of
Memorabilia

Sergeant Joe Cleary at the exact spot where he was found by Alfred Diedams, then a 16 year old. Alkemade was found no more than 200 metres away

Sergeant Joe Cleary with the hill in the background where Alkemade landed as did most of the wreckage and Joe

Sergeant Joe Cleary meeting Lieutenant H. Rokker, who shot
down the Lancaster on that fateful night

Sergeant Edgar William (Bill) Warren

Shot Down Over Germany

FLIGHT ENGINEER KILLED

Several months after he had been reported missing, the news has now been received that Sergeant Edgar William (Bill) Warren, R.A.F., son of Mrs. J. C. Sweetman, of "The Maze," Milward-crescent, has been killed in action.

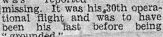

Sergeant Warren, who was 22, was a flight engineer, and it was after an operation over Berlin in the spring that he was reported missing. It was his 30th operational flight and was to have been his last before being "grounded."

Three of the crew of this bomber which, it is believed, was shot down, are prisoners-of-war, and four, including Sergeant Warren, were killed and have been buried at Oberkirchen, Germany.

An old boy of the Hastings Grammar School, Sergeant Warren was employed in the Hastings pay office of the Maidstone and District Motor Services, Ltd. In 1940 he joined the mobile section of the local Special Constabulary.

Early in 1941 he began training on aero-engines at an aircraft factory, and later volunteered as a flight engineer in the R.A.F.

He was engaged to Miss Peggy Dean, of Slough, and was to have been married at St. Paul's Church, Slough, at the end of last April. He attended the Wellington-square Baptist Church.

On Active Service

Death

WARREN. — Edgar William John (Bill), Sergt. R.A.F.V.R., aged 22 years, dearly loved son of Mr. and Mrs. J. C. Sweetman, of The Maze, Milward-crescent, Hastings, previously reported missing in March, now reported killed.

Sergeant Warren was Flight Engineer to Newman's crew and sadly did not return from the op to Berlin on 24th March 1944. The following are obituaries from the Hastings and St Leonards Observer newspaper.

Local author and historian Derek Booth recollects an early encounter with Bill:

During the summer of 1943, my mother, her childhood friend Joy and her half brother Bill Warren (an ex-Hastings Grammar School boy) took me on a picnic to Fairlight Cove, a dip in the Wealden hills on the coast east of Fairlight glen about 3 miles from Hastings. While we were there, one of those violent thunderstorms that brew up on a hot summer's day over the English Channel, menacingly moved over us whereupon we were forced to take shelter on the verandah of a deserted chalet; there was just a handful of these summer residences, a few houses and a hotel which constituted a hamlet at the Cove (today the area is a substantial suburban complex). The story ends with torrential rain and the rotting wooden seat we were sitting on suddenly collapsing under our weight and me being buried under bodies larger than mine!

Bill Warren was on leave as a flight engineer on Lancaster bombers with 115 Squadron based at Witchford near Ely, Cambridgeshire (about 12 miles from where I live today). Sadly, Bill was shot down in a Lancaster over Germany in March 1944 after carrying out a bombing raid on Berlin; he was only 22. Bill was engaged to be married later that spring and fatefully had volunteered to go into the air force without obligation because he was employed in an essential service in civilian life working as an office worker for the Maidstone & District Motor Services Ltd. Bill is buried at Oberkirchen in Germany and his name is entered in a memorial book at Ely Cathedral.

Excerpt taken from:

'Boy of the Wealden Shore: A Hastings Boyhood 1940 – 1960' by Derek Booth. ISBN: 978-0-9569026-0-3

Former Flight Sergeant Harry Rossiter

Wireless Operator to Flight Lieutenant David Jenkin`s crew gives us an insight on what life was like in Wartime Britain and his tour of operation with 115 Squadron based at RAF Witchford.

I once again set foot on my native land on 4th January 1944, after languishing in the Aircrew Transit Pool at Poona, India whence four of us had flown a new Bristol Beaufort torpedo bomber from Cornwall on 13th June 1943 to Jodpur, India, when all Beaufort aircraft had been declared obsolete. We then travelled by rail to Poona to spend time awaiting our fate. Well, what awaited us? Three weeks dis-embarkation leave was next, so on leave we went.

I went home at `Redruff` my home in Laindon Essex and spent a couple of days renewing family ties. I learned that some few months previously, Uncle Bill Aldridge had joined the RAF Now back in 1938, when there was first talk of a possible war he declared that if he was called up again, they would have to fish his corpse out of the garden well. Grannie told me that he had gone to the recruiting centre and taking ten years off his age and had volunteered to be an Air Gunner. Nobody was fooled by his regression in age and as his profession was in culinary matters, he was enlisted as a cook and was at an airfield somewhere in the Midlands. After a brief sojourn at home, I went to see Edna, my girlfriend, at a large Army Ordnance depot in Bicester Oxfordshire. I duly presented myself and Edna was granted a weeks' leave and I escorted her to her home in triumph. We, of course, spent much time together and one evening we went to a dance held at the Crown Hotel. This was situated at the top of Langdon Hill which at the `massive` height of 385 feet was reputed to be the highest point in Essex. Afterwards, we sat on a wooden seat situated at the side of the footpath just outside the `Crown` and after about a quarter of an hour or so, we decided to continue homewards. We hadn't realised just how cold the night was. As we rose from the seat there was the unfrosted outline of our occupation on the seat otherwise covered in frost. Ah! How unconscious is love? The day before Edna was due to return to her unit, I popped the question, would she marry me? I had no shyness in saying this and the reply was equally forthcoming in the affirmative. Doing the right thing, I sought her parents' consent for marriage. Father said, "Yes, you can marry Edna". Mother said, "Yes of course. Remember it is for life". Prophetic words they were. After Edna had gone, time hung a bit heavy. Grannie saw more of me of course and also mother now living back in Laindon. Brother Bill who was still a baker's roundsman, was awaiting call-up and was serving in the local Home Guard.

Then came the postings instructions. I was to go to RAF Station Millom in Cumberland. This unit was classified as No. 2 (O) Advanced Flying Unit. O standing for Observer. I duly presented myself there and was re-united with all the other ex-Beaufort wireless operator air gunners. We learned that we were re-training as Bomber Command wireless operators. We also learned that our reputation as 'trouble makers' had preceded us. Not that we were all guilty of insubordination but there it was. We were all 'tarred with the same brush' as the saying goes. We trained on Anson aircraft and a student navigator would be on the same aircraft. The Anson was roomy enough for this dual function. There was one incident which was not without its humour. The usual thing happened. There was some official who asked to be flown to RAF Wigtown, near Dunfries just across the Scottish border. It was a night exercise. After a perfect landing, the pilot was taxi-ing to the 'drop off' point when he managed to collide with a wooden post which was where it shouldn't have been. A large tear was made in the fabric under the port wing and that meant no more flying for us that night. We had to return to Millom by road and because of the River Solway Firth, we had to travel by way of Carlisle, then westwards to the Cumberland coast. To Carlisle, then by train and then by bus to Whitehaven on the coast. Whilst waiting for the bus, the pilot decided to buy us all a drink.

There we were in full flying kit and carrying parachute packs going into a pub and with curious onlookers, each of us treated to a pint by the pilot with an obvious sense of occasion. We were chuckling over these events (does this happen every night?). An individual approached us and producing a warrant card as an RAF Policeman asked us what the hell we were supposed to be doing. There was the pilot, navigational and wireless instructors, who each assailed him with the facts.

Some of their remarks weren't very polite. "Some of us earn our pay and why aren't you drinking?" Anyhow, he left convinced we weren't Nazi spies. After drinks were finished, we were on our way. We had to change buses at Whitehaven and here another amusing incident occured. The bus was crowded with the locals who were treated to much amusement. The bus conductor, anxious to assist 'our brave boys', went to hand out one of the parachute packs. He commenced to lift it by the nice shiny handle and was immediately assailed by about five voices shouting one word "No". He dropped it as though it was red hot. "That's the rip-cord handle. Don't touch it". The bus was convulsed with laughter and then drove off. We did not have long to wait for our bus that was to carry us to Millom and our 'home base'.

Whilst at Millom, I wrote to the Rector of Langdon Hills, my old friend the Reverend T. Hickson and asked him if he could marry us at short notice. I hastened to re-assure him for the haste as it would be in between courses. He replied reminding me that he knew us both and would be very pleased to arrange the marriage by obtaining a special licence. The date was fixed for 29th March. As it was during Lent, there could not be any bells rung and it was too short notice for any music or choir. I replied with thanks and promised not to be late.

The course at Millom was due to finish about 24th March as far as I can remember. Edna's Aunt Viv made the cake specially and Edna borrowed a wedding dress from one of her A.T.S. friends. I went to the clothing store at Millom and asked if I could be issued with a new tunic for the occasion, as my present one seemed fairly shapeless. I was greeted with a negative response and the result can be seen to this day in my wedding portrait. However, nothing could spoil our magical day. The ceremony was performed at the church of St. Mary on Langdon Hills by Reverend Hickson. It was attended by Edna's mum and dad and her step-grandmother, her uncle Bert and his cake-making wife Aunt Viv, her uncle Harold and his wife and daughter Rosemary. A little girl Iris, the daughter of Aunt Viv was the bridesmaid. My mother and John Ryan, Grannie of course and Aunt Agnes, and Eddie was my bestman. In one of the wedding photos, he stands beside me, a Corporal service policeman, which looks as if I had been 'let out' just to get married. Also attending was my old friend Ken Shaw. At the conclusion of the ceremony, when Reverend Hickson pronounced us man and wife, he prompted me in no uncertain fashion. "Well go on Harry, kiss her", which I did with some enthusiasm. We had a reception at Edna's house, then she changed out of wedding dress into a two-piece suit with a hat perched at a saucy angle and we went to the railway station to go to Southend, where Edna's dad Georgie had arranged for us to stay at a boarding house, which considering the war, was well done.

We had six days for our honeymoon. I was due to report to Number 84 (Bomber) O.T.U. at Silverstone on 4th April 1944. Nothing daunted, I sent a telegram requesting an extension of leave. The reply was swift and to the point, `No. Report as ordered on 4.4.44`, so orf I had perchance to go and Edna, who had been granted a couple of days more than I, went home.

Well there was more `messing about`. At Silverstone we were told to get crewed up. A crew of six was to be formed in the first phase as we were to train on Wellington bombers which had six as a crew. I found myself a pilot, who sized me up with `You'll do` attitude.

Then we acquired a navigator, a hard-headed Yorkshire man, who turned out to be first class at his job. The pilot was Flying Officer David Jenkins, a medical student in 'civvy' street. The navigator was a Flying Officer Bill Ranson who in a former existence was a pharmaceutical chemist (he said). Then we acquired a 'merry' Ulsterman from Dungannon, Flying Officer Bob Patton who was to be our bomb aimer. Following on these, came Sergeant Bill Phillips from Cardiff, South Wales. Now he was a regular, that is, he had known no other existence since leaving school apart from the air force. He was to be our flight engineer. Finally we needed an air gunner. He came in the form of Reg Begon a French Canadian from Vancouver, British Columbia. He was a big lad and boasted of having once been a lumberjack.

There was an introductory address by the Senior Instructor, a squadron leader something-or-other. However he caused some amusement by announcing "One of your number has recently taken a wife and is so much enjoying married life that he applied to have his leave extended". Some hopes. A former Beaufort wireless operator A.G. whom I knew, Peter Barr, sitting besides me gave a nudge in the ribs saying, "I bet that was you". To which I grinned and said nothing. The `curse` surrounding me of being messed about struck again. It transpired that the course

368

was over manned. So two of three crews, including us, were sent to No. 12 (B) O.T.U. at Chipping Warden, whence we were taken by coach. One of the other crews affected was Peter's crew. We became quite friendly with them; they were a cheerful lot and we usually visited the same pubs.

However, we arrived at our new destination, only to be told that we were to be transferred to a satellite airfield called Edgehill, close to the site of a famous 17th century battle. This was to complete what was called pre-O.T.U. Training. Wellington aircraft were used by all aircrew trades to check that efficency had been achieved, before we started the `real stuff`. Now I had a bike with me and when there was any time off, or other spare time, I used to cycle cross country to Bicester to see Edna. Whatever she was doing, she was allowed a few hours to be with me. The nearest town of any size was Banbury, through which I used to cycle on my way to see Edna. We could go to the cinema if we had enough time or, the weather being warm and sunny, we would go for walks in the surrounding countryside.

The course finished about the middle of June. There was a spot of leave and once more I assailed the ears of the A.T.S. hierarchy to success. There was a slight hesitation on their part for a good reason. The invasion of Europe was now under way and ordnance depots were working at full capacity, supplying arms and equipment to the army in the field. Nevertheless, leave was granted and home we came. Now it had been decided that we should have a small room of our own at Edna's home, a bungalow called `Jeanette` in Cecil Drive, Laindon. Leave lasted 7 days, then I was ordered to proceed to what was known as a Heavy Conversion Unit. In other words, flying the `4-engined stuff`.

This unit was at Shepherds Grove, Suffolk and we were to fly Stirling 4-engined bombers. We needed to acquire our seventh crew member, another air-gunner. This proved to be Bill Goulborn, a farmer from Northwich, Cheshire. By mutual agreement it seemed, Reg would be the mid upper gunner and Bill would be the rear gunner. 'Tail end Charlie' as rear gunners were called. The course was simple enough. The flight engineer Bill Phillips came into his own and David Jenkins learned to fly the 'big stuff'. It had large propellers and thus required massive undercarriage. It was something from my wireless operator's position, to see the undercarriage being

369

retracted as the monster took to the air. There followed a turning this way and that, of what seemed steel girders all neatly following their pre-destined course to disappear up their own stowage. This course was 3 weeks long and then we were sent to the final stage of training. This was No. 3 Lancaster Finishing School at a place called Woolfox Lodge in Rutland. Now this was about the 8th of August. It transpired that David Jenkins had his 22nd birthday on the 10th of August. Mine of course was the next day, when I would also be 22 years old.

Down the A1 (Great North Road) was a famous hotel known as the Ram Jam Inn alleged to be a haunt of Dick Turpin and other highwaymen. It was possibly a model for the poem 'The Highwayman' by Alfred Noyes. Anyway, be that as it may, David said he would treat us all to dinner at this hostelry and on the 10th August, we all made our way after a day's flying. It was very pleasant and there were one or two amusing moments at Reg's expense which he took all in good part and a merry time was had by all.

At Woolfox Lodge we were introduced to the Lancaster bomber. By contrast to the Stirling it seemed much neater. Everything was much the same as the Stirling but better designed. One example was the fuel tank system. To change tanks on the Stirling one had to operate levers to select the required tanks and there were seven levers for port wing tanks and seven for the starboard wing. On the Lancaster, all Bill needed to do was to turn two rotary switches, one for the port tanks and one for the other side. The Lancaster sat lower to the ground than the Stirling and was easier to get in and out of. Its bomb load was impressive and versatile. The weight of bombs carried was 13,000 lbs and could be varied to suit requirements of the raid.

So the time of piping peace was over and we were on our way to the sharp end. On the 15th of August 1944 Peter Barr's crew went to 622 Squadron at Mildenhall and we went to 115 Squadron at RAF Witchford near Ely in Cambridgeshire.

Pilot David Jenkins' crew – the crew of KO-C for Charlie 115 Squadron 16th December 1944 at RAF Witchford

Standing left to right:

Sergeant Bill Phillips flight engineer. Flight Sergeant Les Alger mid upper gunner, Flying Officer Bill Ranson navigator, Flight Lieutenant David Jenkins pilot, Flying Officer Bob Patton bomb aimer, Flight Sergeant Harry Rossiter wireless operator/ air gunner.

<u>*Front kneeling:*</u>

Flight Sergeant Bill Goulborn rear gunner and Flight Sergeant Reg Begon RCAF mid upper gunner.

On the 15th August 1944, I became a member of 115 Squadron Royal Air Force and as such was required to take part in operations against our national foe, Nazi Germany. Our crew, led by Flying Officer David Jenkins, was assigned to `A` Flight, comanded by Squadron Leader McFadyean. We were assigned Lancaster HK 578 which was `C` for Charlie. The squadron had the identifying letters KO for `A` and `B` flights and `A4` for `C` flight. Each aircrew trade had its own training leader usually a Flight Lieutenant. The Signals Leader was Flight Lieutenant

Hartley. Each day on the sergeant's notice board and no doubt similarly for the officers mess, there would appear the `Battle Order`, naming the crews who were to fly operations that day or night. By the way, about this time, Edna my wife broke the news to me that I was to be a father about the beginning of March 1945. Every six weeks, we got six days leave and on these occasions, I would collect Edna from the Bicester ordnance depot and go home with her.

Our crew appeared on the battle order of the 26th August. That morning, David phoned me in the Sergeants Mess with the sad news that Flying Officer `Joe` Holdsworth and his crew had gone missing from the previous night's operations. This was Peter Barr's crew. As we had all been 'drinking' partners, this was indeed saddening for us. This was an indication of what to expect in future. The first indication of the briefing for ops was the announcement over the address system that there would be a lecture for navigators. This was usually just after lunch. The time of the main briefing would be on battle orders. Now I do not intend to dwell much on what followed. All our valuables and any means of identification (apart from our identity tags constantly worn round the neck) were deposited in a crew bag and left behind, and we were issued with flight rations, glucose sweets, chewing gum and chocolate. There followed details concerning route, bomb load, flak positions and times. Then about 100 or so young men from most parts of the Commonwealth would gather up their impedimenta and cram into crew buses to be taken their aircraft at various dispersal points around the airfield. `C` for Charlie shared a dispersal point with `G` for George. This was a crew whose captain was a Flight Lieutenant George Dowling. The navigator was Flight Sergeant Ken French who dwelt in the same hut as I did. Mr. Dowling was famed for being able to supply 64 reasons for not doing some particular task or other. We would stand together smoking and chatting until, either him or David would glance at their watches and say "Right boys, let's go".

A few minutes later the silence would be shattered by Merlin engines being started up, and one by one we lifted off into the evening sky, heading for Hitlers Reich. The targets were usually factories or oil plants and mostly in the Ruhr valley, home of Hitler's armaments factories. This first time for us, was the port of Kiel. Suffice it to say, we saw our first enemy anti-aircraft fire we called flak. We were not at all affected by this and we duly deposited our 13,000 lbs of high explosive and came home. From this raid, one of our squadron failed to return. Now it must be said, in my subsequent thoughts, I have realised that our efforts cost the lives of many innocent people. That is the price of waging war, which is the epitome of evil.

At this time we were just young men doing a job which was dangerous but vital to the defeat of our enemy. Bomber Command paid a very heavy price for its role in that war. A total of fifty six thousand aircrew were posted as 'killed in action'. My boyhood friend Vic Nunn was included in this latter category.

The second op' I was part of was with another crew, whose wireless operator, Sergeant Piper, was sick with a severe cold and with such a complaint, flying at 20,000 feet was simply not to be countenanced. This crew, skippered by Flight Sergeant Cooper, asked David's permission to borrow me to make up his crew. After getting my agreement, I duly presented myself for the job. Now this one was to be different from any other op' I took part in. The target was Stettin, on the Baltic coast where a lot of German shipping was repaired and was considered by the enemy to be out of our reach. The route took us over Southern Sweden and the total operational time was nine hours. What was so different was the fact that we had been designated a 'wind finding' aircraft. This entailed the navigator and bomb aimer between them estimating wind speed and direction every half hour or so and sending the results back to base. This kept me busy, when normally strict radio silence was observed.

Despite radio jamming, I contrived to get all my messages through and got a pat on the back from Mr. Hartley the next day. There were some enemy night fighters about, but we were lucky enough not to receive their attentions. From this operation, the squadron lost three aircraft. I should explain 'wind' finding.

From all the information received in these messages, Bomber Command would calculate a good average wind speed and direction and this would be given to the main force half an hour before zero hour to use in their bombing run. I remember that we took off at dusk and landed at dawn. After each op' we would be de-briefed by specialists at their job, we being supplied with mugs of hot coffee laced with rum. There were few who did not down this welcome hot drink and then to bed. There were quite a lot of daylight raids, as at this time, fighter squadrons were based in France and could provide fighter escort for the bombers and very effective they proved. Now a new navigational aid was taken into use. There was already such a device which was referred to as the 'G' box, which gave the navigator a good idea where he was. This updated box was called 'Gh' and gave the navigator and bomb aimer the exact spot in the sky to release the bomb load. This device was set up for a particular target and, having fed into it relevant wind speed and direction, all the bomb aimer had to do was to see radar 'blips' line up and then release the bombs.

There were several targets that we did not see, but dropped bombs above clouds. Our aircraft was desigated a 'Gh' leader and two others would formate on us and copy our bombing manoeuvres. There was no denying however, the accuracy of the enemy anti-aircraft guns. We dropped bundles of metallised strips code named window, to confuse the flak radar. Woe betide any crew who comtemplated taking a short cut as to be first home, which was the custom with those on their final trip, before taking six months rest from ops.

About the beginning of October, we acquired an extra crew member. There was a large hole in the aircraft floor, and over this was mounted a 50 calibre Browning machinegun and this was manned by Flight Sergeant Les Alger. All aircrew not required for ops that day were obliged to report to their respective leaders. To my surprise one day in November, Flight Lieutenant Hartley said to me, "Ross, I'm putting you up for commission. Are you ready for it?" After thanking him for his considerations, I agreed.

I am unable to remember exactly when it was, but one day I received a telegram from Edna which stated, can meet you in Ely Market Place tomorrow about midday. I showed this to Flight Lieutenant Hartley and his remark was, " I don't see how, as you might be on battle order tomorrow". Then, remembering something Edna had told me, that if she could manage such an occasion, she would be staying overnight with one of her colleagues at a nearby village called Wardy Hill. I told Mr. Hartley about this and he said, "Well there you are. Go there this evening and in such a small place it shouldn't be difficult to find her". So that is what happened and going into the village pub enquired among the locals if there was an A.T.S. girl living there. As a result of information received, as they say, I went to the house indicated. I explained my business there, and was welcomed to stay to meet Edna, which I did and she was more than surprised when she walked in the door to be greeted by me. I spent a short while there and if I wasn't flying tomorrow I would come back. As it transpired, I was free to do just that with my chief's blessing and we spent several hours together. An unexpected happy time.

Now about this time, there had been changes in the squadron. The popular squadron commander, who was Wing Commander Devas, was promoted Group Captain and moved on. No longer would we see his cheery on his visits to the Sergeants Mess. His reason for going was however a world better than losing him the other way. Our equally popular Flight Commander, Squadron Leader Castle was lost on ops. It was alleged his aircraft had collided with another of `A` flight piloted by Flight Lieutenant Davidson of the Canadian Air Force. Both aircraft were lost. The wireless operator of Mr. Davidson's crew, Flying Officer Joe Dunford, also a Canadian, was a friend of mine. "Hi-ya Harry", he would exclaim when we met. "Read any good books lately?" This was because he was an avid reader and when off duty, was invariably seen with a book in his hand. I missed him and so many like him. There was another cheery soul who seemed indestructible, Jackie Lynch who, like so many others, just disappeared in those troubled skies.

We did survive two or three fighter attacks during our night operations. In one low level attack on a German position, in a daytime raid, we received a cannon shell in the port outer engine. A Lancaster could and did fly fairly well on three engines, so we were in no immediate danger.

However, I had been promoted Flight Sergeant by this time and on a day appointed, I was interviewed by the Flight Commander, Squadron Leader Gorrie. He was under no misapprehension as to my standard of education, but sent me to be seen by the new Squadron Commander, Wing Commander Shaw, straight from training station, where no doubt he had been enjoying his six months ops break. He was equally cool concerning my prospects of becoming a temporary officer and a Gentleman. However he gave me the following advice which seemed to be equally out of touch with reality. "Find a good officer and see where your shortcomings lie". Later on that one. Anyway, I was comfronted by Mr. Hartley who told me, "They have recommended that you try again in 6 months time, by which period, you might find your 'good officer". Always the wit was Mr. Hartley.

Well, came the day for our final op. Never mind where it was, but the weather closed in and we were all ordered to return to base and jettison our bomb load in designated areas. Now this was 15th December 1944. This a day most remembered by fans of popular dancebands, including Glenn Miller. He went missing in a flight across the Channel when he should not have been allowed to as the weather was appalling, with snow in some places and thick fog in others. It has been established that his light aircraft was brought down into the English Channel by jettisoned bombs. This was not of any of our doings, as our jettison area was The Wash. However the following day, the weather had cleared and we went off to where we should have gone before.

On 16th December 1944, we had survived a tour of thirty operations. In usual circumstances this was only true for the pilot as his first op was with another crew, so the rest of us only did twenty nine. I was different (trust me). I did thirty as I did that odd op with another crew on the Stettin raid. In all the raids that I was involved, the squadron lost twenty four aircraft. I later learned that 115 had a reputation of being the most involved bomber squadron with the consequent heaviest losses. As Bill Phillips said to me in later years, "We were bloody lucky. We must have been saved for some reason. I expect Jenks had something to do with it".

I wish here to refer that earlier reference concerning me being told to 'seek out a good officer to learn my shortcomings'. In the evening following our last op there was a party in the officer's mess. Our bomb aimer Flying Officer Paddy Patton went missing and was found the following morning dead drunk in the officers mess lavatory. Such a good officer.

Incidently, before we left the squadron, the whole crew were summoned before the Station Commander, Group Captain Mac. C. Reynolds. He invited us to volunteer for the Pathfinder Force, but we had to go as the entire crew or not at all.

Now I have said that our navigator, Bill Ranson, was a hard-headed Yorkshireman. He immediately replied, "I don't wish to fly with him any more, pointing to David Jenkins, who incidentally for his troubles was awarded the DFC. So that was that.

We were sent on a fortnight's leave and I went down to Bicester to escort Edna out of the A.T.S. She had been given her discharge 'for family reasons'. It was rather strange this time.

As I walked through the gates through which I had passed several times unchallenged, I was met by a uniformed War Department Constable, who demanded to know, in no uncertain fashion, what business an airman had at one of His Majesty's ordnance depots. He got slightly annoyed at my obvious amusement, until I explained the number of times I had gone unchallenged, athough I had always shown my identity card to the guard room and this was to be my last visit, as my wife was being discharged from the A.T.S. He wished me luck and would I see him on my way out, which I did. Good bloke, doing his job.

I returned to the squadron just after New Year 1945 and we did one last flight together to air test a Lancaster after a major inspection. Then we were sent our respective ways and I never saw any of them again. For some reason, I was sent straight from the squadron to a unit in the North of Scotland, called Brackla, near the town of Nairn. It rejoiced in the title of 'Air Crew Re-allocation Centre'. The weather was severe, all water supplies being frozen solid. Fortunately, the deep snow provided the cookhouse with sufficient water and chemical lavatories were installed, which some unfortunate person or persons were obliged to empty. I had stated my wish to transfer to Sunderland flying boats, but for this situation, I needed to be a wireless operator mechanic. I was given aptitude tests of various kinds and was told I was 'a bright boy'. After two weeks of 'roughing' it at Brackla I, and several others, were given our marching orders. I was to go to an air sea rescue station at the Suffolk town of Beccles.

Flight Lieutenant Archibald Russell

Flight Lieutenant Russell

The following account was written by Archibald's son from his father's dictation.

Full Moon, Cloudless Sky. D-Day, plus 1st - 7th June 1944

Flight Lieutenant Archibald Russell, then a Flight Sergeant, was the Flight Engineer.

The Lancaster in which he was flying set out on the night of 7th/8th June 1944 to attack targets in the Chevreuse-Massey-Paliseau area, just south of Paris. The aircraft bombed the railway to stop the Germans using it for movement of reinforcements.

The Lancaster was attacked by two German fighters, the rear gunner was wounded and all engines set on fire. Archie went to the rear of the aircraft to check on the gunner and saw he had bailed out. He extinguished the fire in the fuselage, spoke to the skipper on the intercom and was told to return to the cockpit and assist him to put on his parachute. They then both bailed out at 700 feet. On the way down, Archie saw the wings of the aircraft break off and the fuselage nose-dive into the ground. All the crew managed to leave the airfraft and land safely. The rear gunner died later.

Archie realised on landing that he had lost a flying boot. He took his parachute to a nearby house, retraced his footsteps and jumped into a bed of nettles about 100 yards from the burning aircraft to gather his thoughts together. He heard German vehicles and troops arrive and decided when the panic was at its height to move out of the nettles and commenced walking down the road. He took off his battle dress tunic and tossed it over a hedge, the verges on both sides of the road were lined with poplar trees which gave excellent cover from oncoming vehicles.

As dawn broke, he left the road and went into a forest intending to hide. Fortunately, he saw a cottage and decided to contact the occupants. A man opened the door and Archie explained in schoolboy French that he was a Sergeant in the Royal Air Force. The forester spoke to his wife, then took him into the forest to hide and await his return. At this point, Archie had no idea whether the forester would assist him or notify the Germans. Within the hour, he returned bringing a mug of goat's milk and explained that he would try to contact the Resistance and have Archie moved from the forest before the Germans launched a full-scale hunt for surviving aircrew. The forest was near a German airfield, Vera Coubley and in fact the Germans searched for the aircrew for two whole days.

At about 7 0'clock that evening, the forester returned and asked if Archie could ride a bicycle. He said that he had contacted the Resistance and two men arrived and gave Archie a pair of shoes and a jacket. They took him along a track where there were three bicycles and said that he was to follow the front man, not to talk to anyone and that the second man would bring up the rear. Before long, they came to the main gate to the German aerodrome and passed without trouble and shortly after, Archie was taken into a house at Vera Coubley, given a meal and afterwards moved into what appeared to be a garden summer house to remain there until contacted.

The next day, Archie was visited by a young woman wanting information about his crew and the aircraft, the only information she got from him was name, rank and service number. The people who were looking after him said that she would come back again and must be given answers to her questions.

Upon her return, she gave Archie a full run-down on the crew by name, the type of aircraft, his name and the information that the rear gunner was dead. This information convinced Archie that he was with the Resistance.

Approximately two weeks later, Archie was escorted to Paris on the Metro. As he emerged from the Metro, he saw a large swastika flag over the entrance to an imposing building. As they came opposite the entrance to the building, they turned at right angles down a road and entered a café where they went into a back room and met four or five people. A lot of talking took place and before long, Archie was taken over the road into headquarters of the Garde Republique, where he was reunited with his mid upper gunner and was informed that the navigator was also in Paris. Unfortunately, the bomb aimer was stopped by a German patrol and endeavoured to run away, resulting in his being shot.

The Commandant of the Garde Republique and his wife, Madeleine, were both members of the Resistance (he was later to be arrested and sent to a concentration camp, but survived) and it was she who took Archie to his first accommodation in Paris and supplied him with a false documentation, identity card and ration card. From that moment, he became Jean Cartier, although he was unable to speak much French!

In order to obtain a photograph for his identity card, he was taken to a booth in one of Paris' railway stations. While waiting to be picked up by the Resistance, he was approached by two German Officers who asked him questions, presumably about the train service. He knew that if he opened his mouth, all would be lost. With incredible presence of mind, he pretended to be both deaf and dumb, touching his ears and mouth and making gurgling noises. The officers retreated in disgust!

In all, he was hidden in three seperate flats in Paris, first at St. Denis, then St. Germain and finally, near the Jardins Zoologiques.

On leaving Paris, he was brought together with the two other crew members and moved by the Resistance to a farm north of Paris. That evening, just about everybody from the village called to see the RAF airmen – which did not seem to them to be very good for their security.

Later in the week, they were visited by an escape route organiser, but nothing came from this, although he returned two days later and asked them what they wanted to do. The resistance had discussed the idea of taking the airmen through the German lines to reunite them with allied troops. But it was not possible. After some discussion, they agreed to make for Dieppe, hoping to get back to England via the Channel.

The next thing was that two youngsters, a boy of 12 years and a girl of 10 years, arrived at the farm with bicycles and escorted them to Beauvais. This was an uneventful journey thanks to the capability of the youngsters. Years later, the boy and girl married and Archie was given a copy of their wedding photograph.

On arrival at Beauvais, they were housed with a family consisting of husband, wife and niece. The crewmen were reluctant to stay put and await liberation and they explained that they wanted to get to Dieppe. The husband said that he would organise bicycles and escort them there, which he did ten days later.

When they arrived in Dieppe, they took cover in a cave in the chalk cliffs where they were told to await instructions. After about two hours, Monsieur le Cure took them to a house in Dieppe, belonging to Mme. Malige. By then, they had realised that the town was full of Germans. Shortly after they arrived at the house, a German soldier knocked at the door demanding a room for an officer. Mme. Malige told the soldier that she did not have an air-raid shelter and that it would be better for the soldier to look for a room elsewhere. The crewmen spent that night on the roof of the house in order to protect Mme. Malige in the event of their being caught by the Germans.

It was clear that the crewmen could not stay in Dieppe. The Maliges and their friends organised a haycart in which the airmen hid. The driver of the haycart took them through three German checkpoints before they were clear of Dieppe's restricted area. Then they were on their own and they decided to return to Beauvais on foot.

Their first encounter came when they walked into a wood to get out of the sun and have a rest, only to find a number of German tanks and their crews were already there. They therefore walked straight on through the wood and did not meet any trouble. Later in the day, they discovered a hay barn and decided to spend the night there.

The following morning when they got up, they were covered with insects so they plunged into a nearby pond to get rid of them. As they got out of the pond, they saw a number of Germans having what looked like breakfast. The crewmen gave them a wave, to which they responded, and carried on.

Later that day, they saw a convoy of farm waggons driven by children under the guidance of two elderly people. The youngsters made signs that they had cigarettes, but wanted matches, they gave them a light and were given three cigarettes. The waggons appeared to be transporting V-bombs! Their next encounter was with a German staff car, which was endeavouring to pinpoint a fighter aircraft that had been shot down. They pointed back towards Dieppe, the staff car turned and drove away.

By now their feet were feeling the effects of the walk and their mouths were extremely dry. By the time they arrived back at Beauvais, at the same house as before, they needed a few days rest to get their feet back into shape.

They were then taken to Les Anderlys, just north of the Seine, to stay with an elderly couple who were looking after another RAF airman, not part of their crew, who had been wounded. The man was a Jesuit who had been a missionary in Algeria before the war and who could not return because of the war. The Jesuit had nursed the wounded airman and he had almost recovered.

Archie and his crewmates stayed at the house in Les Anderlys about a week. The Germans were now in retreat. A Canadian officer arrived at the house as part of an advance party and the next morning British soldiers arrived in tanks and the RAF men were able to make contact with them.

Later, they were escorted to Lisieux, de-briefed by English officers and flown back to England from St. Lo.

They had been on the run for three months, with the help of the Resistance.

Of the six Lancasters that set out from RAF Witchford on that night of 7th June 1944, one was shot down over the Channel, two were shot down over Normandy and two were shot down over the target area. Only one returned safely.

The Wait Back Home

Meanwhile, the family waited back home. Archie's wife, Ena, knew where he was stationed and that he was on operational duties, but never knew just when he would be flying on a mission.

The first she even knew that he was flying on the night of June 7th/8th was when the telegram arrived with the news that his plane had been shot down and he was reported missing. At that stage, Ena had no idea whether her husband was dead or alive, whether he had escaped or was a POW. The telegram was followed up by a letter from Archie's Commanding Officer, but still no definite news one way or the other. All she knew was that the plane had come down in France.

There then followed weeks of waiting for news at the same time as trying to lead as normal a life as possible, caring for their young son. The days turned into weeks and weeks into months and still no news. Then, in September 1944, Ena received two letters. The first from the Commander of the 8th Canadian Reconnaissance Regiment with the news that Archie's name had been passed on to him by the French Underground and that he was alive and well. The second, from a Major in the Royal Artillery, who had promised the Frenchwoman who had sheltered Archie and two of his crew members for eight days, that he would get news through that Archie was O.K.

For the safety of the French Underground, neither letter could give many details. Ena didn't know how recent the news of Archie's survival was, but the letters gave her hope.

Not long after these letters, the long-awaited telegram from the Air Ministry arrived with the news that Archie was safe and well and in England. In fact, Archie had beaten them to it. He arrived home to Ena the day before the official telegram arrived.

Postscript

After some leave at home, Flight Sergeant Russell joined another bomber aircrew. Their task was to drop equipment and supplies to the Resistance in France and other parts of Europe.

At the end of the war, the airmen who had been helped by the Resistance formed an organisation called the RAF Escaping Society. Its purpose was to try to help the men and women of the Resistance who were in need because of their sacrifices during the war. The RAF Escaping Society was wound up after 50 years.

Also, fifty years on from V.E. Day, Archie was able to go back to France and visit Mme. Malige. By then, she was living in the small village of Crillon-le-Brave in Provence near Mont Ventoux. Mme. Malige had kept in touch with some of the airmen whom she had helped and had written to Archie the previous Christmas with an invitation to visit her if at all possible.

Mme. Malige was living on a smallholding, growing olive trees, and living with her was Monsieur le Cure, who was her brother-in-law. By then, her husband was dead. There was chance for a long conversation and Mme. Malige took Archie into her study where she was proud to show him a letter from General Einsenhower thanking her for the help she had given to American airmen. She had also been presented with the Legion d'Honneur.

The Mayor of Crillon gave a civic reception for Archie, where he spoke of Archie's war exploits. Archie found this somewhat embarrassing, but the Mayor was adamant that if it had not been for men like Archie, things would be very different and France would still be under German occupation.

Collated 6th February 2011.

Date	Hour	Aircraft Type and No.	Pilot	Duty	Remarks (including results of bombing, gunnery, exercises, etc.)	Flying Times Day	Night
		115 SQUADRON			WITCHFORD 3 Group Time carried forward :—	41.30	30.30
22.5.44	1045	LANCASTER LL936 "Y"	F/O CAMERON	F/ENGINEER	OPS — TURNED BACK [INTERCOM. U/S.]	1.15	
24.5.44	0009	ND761 "C"	" CAMERON	" "	OPERATIONS — BOULOGNE. N° I		1.50
28.5.44	1145	HK.555	" LAW	"	HK TEST	4.00	
28.5.44	1512	HK.555	" "	"	" (X-Cry)	5.30	
28.5.44	1820	HK.555	" "	"	FERRY Waterbeach to Base.	0.10	
29.5.44	1885	LL.925	" "	"	S.N.R + X-Cry.	2.45	
						7.25	3.05

6.6.44	0030	HK.660 "Y"	P/O LAW	Engineer	OPS. — LISIEUX — N° II	2.50
7.6.44	0220	"	"	"	" MISSING.	1.00

TOTAL TIME ... 55.10 | 44.20

Units at which served						Aircraft in which flown		
Unit	From	To	Unit	From	To	Type	Type	Type
1651 C.U.	25.2.44	3.5.44				WELLINGTON I.C.		
No.1 LFS. Feltwell	3.5.44	20.5.44				STIRLING I.		
115 SQN. Witchford	20.5.44	7.6.44				" III.		
FRANCE	2.8.44					DOUGLAS D.C.3.		
1658 H.C.U. Riccall	9.10.44	2.11.44				OXFORD II.		
297 Sqdn. Earls Colne	2.11.44					LANCASTER I.		
297 Sqdn. " "						" III.		
297 Sqdn. " "						ALBERMARLE VI.		
297 Sqdn. " "						HALIFAX II.		
297 Sqdn. " "						" V.		
Rivenhall	27.6.44					" VII.		

1939-45 Star. France Germany Star. Defence Medal.
1939-45 Victory Medal. Normandy Campaigne.
Bomber Command. Battle of Britain.

Copy of Archie's log book

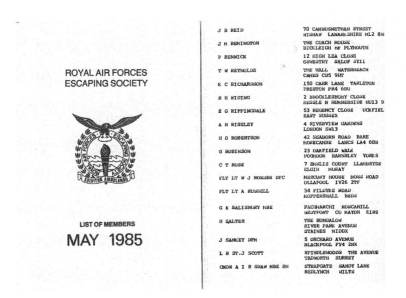

Copy of Certificate of Qualification

ROYAL AIR FORCES ESCAPING SOCIETY

LIST OF MEMBERS

MAY 1985

J B REID	70 CAMBUSNETHAN STREET WISHAW LANARKSHIRE ML2 8N
J M REMINGTON	THE COACH HOUSE BICKLEIGH nr PLYMOUTH
P RENWICK	12 HIGH LEA CLOSE OSWESTRY SALOP SY11
T W REYNOLDS	THE HALL WATERBEACH CAMBS CB5 9HT
K C RICHARDSON	150 CARR LANE TARLETON PRESTON PR4 6BU
R H RIDING	2 BROCKLESBURY CLOSE HESSLE N HUMBERSIDE HU13 9
E G RIPPINGDALE	53 REGENCY CLOSE UCKFIEL EAST SUSSEX
A H RISELEY	4 RIVERVIEW GARDENS LONDON SW13
H O ROBERTSON	42 SEABORN ROAD BARE MORECAMBE LANCS LA4 6BB
G ROBINSON	23 OAKFIELD WALK POGMOOR BARNSLEY YORKS
C T ROSE	7 EMSLIE COURT LLANBRYDE ELGIN MORAY
FLT LT W J ROSSER DFC	MERCURY HOUSE MOSS ROAD ULLAPOOL IV26 2TF
FLT LT A RUSSELL	54 FILDYKE ROAD HOPPERSHALL BEDS
G E SALISBURY MBE	PACIMARCHI ROSCAHILL WESTPORT CO MAYON EIRE
H SALTER	THE BUNGALOW RIVER PARK AVENUE STAINES MIDDX
J SANKEY DFM	5 ORCHARD AVENUE BLACKPOOL FY4 2NX
L R ST.J SCOTT	SPINDLEWOODS THE AVENUE TADWORTH SURREY
CMDR A I R SHAW MBE RN	STEAPGATE SANDY LANE REDLYNCH WILTS

Copy of Royal Air Forces Escaping Society Membership Card

Squadron Leader H.W. Castle

Squadron Leader Castle

At 12.40pm on 15th November 1944, Squadron Leader Castle and crew took off from Witchford in Lancaster MK1 KO-A HK595 to bomb the synthetic oil plant at Dortmund. A total of nineteen 115 squadron aircraft and crews were taking part in this operation. The target was bombed in 10/10 cloud using special apparatus. The P.F.F. markers were well concentrated and crews were confident that bombing was good, although the cloud prevented assessment of results. No fighters were seen and flak was moderate at first, but subsequently developed into a loose barrage and then died away. Two aircraft flying in formation were seen to explode in the air. Squadron Leader Castle and his unusual crew of nine were one of the two Witchford crews that failed to return to base. There were no survivors. Four are buried in the Reichswald Forest War Cemetery, while the rest are commemorated on the Runnymede memorial.

Squadron Leader H.W. Castle	*Pilot*
Flight Sergeant B. Collinson	*Navigator*
Sergeant A. Gribble	*Bomb Aimer*
Flight Sergeant F. Burrows RAAF	*Wireless Operator/Air Gunner*
Flight Sergeant R. Stickland RAAF	*Mid Upper Gunner*
Warrant Officer R. O'Sullivan RAAF	*Rear Gunner*
Pilot Officer G.F. Dawson RCAF	*Mid Under Gunner*
Sergeant G. Sampson	*Flight Engineer*
Flying Officer P.D. Mullet	*2nd Pilot*

The second Lancaster MK1 KO-B NN706 piloted by Flight Lieutenant J.W. Davidson of the Royal Canadian Air Force had taken off one minute behind Squadron Leader Castle and suffered the same fate. All are buried at Reichswald Cemetery.

Flight Lieutenant J.W. Davidson RCAF   *Pilot*
Flying Officer J.H. Powner   *Navigator*
Flying Officer C.D. Dowse   *Bomb Aimer*
Flying Officer J.R. Dunford RCAF   *Wireless Operator*
Flight Sergeant D. Page RCAF   *Mid Upper Gunner*
Flight Sergeant K. Crayston RCAF   *Rear Gunner*
Sergeant A. Gillibrand   *Flight Engineer*

Of the 177 Lancasters from 3 Group that carried out the attack on the oil plant, Squadron Leader Castle and Flight Lieutenant Davidson's crews were the only losses.

Lancaster HK595 was one of 200 Lancaster MK1 delivered between December 1943 and February 1945 by Vickers Armstrongs of Castle Bromwich.

Lancaster NN706, like HK595, was also delivered new to 115 Squadron. One of 400 Lancaster MK1s delivered between July 1944 and February 1945 by Armstrong Whitworth, Baginton.

This scroll commemorates

Flight Lieutenant H. W. Castle
Royal Air Force

held in honour as one who
served King and Country in
the world war of 1939-1945
and gave his life to save
mankind from tyranny. May
his sacrifice help to bring
the peace and freedom for
which he died.

The Scroll

Date	Aircraft Type & Number	Crew	Duty	Time Up	Time Down	Details of Sortie or Flight	References
1944 15th Nov.						DORTMUND was the target today. 19 aircraft were detailed to attack synthetic oil plant in 10/10 cloud. Bombing was carried out by special apparatus. Markers were well concentrated & crews were confident that bombing was good, although cloud prevented assessment of results. No enemy fighters were seen; flak at first was moderate and accurate but subsequently developed into a loose barrage and then died away. 2 aircraft flying in formation were seen to explode in air. BOMB LOAD - Each aircraft carried 1 x 4,000lb H.C. & 16 x 500lb G.P. bombs.	161
	Lancaster Mk.I (KO)A.HK.595	S/L.H.W.CASTLE F/S.COLLINSON,B. Sgt.GRIBBLE,A. F/S.BURROWS,F. (AUS.447830 - R.A.A.F.) F/S.STICKLAND,R. (AUS.430583 - R.A.A.F.) W/O.O'SULLIVAN,R. (AUS.415310 - R.A.A.F.) P/O.G.F.DAWSON (J.89896 - R.C.A.F.) Sgt.SAMPSON,G. F/O.P.D.MULLET	Captain Navigator Air Bomber WOP/Air Mid Upper Rear Gunner Mid Under Flt. Eng. 2nd Pilot	18.40	-	Failed to return from operations - no news being received.	
	Lancaster Mk.I (KO)B.NN.706	F/L.J.W.DAVIDSON (J.25633 - R.C.A.F.) F/O.J.N.POWNER F/O.C.D.DOWEN F/O.J.R.DUNFORD (J.39266 - R.C.A.F.) F/S.PAGE,D. (R.178465 - R.C.A.F.) F/S.CRAYSTON,K. (R.260479 - R.C.A.F.) Sgt.GILLIBRAND,A.	Captain Navigator Air Bomber WOP/Air Mid Upper Rear Gunner Flt. Eng.	18.41	-	Failed to return from operations - no news being received.	
	Lancaster Mk.I (KO)C.HK.578	F/O.D.C.JENKINS F/O.W.F.RANSON F/S.HALL,J. F/S.ROSSITER,H. Sgt.HEGON,R. (R.255689 - R.C.A.F.) Sgt.COULBORN,G. Sgt.PHILLIPS,W. F/S.ALGAR,L.	Captain Navigator Air Bomber WOP/Air Mid Upper Rear Gunner Flt. Eng. Mid Under	12.37	17.23	Located target by G.H., and bombed at 15.41 hours from 18,000 feet. No results were seen due to 10/10 cloud but bombing appeared fairly concentrated. Photo was attempted.	

Page of Ops

392

Former Flight Lieutenant Eric Billson DFC A.E. A. recalls his wartime experiences and answers a few questions:

I did my first tour with 9 Squadron as a rear gunner on Wellingtons from July 1940 to February 1941 after which I was posted to 15 O.T.U. to help train gunners for operational flying duties in Bomber Command. Whilst with the O.T.U., I was sent on one of the first gunnery instructor's courses, as until then when you finished a tour of ops and were posted to an O.T.U. you were classed as a screened gunner. After completing the course I returned to Harwell where I remained until October 1941 when I was asked by Squadron Leader Peter Grant if I would like to go back on ops as his rear gunner, to which I agreed, as I had eight months rest. So we were posted to 115 at Marham, where as a crew we completed our second tour of ops. When I was recommended for a commission by Wing Commander Cousins and Group Captain McKee, I was also recommended for a gunnery leader course at Sutton Bridge.

On completing the course I was duly posted in 1942 to Wymswold O.T.U. as an instructor and flight gunnery leader where I also received commission. After a short period at the O.T.U., I was posted to a heavy conversion unit at Waterbeach who were at that time flying Stirling heavy bombers. In the meantime 115 Squadron had moved to Mildenhall to convert Wellingtons IIIs (which I had done my second tour of ops with) to Stirlings, and for some reason or another 115 Squadron then moved to East Wretham, Norfolk to train on and operate the new Lancaster MKIIs with the Bristol Hercules engines. 115 conversion unit was set up to train crews on this type of Lancaster. I was posted to the unit to organise and train air gunners, where I was appointed gunnery leader of the conversion unit. As the squadrons grew in strength it was realised East Wretham was no longer suitable, so the squadron and the conversion unit was moved to Little Snoring where the facilities were much more suitable and had concrete runways etc; compared with East Wretham which was little more than a field with a pond which had been drained to facilitate a bomb dump. Two weeks after we arrived I was promoted and posted with other officers to Foulsham to form and train aircrews for the newly formed 514 Squadron. After about two weeks after we arrived, I was appointed gunnery leader.

After a few months, 514 and the squadron began to become operational with one flight formed. I was posted back to 115 Squadron who were still based at Little Snoring to take over as gunnery leader, as their gunnery leader did not return from an operation and they needed someone experienced to fill the vacancy. A short time after this, the whole squadron moved in late November 1943 to RAF Witchford, where 115 Squadron remained until the end of the war. I left the squadron in October 1944 after completing my third tour of operations. Some of the crews I flew with were on their second trip. Other times, when I drove around the various aircraft disposal points either on my service motorcycle or with the squadron commander, a gunner may have been taken ill at the last moment, so I would take his place as I always kept flying gear with me in case of such instances, otherwise the aircraft may have to abort from the operation. Officially as a squadron commander or gunnery leader you were only supposed to do a maximum of one trip per month, if absolutely necessary.

After leaving the squadron in October 1944 Eric was sent on a squadron leader's admin course before being posted to the Far East. But, as Eric says, that is another story.

The Eric Billson version: 115 Squadron poem

Motto: Despite the Elements

To be sung to the tune of Lilli Marlene

(Donated by Eric Billson's daughter)

Got a wizard squadron number's 115,
Couldn't find a better, no matter where you try,
I wish you could see them – out on ops,
You surely must agree they are the tops,
Three cheers for 115 boys, three cheers for 115.

Wing Co went on ops once, couldn't understand,
Why he was alone, this was not as he had planned,
Until he discovered in his haste,
He'd bombed Berlin instead of Brest,
Three cheers for crazy Wing Cos, three cheers for 115.

Signal Leader's great, but heed this warning do,
Don't be late for briefing, you'll rue it if you do,
You'll find when you're up there, you've been sold,
His bombing codes are ten day old,
Three cheers for Signal Leaders, three cheers for 115.

If you have a grievance, tell you where to go,
See the squadron Adj. the greatest guy I know,
He's Mum, Dad and Uncle, all in one,
He'll treat you like an only son,
Three cheers for old Adj. three cheers for 115.

Coming back from Essen met some 109s,
Billson swore and shouted "You've had your bloody time",
So crouch' there behind his Browning guns,
He pressed the triggers, no more Huns,
Now Billson is a hero, three cheers for 115.

When the war is over, won't we all be glad,
But we'll miss the fun and frolics we have had,
We'll lift up our heads and proudly say
We've lived to see another day
Because sir, we were members of good old 115,
So come and give a cheer for the boys of 115.

Eric Billson

The Reverend Herbert Murton Hadrill

Vicar of St. Andrews Church at Witchford 1938 – 1948

Photograph of Reverend Hadrill

The Reverend Hadrill was a keen photographer and the photograph above was a self potrait taken in a mirror. The Reverend Hadrill's name appears several times in stories in this book, but one amusing story about the vicar himself was related to me by another Witchford character, the now late Frank Allen. One day the vicar borrowed a camera from Mrs. Allen so that he could go in to Ely and take some photographs of the Cathedral. As can be imagined, cameras could be a very sensitive item to carry in wartime, especially as there were stories of German spies operating in Britain at the time. Later that evening Frank Allen's telephone rang. It was Ely Police Station. "Hello Mr. Allen", said the Police Sergeant, "What`s the name of your vicar?". "Hadrill." replied Frank. "Can you describe him?" asked the sergeant. Frank gave a description of the tall vicar. "Can you come over to the station and identify him, as we have arrested this man on Ely High Bridge taking photographs? He says he is the vicar of Witchford and your wife loaned him a camera to take pictures of the Cathedral". Frank confirmed that his wife had loaned the camera and said that he would drive to Ely and confirm that the vicar was who he was claiming to be. The identification was carried out and Frank and the vicar began the return journey to Witchford. "Bless you Mr. Allen", said the Reverend. "I have saved many souls in my time, but this is the first time anyone has saved mine". This was not to be the Reverend's only brush with the law as the report made by Witchford's village Bobby PC 44 Cecil Sutton reveals.

Although we can now find the previous stories about Reverend Hadrill amusing, tragedy in his own life did not escape him, for his wife was not a well woman and he was to lose one of his own sons to the war while serving with the Royal Navy.

To. Superintendent.F.G.Wells.   Witchford
    Police Office,
    Ely, Cambs.   Ely

                16th August   41

      Rev Herbert Murton Hadrill, age 54, The Vicarage,
Witchford, Ely. During the hours between ½ hour after
sunset and ½ hour before sunrise, causing a light inside
a roofed building to be displayed which was not so
obscured as to prevent illumination therefrom being
visible from outside the building, at Witchford, at 12-5.
A.M. 16th August 1941.
Sir.
      I beg to report that at about 8-30.A.M. on Saturday
16th August 1941. I received a report from Special
Constable No.499, George Sidney Dunham, Witchford, to the
effect that at 12-5.A.M. that morning he had seen a light
showing from a bedroom window in The Vicarage, Witchford,
he visited the premises and called out "Put out that light
receiving no reply he had thrown a handful of gravel at
the window, the light was then put out, he did not get
any reply and he did not see the Rev Hadrill.
      At about 10-30.A.M. this date I saw the Rev Hadrill,
I told him that I had received a report from Special
Constable Dunham to the effect that he had seen a light
showing from his (the Rev Hadrill's) bedroom window at 12-5.A.
M. that morning. He said. "I thought you would do." I
asked him if he cared to give any explanation why he
caused a light to be displayed which was visible from
outside. He said. " I have a shade over the lamp, I think
the light must have been showing through a join in the
shutters. He also said. " I called out to the Special
Constable, I'm sorry, but probably he did not hear me
owing to the wind." I told him that he would be reported.
He then said. "I shall not say anything against that, I
have had my fair share of warnings."
      It is to my knowledge that the Rev Hadrill has been
warned by Special Constables on several occasions about
a light showing from this bedroom window.

                I am, Sir.
            Your Obedient Servant,

                P.c.44.

Police report

399

Leading Aircraftsman Tom Bullman

Tom Bullman was born at Kenny Hill near Mildenhall but spent most of his early years in Ely at Annesdale, near the River Ouse. An only son, he left school to work in the butchery trade for London Central, who had a shop on Forehill in Ely and later for Rayment, who also had a shop on the same hill. At the outbreak of war, Tom volunteered for the RAF and was called up for duty on July 20th 1940. He was first sent to Uxbridge to be kitted out then on to Warrington in Lancashire to do his training as a Cook Butcher. He was posted to Ely, Cardiff in Wales to an RAF Balloon Centre where he stayed till July 1941, when he was posted to Canada, and 35 Service Flying Training Centre at North Battlesford. He stayed in Canada until March 1943 when he came back to Britain with 2,300 British and American Servicemen on board the first `Queen Elizabeth`. The crossing took only five days, which was then a record. On returning to England he was posted to Thorpe Abbot near Diss in Norfolk, to help with the catering facilities for the American 100th Bomb Group and their Flying Fortress crews. At weekends he would bike home to see his wife and family in Ely. After six months at Thorpe Abbot he was transferred to Metfield in Suffolk, to do the same job for the American 353rd Fighter Group, who were equipped with the P47D Thunderbolt.

In early 1944 Tom was posted to RAF Witchford via RAF Waterbeach and Mepal. He was now stationed only 2 ½ miles from home which entitled him to obtain a sleeping out pass, which enabled him to sleep at home with his wife and family when not on duty. During a normal Monday to Friday week at Witchford, Tom would prepare 600lb of meat and on a Saturday 1,200lb. Sunday was his day off. Sadly Tom Bullman died in 1995.

Sergeant Ron Ball recalls being stationed with 115 Squadron at RAF Witchford

Photograph of Sergeant Ron Ball taken in 1940

As senior NCO Engine fitter, my typical day at Witchford in 1943 -1944 was quite different to the more stereotype model elsewhere. Firstly, the main administrative centre was a very long way from the dispersal point, and living on the far boundary of the airfield, I tended to be partially detached from most station activities. Four technical sergeants occupied a former guard house (which was never so used in my memory) set beside the Ely/Cambridge road, as far away as it was possible to be from the main squadron buildings and mess. Because of that, we drew rations from the sergeant's mess for breakfast etc. using said mess for main meals. We had a small kitchen area with an electric hot plate, although breakfast was essentialy cereal based with oceans of tinned evaporated milk. On only one occasion did the orderly officer of the day visit our far flung hut unexpectedly; he took one glance at the table littered with Carnation evaporated milk cans, surrounding a 7lb tin of jam and retreated speechlessly. We were clearly an outpost too far away for military disipline. My personal kite W Willie which later became V Victor DS628 was dispersed quite close to this hut as was the petrol dump. I still shudder to think of the total lack of airfield security; anyone could enter from the main road since there were no guards or patrols as a deterrent. About 8.00 in the morning I walked to the plane where the ground crew, two to three flight mechanics or one or two riggers, according to leave, would have arrived generally on RAF Issue bicycles. Covers would be taken from the engines and cockpit and preparations started for the usual D.I. (daily inspection). If the machine had not been flying recently this was generally a run up of all engines with cockpit checks carried out by me, then a visit to B flight office to see if air tests or cross country flights were scheduled for that morning. Whenever the aircraft flew on operations the night before, the day after would involve complete inspection of engines and aircraft generally. On return from operations the pilot would report any defects or problems experienced during the trip. These would be the first items to be dealt with that day; oil leaks, mag drops, engine faults etc. So each engine would be decowled, the mechanics operating on tall gantries placed beneath each engine.

The mechanics at work

A thorough inspection would be made including all services; engine oil, hydraulic oil, oleo leg pressures etc. would all be checked and serviced as appropiate. Riggers would inspect control services and clean out the fusilies from the night's activities. Engines would be recowled and run up by the NCO to check all obvious functions, such as magneto checks, variable pitch propeller checks, flaps, bomb doors, boost levels, things of that nature. The allocated air crew would come out for a general chat and perhaps an air test, although the latter was relatively infrequent if the squadron was on continuous operations. Some technical faults were reported as only occurring at altitude. In such cases I would accompany the crew on air test to endeavour to diagnose the defects. As a rule by lunchtime it would be known if operations were on that night. Fuel loads would be known and the big 2,500 gallon petrol tankers would arrive for the ground crew to top up the tanks to the specific amount. Accuracy was important; the total bomb loads depended on the weight of petrol which together tended to be near the maximum. Too much fuel and the take off might be dicey, not enough and the crew would not make it back, especially if the weather deterioration set in. The Armourers would arrive to bomb up and various other trades and the aircrew as well would arrive to check their particular functions. Some air gunners liked to load or supervise the arming of their turrets. Generally speaking the kites would be ready by 16.00 to 17.00 hours unless, as often happened, there were particular technical problems yet to be completed. A team of NCOs and ground crew would be on duty at evening and night until the air crew came out by lorry or bus, about an hour before they were due to fly and would check their particular functions in the aircraft. Then a general chat with them until time to go. Engines were individually primed from each Nacelle and started by the skipper using external trolley accumulators to save the aircraft's own batteries. All engines were run up and checked, turrets rotated and bomb doors closed. No aircraft could fly without a completed form 700, which was the maintenance history etc. of each individual aircraft. All relevent trades would have checked and signed for such inspections during the day and finally the ground NCO would sign the aircraft form as fully serviceable. I would take this up to the cockpit where the pilot, if satisfied with the checks, would sign in acceptance. The 'C' chocks were then pulled away and Pitot head cover removed and we would wave them off when control tower so signalled. The ground crew not on night duty were then finished for that day. I always saw my machine away and although under no duty to do so, return to welcome the crew back whatever time during the night they returned. Such was the bond between us, strangely enough conscientious ground crew, the majority, regarded their kite as personal property, only on loan to the air crew. So my main duties were the overseeing of servicing and dealing often personally with more difficult, technical, renewal or adjustments to the engines on kite generally. There were of course duties away from the flights for senior NCOs like orderly sergeant and station defence exercises, but activities were generally confined to the flights. Squadron parades were held from time to time at the main buildings but they were relatively rare.

My lasting memory of 115 is that it was a bomber squadron first and foremost so that `Bullshit` activities were always minimal. Being so far from the main buildings the obtaining of spare parts, special needs for the aircraft was quite difficult; they had to be obtained from the squadron stores after much paperwork,

405

which meant of course a long cycle ride. All renewals and unusual services had to be recorded on the form 700, so they formed a complete record of all that had been done to the aircraft including fuel, flying times on operations and airtest etc. So that formed a normal day. There were other advantages. It was possible to be sent off on courses to aircraft manufacturers. I was lucky enough to have a fortnight at Derby with Rolls Royce and also a fortnight at Bristol learning all there was to know about their Hercules engine, and at least two or three courses on various airscrews, electric or otherwise, so that we were very, very up to date. I was lucky enough to be trained early in the war 1940, beginning of 1941. I found that the technical instruction was to a very, very high standard indeed which I think produced as it did, many capable and conscientious technical staff who came as they did from all walks of life, completely unconnected with flying in any form.

Leonard Stores, Main Street Witchford

Leonard Stores Photo via Madge Baxter

The above photograph shows the bungalow stores as the construction workers and RAF Personnel would remember it. The date of the photo is uncertain but is either during or just after the war, as the blackouts for the windows can be seen next to the Lyons ice cream advertising board. The shop much extended and now including a Post Office is still serving the people of Witchford today.

Witchford Shop and Post Office 1998 - Formerly Leonard
Stores. Photo: Author

The shop in 1998, with its new owners was still serving the
people of Witchford although hardly recognisable from the
previous photograph.   Only the arch over the bricked up
doorway where the Irishmen queued for bread and bacci is still
recognisable from the old building.

The population of Witchford just before the war was under five
hundred. Steadily over the years the village has grown as most
of the old RAF domestic sites have been demolished and
developed as housing estates.   Shortly, the dilapidated
remaining buildings of site 3 which includes the Commanding
Officer's bungalow and the Officers Mess will disappear forever
as the builders move in, but at least this will ensure increased
trade for the local store for many years to come.

Witchford Shop and Post Office with new extension to the left, which is now Witchford Chinese Takeaway

Photograph taken in May 2013

Madge Baxter

Madge Baxter

Madge Baxter died unexpectedly on 2nd August 2008 age 88 years. She was one of several Witchfordian`s who encouraged me to write this book. She was a lovely lady and loved to relate stories of Witchford's wartime role. She put me in touch with many airmen, who provided information on the roles that they played in the day to day running of the operational wartime airfield.

After the war Madge continued to run the village shop with her parents Will and Ada Leonard and her first husband Walter. Madge later became Postmistress and continued to run the village shop and Post Office with her second husband Gordon, who was at one time the village policeman.

Gordon died in 2005.

The Isle of Ely and the War

Ely and its surrounding area escaped quite lightly during World War II with regard to damage to property and loss of life, unlike Cambridge and Newmarket 16 and 14 miles away. This is quite surprising, especially with the close proximity of so many airfields and the amount of troops billeted in and around the area. The Witchford Intruder Incident on the 19th April 1944 cost the lives of fourteen airmen; the largest loss of life in the Ely area during World War II.

Many other incidents took place. The following stories briefly describe some of them.

On the 19th June 1940, Ely had its first air raid, when ten enemy Heinkel IIIs passed over Ely between 11.40pm and 1.40am.

Eight bombs fell at twelve minutes passed midnight, from 20,000 ft, at West Fen, killing one person, damaging a hut and killing thirty cattle.

At twenty minutes past midnight another ten bombs fell in the vicinity of St. John's Road and Mill Pits, breaking several windows.

In the late summer of 1940 three Hurricanes from RAF Duxford were flying over Ely when one, piloted by Czechoslovakian Jan Chalupa, developed a problem and began to loose altitude. Pilot Officer Chalupa baled out but was hit by the tail plane. His lifeless body coming down in Barton Fields, now part of Ely Golf Course. The pilotless aircraft crashed into the river bank on the Ely side of the River Ouse, not far from the Ely High Bridge.

Sergeant Jan Chalupa

Photo of Jan Chalupa

Sergeant Jan Chalupa was born in Czechoslovakia at Brno on 5th May 1919.

He was trained as a pilot at the Military Air School at Prostejov from October 1938. As the German army advanced, Jan crossed the border into Poland and reported to the Czech legation at Krakow. On 26-7-39 he escaped to France where, on 13th September, he enlisted in the French Foreign Legion. In October he was sent to the Air School at Bourges and by the 20th May 1940 he was in Combat with the French Air Force based at La Rochelle. When the Germans advanced into France he escaped to Northern Ireland, via Bordeaux, and arrived in Liverpool on 26th June 1940. On 2nd August he was accepted by the RAF (V.R.) and given the rank of Sergeant. He was then sent to No. 6 Operational Training Unit at Sutton Bridge, after which he was posted to No. 310 Czech Squadron at RAF Duxford.

After his death aged 21 years at Ely on 16th October 1940, he was buried at the Brookwood Military Cemetery in Surrey.

Sergeant Chalupa's grave, No. 10, Plot 28, Row D

(Extracts from AM. Forms:- 1180 & 78)

DATE			TIME	UNIT	BASE	CODE	GROUP	COMMAND
16	10	40	1500 hrs	310 sq.	Duxford	NN-D	24	Fighter

A/C TYPE & MARK				No.		CAT.	LOCATION		
Hawker Hurricane MK 1				P 3143		E	Middle of R. Ouse		

ENGINES TYPE & MARK	1	R.Royce Merlin ▭			E	400 Yards From
	2					Railway Station
	3					Ely, Cambs.
	4					MR:

DUTY	NAME : INITIALS	RANK	No.	NAT.	CAS.	SOLO TOTAL	SOLO TYPE
Pilot	Chalupa J	Sgt	787659	Czech	K	300	

	IN A/C	OTHER A/C	OUTSIDE A/C
K	1		
M			
I			
U			
TOT	1		

OTHER A/C TYPE & MARK	No.	CAT.	UNIT
None			

TIME AIRBORNE: 14:30 Hrs   FROM (DROME): Duxford

DUTY: Training Flight

HISTORY OF ACCIDENT: Aircraft took off from duxford in a section of three Hurricanes for a training flight and altitude test (between 600-4000 feet)

After approx 30 minutes in the air this aircraft started losing height and the other pilots believed that Sgt Chalupa was going to attempt a forced landing. At 2,000 feet the pilot abandoned the aircraft, during the course of which, he hit his head on the tail unit. It is believed that as a result, he lost consciousness and was unable to open his parachute.

The Aircraft went into a steep dive and crashed into the river at Ely.   Cause:- Engine Failure.

CONTRACTOR:

UNIT				
TOC				
UNIT				
TOC				

SOC: | TOTAL HOURS: |

Flying accident technical report

Photo of Jan Chalupa's Hurricane at Duxford

The Citation of Corporal Terence Henry King

In 2003 I was contacted by the daughters of the late Cpl. Terence Henry King who was stationed at RAF Mepal during the Second World War. They informed me that their father had received the B.E.M. from the King in 1944, for his bravery during an incident which took place on the airfield on September 8th 1943. I was shown the citation that appeared in the London Gazette, a copy of which can be seen below.

610334 Corporal Terence Henry KING, Royal Air Force Volunteer Reserve.

In September, 1943, an aircraft, which was taking off with a load of bombs, crashed into two houses on the edge of an airfield and burst into flames. Corporal King hurried to the scene and, although fully aware that high explosive bombs were likely to explode at any moment, he went to the cottages a few yards from the burning aircraft to warn the occupants of their imminent danger and render assistance. An injured man was found and whilst Corporal King, with the help of a civilian, was taking him to safety a bomb exploded. The bravery shown by Corporal King was instrumental in saving a life, and many more lives might have been lost had it not been for his prompt action in helping to warn occupants of the nearby houses.

Citation, London Gazette

Shortly after receiving his medal, Corporal King who had been in the Air Force for six years was taken ill and had to go into hospital. His illness was so serious that he had to be invalided out of the Air Force.

Photograph of Corporal King's wedding

American Flying Fortress crash at Prickwillow

Another tragedy occurred on 6th February 1945 when an American Flying Fortress from the 490th Bomber Group crashed on to a bungalow and a cottage at the village of Prickwillow, near Ely, after being abandoned by its crew, after a collision with another Fortress.

The Fortress had taken off from Eye, near Peterborough, at 05.45 piloted by J.W. Hedgecock. Shortly after take off at 4,000 feet and in thick fog a collision took place. There was a loud bang and one engine stopped. Hedgecock sounded the bale out alarm and the crew vacated the aircraft, all survived except the tail gunner Ed Tijan.

The other Fortress from the 388th BG lost a section of wing and crashed at Bracks Farm, Soham, Cambridgeshire. All the crew baled out, but the co-pilot died when it is believed his parachute failed to open properly.

Tragically, Hedgecock's aircraft came down on the bungalow of the Legge family, and then flipped over the road into the cottage occupied by the Howes. Mrs. Legge was seriously injured; her baby and ten year old girl evacuee from London were killed. Mrs. Gladys Howe, her mother, daughters Doreen and Janet all escaped the terrible blaze which engulfed the cottage. Thanks to the brave help from brother-in-law Reg Howe, who walked through blazing fuel to help them out.

Crash site at Prickwillow

Bombing of the Sugar Beet Factory at Queen Adelaide

At 7.00am on 1st November 1940 German bombers appeared in the bright early morning sky* to bomb the Sugar Beet Factory on the outskirts of Ely at Queen Adelaide. Nineteen bombs were dropped from 10,000 feet. Nine of which hit their target. The roof of the main building was hit, as well as the boiler room, workshops and sugar stores. Sixteen workers were injured but amazingly there were no fatalities. The factory was out of production for a month.

*During the war, double Summer time was in operation, hence bright morning sky at this time of day.

The sugar beet factory at Queen Adelaide during its construction in 1925

Spitfire Crash at Little Ouse

On the 18th February 1939 Ian Gleed, a Flight Commander with 266 Squadron based at Sutton Bridge, took off to air test a Spitfire. While flying over the fens, the aircraft started to break up in the air. Ian, or `Widge` as he was called, managed to bale out from the aircraft which crashed at Little Ouse. Injuries received during the incident prevented him returning to the squadron until April 1940.

Gleed would go on to play an important part in the Battle of Britain after he joined 87 Squadron. He joined the squadron while it was based in France on May 14th 1940 and would remain with them till the Battle of Britain was over. During the Battle of Britain he shot down three enemy aircraft, shared a kill with another pilot and damaged two others. Gleed was given command of 87 Squadron on 24th December 1940.

In 1941 our fighters began taking the fight to the enemy, attacking German targets in Northern France. On the 14th/15th March 1941 Ian Gleed took part in an attack on Caen airfield where he destroyed one aircraft and damaged two others.

On the 7th May he shot down a DO 17 and shared kills on 24th and 28th of May.

During an attack on another enemy airfield on August 6th, he damaged two aircraft. On November 18th 1941 he was appointed a Wing Leader and was relocated to Middle Wallop in Wiltshire.

In 1942 his combat skills brought him more success, when he destroyed three more enemy planes and damaged another between March and May.

On the 22nd May, Ian Gleed was awarded the D.S.O. for his courage and bravery. On the 16th July 1942 he was posted to Fighter Command Headquarters as Wing Commander Tactics before becoming Wing Commander Operations on December 7th.

In January 1943 he was posted to North Africa to gain experience of desert conditions, before becoming Wing Leader of 244 Wing on January 31st 1943. His last victory was claimed when he shot down a BF 109 while flying with the Wing on 17th March 1943.

Gleed was awarded the Croix De Guerre (Belgium) on April 1943.

During a patrol on 16th April, Gleed's luck ran out, when he was attacked by German Fighters, over the Cap Bon area and received several hits. Gleed tried to get his damaged Spitfire back to Tunisia, but the aircraft crashed on the Tunisian Coast and he was killed.

He was posthumously awarded the Croix De Guerre (French) on June 5th 1946.

Ian "Widge" Gleed

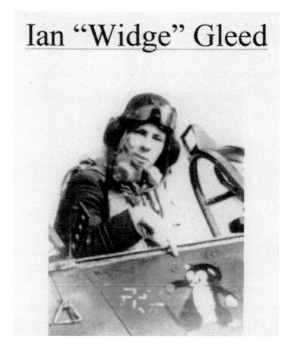

Photo of Ian Gleed

Stirling crash at Sutton

At RAF Mepal on the evening of 8th September 1943, seventeen bombers were taking off to bomb the site of a long range gun battery at Boulogne.

Stirling BK 809 AA-T was taking off when it swung violently to starboard. The aircraft hit a petrol tanker and crashed into a pair of houses at Park Road, in the village of Sutton, Cambridgeshire, situated on the edge of the airfield, and burst into flames. Fifty eight year old Mr. Randall of No. 18, Park Road, who had been standing in his garden watching the aircraft taking off, was killed and his wife injured. WAAF Section Officer Joan Marjorie Easton and Flight Sergeant Peter Gerald Dobson, a Navigator on leave, were killed when bombs started to explode while they were trying to help with the rescue. Fireman Albert Kirby was also killed and a Special Constable injured.

The Pilot, twenty one year old Flying Officer Ian Robert Menzies of the RNZAF was killed instantly, as was Bomb Aimer Flying Officer Gale. The Flight Engineer Sergeant Mellor died of his injuries the next day. Pilot Officer Cordry and Sergeant Barker Wireless Operator and Navigator were injured, but Mid Upper Gunner Sergeant Bullivant and Rear Gunner Sergeant Muir escaped.

Park Road, Sutton, 1999

The pair of houses at the end of the cul-de-sac was built to replace those demolished by the Stirling. No. 18 is on the left. The eight other houses survived but had to be braced and repaired. Seven months later Park Road again received damage, when several houses, including No. 19 the home of Mr. & Mrs Nunn, were involved in another incident, the details of which can be read later in the book.

Stirling BK809 AA-T receiving an engine inspection on dispersal at RAF Newmarket shortly before 75 Squadron moved to its new base at RAF Mepal. Photo via K.D. Mitchell

Twenty one year old pilot, Flying Officer Menzies was the son of Mr. & Mrs. D. Menzies of Auckland, New Zealand and was buried with full military honours at Cambridge City Cemetery. Bomb Aimer Pilot Officer Norman Hatherway Gale aged thirty years was the son of Mr. & Mrs. T.R. Gale of Bristol and the husband of Ellen Gale of Bishopton, Bristol and was buried at Bristol (Canford) cemetery. Flight Engineer, Sergeant A.L. Mellor, suffering from a fractured femur and severe shock, died two hours and forty minutes after the crash in RAF Mepal sick quarters. Thirty year old Sergeant Mellor was the son of Mr. & Mrs. A. Mellor of Buxton and husband of Gladys Mellor also of Buxton. He was buried at Buxton cemetery, Derbyshire. WAAF Section Officer Joan Marjorie Easton was buried at Greenwich (Charlton) cemetery, London. Flight Sergeant Peter Gerald Dobson and Section Officer Easton were off duty and died while trying to help save lives at the crash site. Dobson was the navigator for another of Mepal's crew, that of Sergeant Whitehead. The son of Mr. & Mrs. H.B. Dobson of Blenheim, Marlborough, New Zealand, he was buried at Cambridge City Cemetery.

On Friday 17th September the local weekly newspaper The Ely Standard and Cambridgeshire Times, reported on the terrible events of the 8th September. Due to security, the report did not mention the village in which the incident took place, or the deaths of the RAF personnel. The Stirling had started its take off at 21.35 hours and before the crash had successfully completed thirty operations.

The photograph below was taken in late 1942 at Stoke Holy Cross Chain Home Radar Station, where Joan Marjorie Easton was serving as a WAAF Section Officer. In 1943 she was transferred to RAF Mepal where her bravery led to her untimely death.

Left to right:
Pilot Officer Harper, Section Officer Cantrell, A/S/O. Merwood an Officer from the Royal Norfolk's, Section Officer J.J. Easton and Pilot Officer D. Slight.

Flying Officer Menzies

Flying Officer Menzies

This photo of Flying Officer Menzies of Auckland New Zealand was probably taken during training as a Pilot at No. 1 Elementary Flying Training School at Taieri flying the DH 82 Tiger Moth. He would then have most likely moved on to No. 1 Flying Training School at Wigram where he would have continued his training with the twin Engined Airspeed Oxford, before leaving for England.

Sergeant George Stokes who was the mid upper gunner in Sergeant Don Whitehead's crew recalled in Norman Frank's excellent book `**Forever Strong`** the story of 75 Squadron

RNZAF 1916 – 1990, how his comrade and crew mate Peter Dobson came to be in the wrong place at the wrong time:

"At this stage of the war, aircrew had six days' leave every six weeks, a block of six crews taking it in turn. If a crew got shot down, the other crews stepped up a week, so you would get leave after five weeks. I had arranged to get married on 14th September which was when we were due leave, but unfortunately, a crew went missing, so leave came a week early.

We had only got a couple of ops to do to complete our tour, so I elected to stay and fly as a spare gunner if required. Peter Dobson our navigator said he would take his leave but would stay on camp and help on the local farms, saying we would be on end of tour leave in a fortnight.

On the night of the 8th September he left our hut to go to the farm and the squadron was operating that night. As one of the Stirlings was taking off, it swung and crashed into a small housing estate in Sutton village and later the bombs exploded.

The following lunchtime Peter's body was found in the rubble of the houses, along with a WAAF officer. He had earlier borrowed a bike and this had been found, but the owner of course was on leave. It was only then I knew it had to be Dobbie who had been killed. It was typical of him to have gone to help. They had both gone to ensure there was no one alive and trapped in the houses when the bombs went off. Two civilians were also killed, with others injured.

The pilot of the Stirling, Flying Officer Menzies also died and so did two of his crew. The WAAF officer was Section Officer J.M. Easton.

Flying Officer Menzies' aircraft was one of seventeen Mepal based Stirlings that 75 RNZAF squadron were sending to make up a force of two hundred and fifty seven aircraft detailed to bomb a German long-range gun battery situated at Boulogne. A new marking technique was being tried which proved unsuccessful and so was the raid".

Plane Crashes On East Anglian Village.

HOUSES WRECKED: TWO PERSONS KILLED.

Splendid Work by Civil Defence Services.

THE PEACE of a little village in East Anglia was shattered on Wednesday week, when an aircraft crashed on two Council houses and two villagers lost their lives.

The crash occurred at night when people were in bed or were preparing to retire, and the fact that there were few casualties is a tribute to the magnificent work of the men on the spot. 'Plane and houses burst into flames, and special constables and wardens, showing great heroism, shepherded the women and children to safer zones before terrific explosions completely demolished the two houses involved and severely damaged many others. Grand work, too, was done by the N.F.S. in preventing the spread of the fire, and in assisting with rescue work.

There was a splendid response on the part of all civil defence services, and a true neighbourly spirit was shown by the people of the village in attending to the needs of the families who were rendered homeless.

The people who were killed were Mr. John Randall and Fireman A. E. Kirby. Their wives and a special constable who were injured, were the only other casualties.

The aircraft struck the backs of the two houses, which were immediately enveloped in flames, and a few minutes later came the explosions which completed their destruction. But in that brief interval between, stirring deeds were done by these villagers who lay no claim to being heroes.

LED TO SAFETY.

Mrs. Randall was sitting in her house when the crash came, and as her legs were imprisoned by falling debris, airmen from the 'plane leapt down into the room. She left her shoes behind in struggling free from the rubble and led the way to safety, making exit through a window. With stockings torn to ribbons and her feet, cut, she reached the roadway . . . her first thought was for those members of the crew.

As Mrs. Randall left the blazing house, a man approached; she voiced her concern to him, and recognised Fireman Kirby in the lurid glare . . . He went on . . . his body was discovered the following day.

Elsewhere, Mrs. Kirby was carrying out her duties and was attending to Mr. Randall, when there was an explosion, and she became a casualty.

Mr. P. Smith, the occupant of the second house, was in his garden and saw the aircraft approaching. He ran into the roadway, shouting a warning, and as a result the people in the adjacent houses were able to get clear before the explosions. Mr. Smith was alone at home, and he told how his wife had left him for the first time in 26 years, to spend a short holiday with relatives. His family also were away.

WARNING IGNORED.

One of the first to arrive on the scene after the crash was Special Constable Sergeant R. P. Humphrey. He found the aircraft and houses a raging inferno, and as he approached, he stumbled over an airman lying in the front gateway of one of the houses. Mr. Humphrey stooped to assist him, and the man, although gravely injured, urged the special to get to safety, with a painfully whispered "Get out." Ignoring the warning, Mr. Humphrey was preparing to drag the airman to safety when there was a terrific crash.

"Something struck me on the shoulder," he said, "and I think I must have gone to sleep for a short time. When I came round it was raining fire, and, brushing the sparks off the airman, I dragged him away." Despite his injury, Mr. Humphrey carried on for some time with rescue work, until persuaded by a doctor to take a rest.

Near the fire the wire of a chicken run still stood, and there, in a space restricted to about two yards, a hen walked up and down. A fireman rushed up and endeavoured to tear down the wire, but he was obliged to retreat owing to the terrific heat.

Families who were removed from threatened houses spent the night in a rest centre, established in the village school, where blankets and food were provided. Women who staffed the centre worked untiringly until four o'clock the following morning. They went home for a couple of hours and were back again on duty at six. Such was the spirit of service shown by these villagers; a devotion to a job of work with personal danger ignored.

VICTIMS LAID TO REST.

Large Gatherings in Village Churchyard.

The parish church was filled to capacity on Saturday afternoon when the remains of Mr. John Randall were laid to rest.

About 50 R.A.F. officers and men attended, and together with members of the Special Constabulary, the N.F.S., wardens and the Royal Observer Corps, formed a guard of honour which extended along the entire route taken by the funeral cortege, from the residence of Mr. G. Randall, brother of deceased, to the church.

The coffin, which was borne by neighbours, was met at the entrance to the churchyard by the Vicar, and a R.A.F. chaplain and the Bishop of the Diocese, with members of the choir.

The family mourners were: The widow; Miss Molly Randall, daugh-

(Continued on Page 4).

[Continued from Page 1]

ter; Mr. G. Randall, brother; Mrs. G. Randall, Mrs. Cumberland, Messrs. A. Warren, F. Warren, Molly, brothers-in-law; Mrs. G. Randall, Mrs. Moir, sisters-in-law; Misses J. Warren, H. Warren, nieces; Alan Warren, nephew; Mr. and Mrs. A. F. Ibbott, Mrs. R. W. Ibbott, Master Max Ibbott, Mr. H. Ibbott, cousins; and Mr. J. Bamenck.

Among the many others present in church or at the graveside were representatives of the Parochial Church Council, School Managers, Parish Council, District Council, British Legion, Police, and all sections of the community.

The first portion of the service in the church was conducted by the Vicar, and included the hymn "Jesu, Lover of my soul," and Psalm 23.

Prayers were offered by the Bishop, who also officiated at the graveside.

The funeral rites at an end, R.A.F. officers and men and members of the civil defence services advanced, one by one, to the foot of the grave, there to stand at attention and salute.

There was a wealth of beautiful floral tributes.

A native of the village, Mr. Randall was the son of the late Mr. and Mrs. Joseph Randall. For some time previous to 1914 a member of the Bedfordshire Yeomanry, he joined the 19th Hussars in 1914, and with that Regiment served in France from 1915 to 1918. For many years a member of the church choir, he was a school manager. Of a quiet, unassuming disposition, and upright in character, he earned the respect of all with whom he came in contact.

IMPRESSIVE SCENES AT FIREMAN'S FUNERAL.

Hundreds of people attended the funeral of Edward Kirby on Tuesday afternoon. The cortege of mourners was a most impressive one, fellow members of the N.F.S. nearly 100 strong (including the area and divisional officers) formed a guard of honour and members of the service acted as bearers. The coffin was draped with the Union Jack and bore the dead fireman's service steel helmet, with floral tributes from his near ones.

The immediate mourners were: Master Roy Kirby, son; Mr. Wm. Kirby, brother; Mrs. W. Kirby, sister-in-law; Mr. and Mrs. A. Purell, Mr. and Mrs. T. Waters, Mr. B. Sykes, Mr. and Mrs. J. Sykes, Mr. R. Casbon, Mr. F. Sykes, brothers-in-law and sisters-in-law; Mrs. B. Nunn, Mrs. D. Goodjohn, Mrs. Kirby, Mr. and Mrs. A. Spencer, Mr. and Mrs. G. Burgess, Mr. O. Casbon, Mr. G. Purrell, nieces and nephews. A large number of sympathisers followed, together with strong contingents representing the R.A.F., the Wardens' service, the Royal Observer Corps and Special Constables. Also represented were the St. John Ambulance Brigade, Home Guard, Rural District Council, Parish Council, British Legion and other village organisations, with neighbours and all sections of the community.

Newspaper cuttings reporting the crash (Ely Standard)

Photo of A.L. Mellor who died from his injuries

GUARD OF HONOUR.

From the highway to the church doors members of the N.F.S. formed a guard of honour and through their lines the funeral procession passed into the church by the west door. The church was filled; the first portion of the service was conducted by the vicar, supporting clergymen being the Assistant Bishop of the diocese, and a R.A.F. chaplain. Members of the church choir were present. The hymns, "Fight the Good Fight," and Abide with me" were sung with great feeling by the large congregation. The service also included Psalm 23. Prayers were offered by the R.A.F. chaplain. The final rites of commital were performed by the Assistant Bishop.

The ceremony concluded, officers in charge of the service contingents stepped forward to stand at the salute by the grave.

There was a wealth of beautiful flowers.

Aged 50 years, Edward Kirby was respected by all who knew him. Of a cheery disposition and sterling character and well known over a large area, he served for a period in the A.S.C. during the last war.

To the widow who was unable to attend the funeral, sympathy and hopes for a speedy recovery from her injuries is extended; as is also heartfelt sympathy to Mrs. Randall, to Master Roy Kirby and to Miss Molly Randall.

MEMORIAL SERVICE.

Every pew in the Parish Church was occupied on Sunday evening, for a service of remembrance of those who lost their lives in the crash and of thanksgiving for those who escaped the dangers of the previous Wednesday night.

The Vicar conducted, and the opening hymn, 'O God our Help in ages past" was followed by Psalm 121, "I will lift up mine eyes to the hills."

The lessons were read by Mr. Scott and were followed by the hymn, "Blessed are the pure in heart."

Special prayers were offered, remembering the injured, asking that they be restored to health; both in body and mind; the bereaved were remembered, and thanks were given for the lives of the deceased.

Following the singing of the hymn, "Alleluia, the strife is o'er," the Vicar stated that many offers of help for those distressed had been received, and, as a result, after consultation with the Chairman of the Parish Council, a fund to aid those who had sustained loss was to be raised. The collection at that service would be devoted to this fund. He pointed out that only direct gifts of money would be accepted.

TRIBUTES TO DECEASED.

In an uplifting address, the Vicar referred to the sorrow and the tragedy of the Wednesday night and to the loss of the lives of two neighbours, two friends who worked and lived for their homes and families and to do a good turn for their neighbours. John Randall met his death in the garden he loved so well. He served in the last war and gave much for his country; now he had been called to give all. Edward Kirby walked away from all he loved into a blazing inferno to the rescue; his body was found later. "Greater love hath no man than this . . . ." Calling upon his listeners to offer thanks for the life that he gave, the Vicar went on, "Our hearts go out with love and sympathy to those that mourn; to Mrs. Randall and her daughter Molly; to Mrs. Kirby, sorely smitten and injured, and to her son Roy, who will miss his father so much." The village, he said, had witnessed a great tragedy; many deeds of great risk, courage and devotion to duty. The deeds of these men would stand as a light in the darkness to help those who were left.

The address was followed by the hymn "Abide with me" and the service concluded with the singing of "Now thank we all our God."

AN APPRECIATION.

Admiration for the valuable assistance rendered by the civil defence services of the parish and the unselfish way in which the parishioners helped to evacuate and accommodate those affected by the accident, is conveyed in a letter received by the Chairman of the Parish Council. The letter also expresses the deep sympathy felt by officers

Lancaster crash at Downham Road, Ely

On 30th April 1944 Lancaster ND553 of No. 460 Squadron was flying over Ely, having taken off from Binbrook on a training flight with a scratch crew when a CO_2 bottle discharged itself, causing the dinghy to be released. The dinghy wrapped itself around the tail plane causing loss of control. The aircraft crashed close to the Downham Road, between Ely and Little Downham, at 16.55 hours. All crew members were killed including Flying Officer Jagger who had taken part in the Dams raid with 617 Squadron in May 1943.

The crash report on ND553

Those who died were:

> *Flight Lieutenant W.A. Healey DFC RCAF*
> *Sergeant F. Boardman*
> *Flying Officer R. Bailes*
> *Sergeant J. Jones*
> *Sergeant T.A. Hutchinson*
> *Flying Officer B. Jagger DFM*

Flying Officer Jagger won his DFM while serving with 617 Squadron and had flown as front gunner in Flight Lieutenant Shannon's aircraft on the Dams raid.

Lancaster explosion on RAF Mepal Airfield

The 29th April 1944 saw the last Stirling bomber leave Mepal destined for 1653 Conversion Unit. 75 NZ Squadron were now completely equipped with the Lancaster.

On 29th June the Lancasters were bombed up for an operation to attack the Railway Yards at Vaires on the outskirts of Paris, when orders were received postponing it. The bombs were left on the aircraft which were standing on their dispersal points around the airfield. At 04.20 hours on 30th June Lancaster LL 942 AA-C exploded, damaging five other aircraft. The villagers of Mepal, Sutton and Witcham bordering the airfield had a narrow escape as bits of aircraft were blasted over a wide area. At first light, ground crews were out retrieving the debris. One wheel was found in Sutton church yard, the mid upper turret was found in the motor transport section and an airscrew imbedded itself in the middle of the airfield. An A.E.C. petrol tanker was holed by shrapnel and one thousand gallons of fuel was lost. Park Road, Sutton again received damage as it had in September 1943 when the Stirling crashed, but this time there were no casualties.

Mrs. Daisy Nunn and husband Fred were tipped out of bed by the blast and Mr. Nunn's suits were shredded when they were blown through the ceiling. All the chickens in the garden were also killed and all the surrounding houses had to be strengthened with tie bars. It was twenty eight weeks before the Nunn's were able to return home.

It was believed that a fuse on a 500 lb GP American bomb had malfunctioned causing the explosion.

The aftermath of the explosion: Bits of Lancaster were spread all over the airfield. Photo via Ken Wooton

Stirling crash near Ely Railway Station

With so many airfields in the area, crashes would be inevitable. Some, like Sergeant Weaver, Pilot of Stirling MKII BK663 ZO-K of 196 Squadron and his crew were lucky. The aircraft took off from Witchford at 19.54 on 27th September 1943 to bomb Hanover. Due to an electrical fault the bombs could not be released over the target, so Sergeant Weaver turned for home. Crossing the Dutch Coast the aircraft was hit by Flak. Sergeant Weaver maintained control but their problems increased when they encountered bad visibility approaching the airfield. The Stirling flew into the ground, two miles short of Witchford airfield, on land between the village of Stuntney and Ely Railway Station at 01.15. Sergeants Weaver, Perry, Rouse, Wooten, Oakes (RAAF) and Pepall, all escaped unhurt. Sergeant Stearn was injured.

BK663 was written off; this was its second crash in 63 flying hours. The aircraft had originally been delivered to 214 Squadron at Chedborough and put on charge on 9th March 1943.

On 28th March the aircraft took part in a raid on Berlin. On returning to Chedborough it collided over the airfield with Stirling EF362 BU-N, which had returned early due to severe icing.

The pilot of EF362, Flying Officer Cooper, was killed when the aircraft crashed near Hadleigh, Suffolk. BK663 crash landed, but after originally being written off was repaired and sent to Witchford.

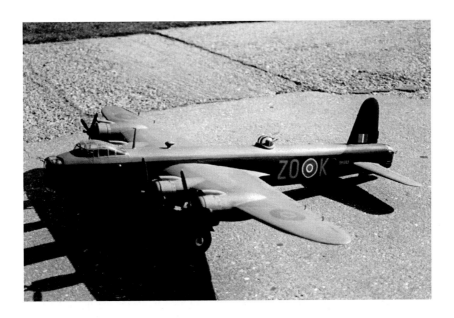

A model of ZO-K663 stands on a remaining section of runway at Witchford, before joining the display of memorabilia on the old airfield

Wellington Crash at Stuntney

On the 23rd August 1944 there was trouble in the skies over the village of Stuntney, situated just two miles from the Cathedral City of Ely. Wellington Bomber MF 520 TYG of No. 24 Operational Training Unit had taken off from its base at Honeybourn, Worcestershire for an evening cross country flight with an all Canadian crew and a second pilot. Control of the aircraft was lost in heavy cloud, but was quickly regained by the pilot Flight Sergeant Murry, but almost immediately he was faced with a total engine failure. As the Wellington started to break up, two men, Sergeants Hobbs and Jones managed to bale out and deploy their parachutes. The wreckage crashed into the ground at 22.15 hours at Nornea Farm Stuntney, on Middle Fen, two miles South East of Ely.

Personnel from nearby RAF Witchford were involved in the search for the bodies of five other members of the crew, while the two survivors were taken to the RAF Witchford Sick Quarters suffering from shock and abrasions.

Those who died along with the pilot were Flying Officer J.M. Rinahan, Sergeant W.S. Paton, Sergeant A.D. Daniels and Sergeant R.C. Green. All were buried in the Brookwood Canadian Military Cemetery.

The Case of the Stray Bullet

On Friday 21st April at 5.58pm, twenty eight year old Mrs. Edith Young of Cambridge Road in Ely was about to leave the office in Main Street, Witchford where she worked as Clerk for the Builders of the airfield; Holland, Hannon and Cubits. About to walk through the door she heard a loud crack and felt something hit her in the back. Turning round she saw a bullet lying on the floor of the office. The bullet caused no injury to Mrs. Young as it glanced off her clothing.

On Saturday 22nd April, Witchford's PC Sutton was called in by Mr. Albert Edward Jackson, agent for the building firm to investigate. Mr. Jackson handed the 303 bullet to PC Sutton who observed rifling marks, and was in no doubt that it had been fired by a rifle from some distance, especially as it had left a hole in the corrugated iron roof, some 9 feet from the floor.

PC Sutton's investigations eventually led him to the crash site of Flight Lieutenant Eddy's Lancaster in a field to the side of Beald Drove owned by Herbert Johnson. Mr. Johnson informed PC Sutton that he had been working in the field all day on Friday 21st April, but had left before 18.00 hours. He did remember that at dinner time after the men who came to take the wreckage away had gone to dinner, there were two guards lying down against the aircraft, firing their rifles across the drain. He saw two officers get out of a car near the gate and walk along the road way in the direction of Coveney. When they came into line to where the men were firing they turned back. PC Sutton observed that the gate mentioned was about quarter of a mile from the crash site. PC Sutton contacted Corporal Smith of the RAF Police and was shown a report made by the two officers on the incident.

At 10.00 hours on Thursday 27th April PC Sutton and Corporal Smith interviewed the two men who were on guard at the crash site at the time the bullet came through the office roof. Both men denied they fired any shots during the time they were on guard, but claimed there were one or two explosions from the wreckage. In his report to Superintendent Wells at Ely Police Office, PC Sutton stated that the bullet cases he found at the crash site had been fired by a gun and had not exploded in a fire. He also said that in his opinion that, if shots were being fired at 13.00 hours, it was possible that the stray bullet that glanced off Mrs. Young at 18.00 hours had probably also been fired from the same spot. He informed the Station Adjutant of the incidents and respectfully requested that Superintendent Wells forwarded a full report to the Commanding Officer of RAF Witchford.

This incident involving Mrs Edith Young should not be confused with an earlier incident in 1941 when Lilian May Youngs was accidentally shot during a training exercise.

Tuesday 19th August 1941

An unusual incident took place at Wayhead near the village of Coveney, Cambs.

Photo of Lilian May Youngs taken in 1938

The following report was made by Witchford's village policeman
to Superintendent F.G. Wells at Ely Police Office.

To. Superintendent.F.G.Wells.   Witchford
    Police Office,
    Ely, Cambs.   Ely

                      19th August   41

          Woman hit in the back by a machine gun bullet.
Sir.
        I beg to report that at 11-45.A.M. on Tuesday 19th
August 1941. I received a telephone message from P.c.
Hudson,Sutton, to the effect that he had received a
message from Dr. Young, of Sutton, stating that he had
received a message from Wayhead,Coveney, to attend a
woman named "Youngs" who had been hit in the back by a
bullet from a machine gun fired from an aeroplane. I
proceeded to Wayhead and on the way I met Dr. Young in
Coveney, he informed me that he had ordered the woman's
removal to Addenbrookes Hospital, Cambridge. I obtained
a statement from the Doctor to the effect that the bullet
entered on the right shoulder and was lodged in the
woman's back.
        I was unable to see the injured woman she having
been taken away before I arrived.
        I made enquiries at Wayhead and found that the woman
(Mrs Lilian May Youngs, age 22, wife of Cyril Youngs,of
Wayhead farm, Coveney) had been engaged in potato picking
and had stopped for lunch and in company with several
other women was sitting on a tree trunk on the Witcham
Fen Drove, Wayhead, with their backs towards the Wash,
where apparantly some aeroplanes were at target practice,
one of the women Mrs Alice Lucas,of Wayhead, stated that
she heard a sort of crack, Mrs Youngs screamed and said,
"What's that" and with her hand up to her back fell face
downwards across Mrs Lucas's feet. Statement from Mrs
Lucas attached.
        The injured woman was conveyed home by Mr John Lucas
of Wayhead, and attended by Dr Young.
        The distance from where the women were sitting to
the wash would be approximately 1 mile.
        Dr David Ernest Young, Cambria House, High Street,
Sutton. States. At about 11-45.A.M. on Tuesday 19th
August 1941. I received a telephone message to the effect
that a woman by the name of Mrs Youngs, had been hit in
the back with a machine gun bullet. I proceeded to Wayhead
and examined the woman and found a bullet lodged in her
back which had entered on her right shoulder. I ordered
her removal to Hospital.
        Alice Lucas, States.
                I am the wife of Horace Lucas
and reside at Wayhead, Coveney. At about 11-30.A.M. on
Tuesday 19th August 1941. I was sitting on a tree trunk
on Witcham Fen Drove, Wayhead, in company with several
other women, having my lunch, there were several aeroplan .
aeroplanes about at the time and there were some planes
behind us over the Wash firing with machine guns,
suddenly I heard a sort of crack, and one of the women
Mrs Lily Youngs screamed out and said "What's that" and
fell across my feet and put her hand up to her back. She
was taken to her home by Mr John Lucas.
                I am, Sir.
          Your Obedient Servant,

439

After reading the report made by PC Sutton, I often wondered what had happened to Mrs. Youngs. No further reference was made to this incident in the collection of records kept by the late PC Cecil Sutton and donated to the RAF Witchford Display of Memorabilia in 1997 by PC Sutton's son.

In 2002 I was contacted by a Mr. Colin Stearn, someone I had known for most of my life, who asked me if, among my records, there was any mention about a woman being shot in the back in 1941. On replying `Yes`, to his question, I was amazed when he told me that the lady in question was in fact his wife Ann's mother. I had known this lady for many years and often used to have a chat with her whenever we met, but I had no idea that this was the lady mentioned in PC Sutton's report. Sadly Mrs. Youngs had died on 25th December 2001, and Colin asked me if he could have a copy of the report and said, that if I would like to drop it round to him he would show me something of interest relating to his mother-in-law's accident. When I called to see Colin and Ann a day or two later, I was shown a small box which they had found after Mrs. Youngs' death, containing a 303 bullet and the remnants of a letter from the Canadian pilot whose Wellington Bomber had accidentally shot Mrs. Youngs during training over Welney Wash. The Bomber was from an Operational Training Unit based at RAF Bassingbourn. The letter was an apology for what had happened with the stray bullet. Mrs. Youngs had to undergo surgery to remove the bullet at Addenbrookes Hospital, Cambridge and had two blood transfusions during the operation.

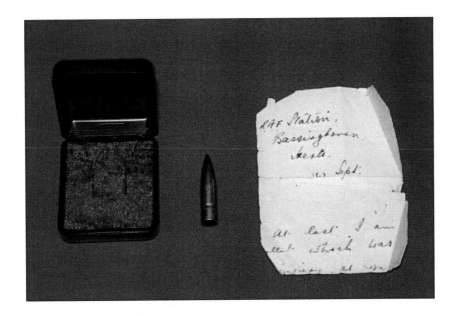

The small box which contained the 303 bullet which was removed from Mrs. Youngs' back and the remains of a letter of apology from the Canadian pilot

The Soham Explosion

Probably the most famous incident took place on Friday 2nd June 1944 at 1.43 am, when an ammunition train blew up, demolishing Soham Railway Station. But for the bravery of driver Ben Gimbert and fireman James Nighthall, who uncoupled a blazing wagon and pulled it clear of the other wagons before it exploded, things could have been worse.

Ben Gimbert survived, despite being blown over the station building, but fireman James Nighthall and signalman Frank Bridges died in the explosions. Although the station was demolished in the massive blast, the bravery of these men prevented probably the total destruction of the town of Soham.

This story is told in detail in Anthony Day's book, `**But for Such Men as These`**.

The aftermath of the explosion can be seen as the clearing up operation takes place. This photograph shows only a small part of the devastation caused by the explosion. Photo: The Cambridge Collection. W. Martin Lane

After the war the Nissen huts were used for Civilian use

In October 1953 one of my wife's relations got married. They lived with his Mother for 8 months before moving into their own first home. This was a prefab at No. 9, WAAF Site 11, Common Road, Witchford, near Ely, Cambridgeshire, which previously was a WAAF Dormitory.

They describe their time living there

The site was taken over by Ely Rural District Council, and rent including rates was 7s 6d (37 ½ p) per week. To make the prefabs suitable for civilian use, a concrete wall panel was built making 2 bedrooms, living room, kitchen and lavatory. The

walls were panelled inside the bedrooms and living room, 5 feet in height for extra warmth, and the panels were painted cream. They had corrugated roofs with one centre chimney. All windows had metal frames and frosted glass. All floors throughout the prefab were covered with lino, black and white in the kitchen, flower design in the living room and brown in the bedrooms.

There was no central heating, only a cooking range in the kitchen which had a switch that could be turned to heating or cooking. It was kept clean by rubbing it with `Zebra black lead` polish. Also in the kitchen was a bath with a lid over it, so when not in use this was used as a work top. A deep white Belfast sink, a black copper and a cabinet with a drop down leaf was installed. There was no washing machine, we only did hand washing, and would send our sheets to the laundry in Ely.

In the living room was a sideboard, a gate leg table with 4 chairs and 2 fireside chairs. We had no television, only a wireless. In the bedroom there was just enough space for a double bed, wardrobe, dressing table and Lloyd Loom chair. When it was very cold weather, the ceiling was so icy that we moved our bed into the living room. Each prefab had its own garden all round with a fence between neighbours.

There was no fridge or freezer, so groceries were more or less purchased daily from Leonard's Stores in the Main Street in the village of Witchford, which was also the Post Office. Further down the main street in one of the houses, the front room was a hairdresser's. There were no telephones in the homes or mobile phones, just a telephone box down the road.

Three bags of coal were delivered each week by Coote & Warren coal merchant. The Milkman came round regularly, also the Butcher and Paperboy. There were no street lights, so Common Road was very spooky to walk down in the dark. Mice were often found in the bath and the biggest spiders ever, were seen due to the open fields around the site.

Although we had no mod cons. as we have today, they were very happy times with all the neighbours being very friendly and everyone helped each other. They would get each other's washing in, if it started to rain while you were out and even ironed it, and they would cut each other's grass.

We were eventually offered a brand new council house at High Barns in Ely. We moved out of our little prefab in May 1957, quite sorry to leave, but we were getting a 3 bedroomed house with a fire and back boiler and a proper bathroom.

Photo of Nissen hut

Forces Sweetheart Dame Vera Lynn visits RAF Witchford Display of Memorabilia

On Sunday December 9th 2007, Forces Sweetheart Dame Vera Lynn visited RAF Witchford Display of Memorabilia, having attended a Charity concert in Ely Cathedral the previous evening. Dame Vera was greeted by some of the people who have helped in setting up and running the display of memorabilia, dedicated to those who served at Witchford and nearby Mepal airfields during World War II. Among those in the photograph are Mr. David Brand and his wife Ann who owns a large part of the old airfield, now Lancaster Way Business Park, and without his generosity of the use of his office foyer, the display of memorabilia would not exist. Also attending were the Squadron Presidents of 115 and 75 N.Z. Squadron Associations. Mr. Frank Leatherdale and Mr Jack Richards, joined by their wives and members of the RAF Association and Royal Naval Association who help man the display.

Group photo with Dame Vera Lynn

Barry Aldridge welcoming Dame Vera Lynn. Also present: Terry
Strawson

115 Squadron Memorial

The Memorial

Unveiled and dedicated by the Bishop of Ely on May 21st 1989.
This fine memorial stands on the Lancaster Way Business Park,
off the A142 roundabout between Ely and Witchford.

No. 115 SQUADRON
MEMORIAL
SERVICE OF DEDICATION

LANCASTER WAY WITCHFORD
ELY CAMBRIDGESHIRE

SUNDAY 21ST MAY 1989
AT NOON

Service of dedication booklet

PART 5: Present & Future

Carrying the flame forward

Having been so closely involved with the memories shared in this book, we have all been affected by the events and the sacrifices made during those three brief years. I hope we have given you a glimpse into the life of these young servicemen and women and that you too feel you have got to know them as we have.

Since the original exhibition in Ely Museum and the opening of the Display of Memorabilia on the former RAF Witchford Airfield in 1995, there has been a steady stream of visitors, letters and information about the site and personnel.

Barry has spent many years sorting through the stories and tales and researching additional information, always intending to pull them together in a book to remember the brave men and women who were based at Witchford and Mepal during the war.

Every November ex 115 Squadron Men and their families come back to their old wartime base and we have a short Remembrance Service around the Memorial addressed by the Vicar of Witchford. It is our hope that this will continue for the foreseeable future.

Sadly, in October 2012 Barry became a resident at Soham Lodge Care Home and was no longer able to continue with his project.

By getting Barry's book finished and published, with the help of Beth and friends, I hope it will serve as a memorial to Barry and all those courageous young people (really only young boys & girls) who will never be forgotten and hope too that it will be read by the generations to follow.

And so, I continue to keep the flag flying.

The Display of Memorabilia contains many of the artefacts described in this book and is well worth a visit. It is housed in the foyer of Grovemere House on the Lancaster Way Business Park and is open to the public on weekdays during office hours and by appointment at the weekends. At the time of publication, appointments can be made by telephoning me on 01353 664934.

Sue Aldridge, August 2013

And finally: . . Do come and visit our display

A display of memorabilia

RAF Witchford
1943 - 1946

Supported by City of Ely Council

RAF Witchford Display of Memorabilia, Grovemere House,
Lancaster Way Business Park, Ely, Cambridgeshire

CB6 3NW